Emoji and Social Media Paralanguage

Emoji are now ubiquitous in our interactions on social media. But how do we use them to convey meaning? And how do they function in social bonding? This unique book provides a comprehensive framework for analysing how emoji contribute to meaning-making in social media discourse, alongside language. Presenting emoji as a visual paralanguage, it features extensive worked examples of emoji analysis, using corpora derived from social media such as Twitter and TikTok, to explore how emoji interact with their linguistic co-text. It also draws on the authors' extensive work on social media affiliation to consider how emoji function in social bonding. The framework for analysing emoji is explained in an accessible way, and a glossary is included, detailing each system and feature from the system networks used as the schemas for undertaking the analysis. It is essential reading for anyone wishing to investigate the role of emoji in digital communication.

Michele Zappavigna is an Associate Professor at the University of New South Wales. She is co-editor of the journal *Visual Communication.* Her key books include *Searchable Talk: Hashtags and Social Media Metadiscourse* (2018, Bloomsbury) and *Discourse of Twitter and Social Media* (2012, Bloomsbury).

Lorenzo Logi is an early career academic based in Sydney, Australia. His major research interests include social semiotics, digital communication, paralanguage, and humour, and he has published numerous articles in top-rated journals and book chapters on these subjects.

T0382456

Emoji and Social Media Paralanguage

Michele Zappavigna

University of New South Wales, Sydney

Lorenzo Logi

University of New South Wales, Sydney

CAMBRIDGE
UNIVERSITY PRESS

CAMBRIDGE
UNIVERSITY PRESS

Shaftesbury Road, Cambridge CB2 8EA, United Kingdom

One Liberty Plaza, 20th Floor, New York, NY 10006, USA

477 Williamstown Road, Port Melbourne, VIC 3207, Australia

314–321, 3rd Floor, Plot 3, Splendor Forum, Jasola District Centre, New Delhi – 110025, India

103 Penang Road, #05–06/07, Visioncrest Commercial, Singapore 238467

Cambridge University Press is part of Cambridge University Press & Assessment, a department of the University of Cambridge.

We share the University's mission to contribute to society through the pursuit of education, learning and research at the highest international levels of excellence.

www.cambridge.org
Information on this title: www.cambridge.org/9781009179812

DOI: 10.1017/9781009179829

© Michele Zappavigna and Lorenzo Logi 2024

First published 2024

A catalogue record for this publication is available from the British Library.

Library of Congress Cataloging-in-Publication Data
Names: Zappavigna, Michele, author. | Logi, Lorenzo, author.
Title: Emoji and social media paralanguage / Michele Zappavigna, University of New South Wales, Sydney, Lorenzo Logi, University of New South Wales, Sydney.
Description: Cambridge, United Kingdom ; New York, NY : Cambridge University Press, 2024. | Includes bibliographical references and index.
Identifiers: LCCN 2023027009 (print) | LCCN 2023027010 (ebook) | ISBN 9781009179812 (hardback) | ISBN 9781009179805 (paperback) | ISBN 9781009179829 (ebook)
Subjects: LCSH: Emojis. | Social media. | Language and the Internet. | Communication – Technological innovations.
Classification: LCC P99.63 .Z37 2024 (print) | LCC P99.63 (ebook) | DDC 302.2–dc23/eng/20230816
LC record available at https://lccn.loc.gov/2023027009
LC ebook record available at https://lccn.loc.gov/2023027010

ISBN 978-1-009-17981-2 Hardback
ISBN 978-1-009-17980-5 Paperback

To Yaegan Doran for his ongoing interest in and generous feedback on this book, as well as his inspiring work on modelling tenor.

Contents

Figures

Tables

Acknowledgements

We would also like to thank our colleagues Shooshi Dreyfus, Aurélie Mallet, and Josh Han for their contribution to the early stages of gathering and analysing data about emoji. And to all our friends and loved ones, thank you for your indulgence and opinions when the subject of emoji comes up around the dinner table.

Emojis used under a creative commons licence, © X Corp. Full details:

Copyright 2023 X Corp and other contributors

Code licensed under the MIT Licence: http://opensource.org/licenses/MIT

Graphics licensed under CC-BY 4.0: https://creativecommons.org/licenses/by/4.0/

Part of this work was funded by the Commonwealth of Australia.

Note on the Text

The following conventions are adopted in this book when explaining the analysis:

1 System networks are drawn using the conventions defined in Systemic Functional Linguistics. References to the names of systems occur in SMALL CAPS and features occur in [square] brackets.
2 Bonds identified in affiliation analysis are shown in ALL CAPS and square brackets and IDEATION-ATTITUDE couplings are also shown in square brackets.
3 Emoji are referred to using the Common Locale Data Repository (CLDR) Short Names, which are presented in ALL CAPS.
4 Realisation of features from system networks are shown using –>[1]
5 ' ... ' is used to indicate text has been abridged.
6 Anonymised information is shown in braces.

---

[1] The more traditional notation of a downward slanting arrow was not used in order to avoid confusion with the DOWN-RIGHT ARROW emoji.

Abbreviations

API	Application Programming Interface
CLDR Short Name	Common Locale Data Repository Short Name
JSON	JavaScript Object Notation
SFL	Systemic Functional Linguistics
ZWJ	Zero Width Joiner
NSW	New South Wales

1 Social Media Paralanguage and Emoji

1.1 Introduction

This book explores the kinds of meanings that can be made with emoji, small graphical icons encoded as Unicode characters. Emoji are a frequent feature of digital communication and, as we will see, can enact a wide range of functions in tandem with language and other semiotic resources. We began writing at home during lockdown in Sydney in the midst of the third wave of the COVID-19 pandemic in Australia. At 11 o'clock each morning, the New South Wales State Premier Gladys Berejiklian provided a televised update on the COVID-19 case numbers. These addresses generated large volumes of social media reaction on platforms such as Twitter. Emoji proliferated in these reactions, appearing in the ambient audience's responses to the case numbers, and in their criticism or praise of the government's policies. For example, journalists made use of emoji to encapsulate, categorise, and evaluate information provided during the premier's press conference, as in Text (1.1).

Text (1.1)   🖥 1431 new cases in NSW
              ⚰ 12 deaths (119)
              ⚰ Woman in her 30s died (unvaccinated)
              @ 7.2 M 💉
              🚑 Ambulance 160 in ICU (☐0)
              🏥 979 in Hospital (☐62)
              🦠 7 new cases in Wilcannia (88)
              🦠 53 new cases in Western NSW (⚕ 11 Burke)
              🗣 @gladysB says 'The next 2 weeks will be the worst'

Not only do the emoji in this tweet[1] visually organise the message into a list, they articulate both key content (e.g. 🦠 + '*cases*') and key feelings (e.g. ⚰ + '*deaths*'), together with the written verbiage in the post.

Everyday social media users also discussed their reactions to the daily updates in Twitter interactions such as Exchange 1.1.

---

[1] Tweets are short character-constrained messages posted to the social media service Twitter.

Exchange 1.1

Text (1.2)   **User 1:** Anyone else feel like the day doesn't start until @gladysB tells us exactly how screwed we all are?

Text (1.3)   **User 2:** Same, about to get my 11am presser coffee made☕

Within this exchange, there appears to be a relationship between '*coffee*' and the HOT BEVERAGE ☕ emoji. However, this emoji also seems to be important in terms of how interpersonal alignments are negotiated in the exchange, hinting at solidarity among the interactants and perhaps even some ironic enthusiasm. This book aims to deal with these kinds of relations – of emoji to any co-occurring text and to the interactive context – that are so central to how emoji make meaning in social media discourse.

1.2   The Semiotic Flexibility of Emoji

In order to function in a wide variety of discursive arenas, emoji need to have high semiotic flexibility. By virtue of their technical encoding, emoji are treated by social media platforms, and the devices on which they are navigated, as characters. This means that they can integrate seamlessly with the rest of the Unicode characters in the body of a social media post. This property also contributes to their semiotic capacity to make meanings relatively seamlessly with the written verbiage in the rest of the post, hereon the 'co-text'. For example, as a prelude to the discussion in the chapters that follow, let us consider the sorts of meaning emoji realise in the example tweets: Text (1.4), Text (1.5), and Text (1.6).

Text (1.4)   Lovely chatting with {Name} from @{Username} about the insane endurance feats of @{Username} & @{Username} and the approach to supporting such giants.

Grab a cuppa & have a listen! ☕

[tiny URL]

It comes after brill insights from {Name} on his PW record

Text (1.5)   I drink so much ☕ I feel like 🐝 even thinking ☁ bout it

Text (1.6)   Good Morning Tweepies!..✔️.Monday Morning!.☺.Slept in!.😴 😋.. have to say hello and Goodbye.☁ ... see you this arvo! ... ☁ 😁 ☕ ☕ ☕ ☕ ☕ [GIF]

In Text (1.4), we see how the ☁ emoji is used as a visual deictic, pointing to the location of the 'tiny URL'[2] in the text. The emoji also potentially references

---

[2] A 'tiny URL' is short alias linking to a longer URL (Uniform Resource Locator) used to locate resources on the internet such as a web page.

the implicit call to action of 'clicking on' the URL since it resembles the mouse pointer icon of some operating systems. We thus have an emoji making meaning by visually depicting a material action and by referencing how a stylised rendering of that hand gesture has been adopted in another mode. In Text (1.5), the ☕ and 🤮 emoji are used to directly represent the entity (a hot beverage) and action (vomiting) they depict, thereby effectively replacing the written text for these. Noteworthy here, however, is that while the ☕ emoji depicts a category of things, when interpreted in combination with linguistic co-text a reader would supply just one example of that category, such as 'coffee' or 'tea'. Lastly in Text (1.6), the 💨, 😵, 😣, 😵, and 😓 emoji act to imbue the text with various emotive inflections. Unlike in Text (1.5), however, we are unlikely to interpret the emoji as indexing the expressions or gestural paralanguage of the author or of other textual participants. Rather we recognise that in this context the emoji coordinate with the affective and convivial meanings made in the text, contributing to the inclusive solidarity enacted. In these small examples alone, we can see evidence of the semiotic suppleness of emoji.

On their own, emoji are rather under-specified and stylised representations that hint at a range of ideas. However, in combination with their co-text, they can make a range of complex meanings. Emoji can optionally involve themselves in the organisation of the text as a coherent semantic unit, can contribute to the articulation of entities and activities, and can resound with the emotional implications of the text, as we will explore in detail in Chapters 4, 5, and 6. In addition, each of the examples we have just explored offers a potential 'bond' to any interactants in the ambient social media audience through the way that emoji and language are used to share and position particular values. We will deal with such social affiliation in Chapters 7 and 8, considering both interactive exchanges and ambient communing. Emoji also enter into relationships with multimedia beyond the written co-text, such as digital stickers, memes, and simple animations. For example, Text (1.6) includes an animated image (a GIF), created from a snippet of a 1966 episode, 'Atlantic Inferno', from the British TV series *Thunderbirds*. The GIF depicts the electronic marionette puppet character, John Tracy, sitting up abruptly in bed. In terms of the meanings the tweet makes as a multimodal text, the GIF appears to coordinate intermodally with broadly shared ideas about coffee, mornings, and alertness that we will explore in Chapter 9.

1.3   The Semiotic Complexity of Encoding and Rendering 'Picture Characters'

Emoji are fascinating in their capacity to involve themselves in intricately specific meanings made within localised social media subcultures, at the same time as being malleable and under-specified enough to make meanings across a vast array of social contexts. In terms of their visual appearance, they are presented to users of social media platforms such as Twitter, Instagram, Facebook, and TikTok as small, coloured glyphs. While it might be tempting to interpret the meaning-potential of emoji in terms of their visual appearance alone, they are complex semiotic resources. As we will explore in Chapter 2, emoji are 'picture characters' with some of the affordances of written characters and some of the affordances of images. One way of conceiving of this is to treat emoji as an iconographetic mode:

> … the element *icono* (from the Greek for *image*), generally refers to pictorial characters; it does not matter whether these are iconic or symbolic characters in isolation. The second part of the term, *graphetic*, is understood in terms of the Greek word *graphé* (or writing) and will hence refer to all kinds of written characters: *typed* characters in the case of digital communication. (Siever, 2019, p. 129, original formatting)

The concept of a picture icon used for interactive digital communication arose with the practice of mobile text messaging in Japan. The popular term 'emoji' is itself derived from the Japanese 絵文字 ('e' = 'picture'; 'moji' = 'written character'). However, just what constitutes a 'picture' or the property of pictoriality can be difficult to establish (Wilde, 2019). Studies have noted a range of analytical quandaries regarding how emoji, as picture icons, can represent apparently complex concepts via a visual shorthand that is both imprecise and expansive enough to range across the multitude of meanings needed in a wide range of communicative situations. Some studies appeal to a contrast with visual images to understand this semiotic potential: 'the specifics of the individual representation is often incidental to the underlying meaning of the ideogram [i.e. an emoji] – this is unlike images where the particulars of a given image are often more crucial than what it is representing generally (i.e. it is a photo of your dog, not just a photo representing the semantic notion of "dog")' (Cappallo et al., 2018, p. 2, clarification added). By this logic, there is an inherent difference between an image of a dog and the DOG 🐕 emoji.

In order to meaningfully account for how emoji make meaning as picture characters, we also need to factor in the way they operate inside 'semiotic technologies' (Zhao, Djonov, & van Leeuwen, 2014) such as social media in which they are deployed. We thus need to isolate each relevant semiotic mode and resource, as well as their particular affordances and functions. Part of this involves understanding exactly what emoji are as technical constructs and the implications this has for how they can be analysed. Emoji are 'encoded' as characters with unique code points in the Unicode Standard. This standard is widely adopted worldwide as a consistent method for encoding typed information in software, enabling cross-platform interoperability. In terms of their visual representation, emoji are 'rendered' by software as glyphs which gives them their distinctive appearance and 'colorful cartoon form' (Davis & Edberg, 2018).

This process is controlled by the software companies who own the platforms and is not standardised by Unicode. For instance, consider Text (1.7).

Text (1.7)　　Day 5 of covid. Feeling a little better. Still no taste or smell. Does anybody know how long that takes to come back I can't taste my coffee☕ 😭

The first emoji in the sequence ending Text (1.7) is the HOT BEVERAGE, which has the unique hexadecimal code point U+2615 and is rendered as the glyph ☕. The final emoji, LOUDLY CRYING FACE, has the code point U+1F62D and is rendered as 😭.

As Unicode characters, emoji form part of a designed and institutionalised pictographic lexicon defined by the Unicode Consortium's bureaucratic processes. This consortium is a conglomerate of entities that controls which characters are added to the Unicode Standard. A total of 674 emoji were added to Unicode in 2010 and their numbers have increased with each new version of the standard. The consortium's voting members include technology companies such as Adobe, Apple, Facebook, Google, Microsoft, and Netflix, institutional members like the Ministry of Endowments and Religious Affairs of Oman and the University of California at Berkeley, supporting members like Emojipedia, and a variety of associate and individual members (Unicode Consortium, 2021a). The Emoji Subcommittee, a part of Unicode's Technical Committee, evaluates proposals for new emoji based on various inclusion criteria, which will be discussed in further detail in Chapter 2.

Emoji's visual presentation as coloured glyphs also depends on the communicative channel used to create or read a social media post. Unlike encoding, the visual 'rendering' of emoji is controlled by the particular vendor (operating, software system, or platform) applying the font to the Unicode characters. For instance, if I enter the HOT BEVERAGE emoji from Text (1.7) into Twitter, the emoji will be rendered as a Twemoji, the distinctive rendering style used by Twitter, and displayed as: ☕. Therefore, it will have a different visual appearance compared to the emoji typed in Microsoft Word, which would display as ☕. Twemoji were created by Twitter designers working in collaboration with the company Iconfactory (Twitter, 2020). Vendors display emoji differently to showcase the unique branding and visual style they wish to project. According to its designers, the flat, gradient-free visual design of Twemoji aims to convey 'light-hearted, fun versions of the familiar icons users around the world know and love' in a visual style 'that would be easily identified as uniquely Twitter's' (Iconfactory, 2022). Twemoji have a minimalist, 'flat' design, with rounded shapes, dots, and lines used to articulate facial expressions, and without shading or 3D effects. In terms of colour palette, Twemoji 'tend to use colors that are similar to – or at least complement – the Twitter logo' (Gray & Holmes, 2020, p. 16). Figure 1.1 shows instances of Twemoji

Figure 1.1 Examples of Twemoji rendering of emoji from the Unicode 'Smileys and People' category

from the 'Smileys and People' category in the current version, Twemoji 14.0 v. This release of Twemoji includes 3,245 emoji which map to Unicode 14. All emoji in this book will be presented in this style as it is open-source and our main corpora were collected from Twitter.

To refer to emoji, we will use the naming convention adopted in Unicode, the Common Locale Data Repository (CLDR) Short Name, for instance, 'HOT BEVERAGE' for '☕'. The Common Locale Data Repository (CLDR) project, run by the Unicode Consortium, aims to provide locale data (e.g. relating to different languages) in an interoperable XML format so that it can be used in a variety of computer applications. For instance, emoji will have different CLDR Short Names depending on language, and these may be provisional for new emoji and change with version releases. However, CLDR Short Names should not be confused with the meaning of an emoji, which will instead be analysed using close text analysis and corpus-based methods. As visible in Text (1.1) and Text (1.7), because emoji are technically characters, they appear in-line with the rest of the written characters in the post (e.g. letters, digits, and symbols). This also means that the user can enter emoji through the keyboard, or a palette menu, without the author leaving the post's preparation window.

While emoji in their rendering as glyphs are images, their visual meaning potential is constrained. They cannot incorporate free-form components and are limited to the small size of accompanying textual characters. Their visual rendering also tends to be stylised rather than realistic, as seen in Figure 1.1. Emoji tend to have a limited degree of visual specificity, in part due to their constrained size. Paradoxically, it is this under-specification that means they are open-ended enough to enter into distinct relations with their co-text, and, in effect, make more complex meanings. We will return to these ideas about emoji encoding and rendering in Chapter 2, where we consider some of the technical dimensions touched on here in more detail, as well as reflect on their important implications for creating and processing corpora containing emoji.

1.4   Emoji as a Social Media Paralanguage

Our approach in this book is driven by observation of the close relationship between emoji and the linguistic meanings in social media posts; in other words, how intertwined emoji appear to be with the meanings made in their co-text. This perspective aligns with a shift in emoji research from attributing independent linguistic meanings to emoji towards analytical frameworks that prioritise the relationship between emoji and language. Research exploring the consistency of emoji interpretation (without the provision of contextual information to interpreters) has found that only a few emoji have completely unambiguous meanings (Częstochowska et al., 2022). As emoji have proliferated and become ubiquitous across digital communication, their apparent pragmatic meanings have become diluted (Konrad, Herring, & Choi, 2020) or have undergone semantic drift (Arviv & Tsur, 2021). Accordingly, an individual emoji may be considered a resource that is 'graphematically ambiguous, as the specific linguistic unit it refers to is not fixed but variable and determined by the context' (Dürscheid & Meletis, 2019, p. 174). As such, emoji are heavily dependent on their linguistic co-text, which acts as 'a clear verbal anchorage' (Sampietro, 2016, p. 110) for the meaning made by the multimodal text as a whole.

As our brief suggestions about the meanings made in Text (1.4), Text (1.5), and Text (1.6) at the beginning of this chapter have suggested, emoji may enact a range of semiotic relations with their co-text. For example, they can serve either a referential role (replacing words) or a modal role (modifying or complementing the surrounding text) (Siever, 2019). Some studies analogise emoji with co-speech gesture and suggest that, like beat gestures accompanying speech, emoji 'are not taking on the function of grammar, but acting in relation to written text' (McCulloch & Gawne, 2018). Other studies broaden the scale of context to consider cultural meanings, and argue that interpreting emoji requires a degree of 'familiarity with the cultural conventions of various aspects of contemporary society, along with an eclectic range of knowledge from

Eastern and Western written and gestural languages, sign languages and even fictional communication systems' (Seargeant, 2019, p. 25).

Given their strong connection to the meanings conveyed in their written co-text, we approach emoji as a form of paralanguage. Paralanguage is semiosis, such as gesture, which is dependent on language (Abercrombie, 1968). This dependency is sometimes described as 'parasitic' since it depends 'on the fact that those who use them are articulate ("linguate") beings' (Halliday & Matthiessen, 1999/2006, p. 606) and will vary depending on the kind of expression plane involved. For instance, in the case of paralanguage where the body is used for expression, this dependency might be 'sonovergent' with spoken language, that is, in-sync or in-tune with the phonological patterns of co-speech, or 'semovergent', that is, coordinating with linguistic meanings made in the co-speech (Martin & Zappavigna, 2019). Thus, rather than attempting to catalogue emoji as a kind of visual lexicon, we focus our attention on modelling the meaning-potential that emoji realise in concert with language.

Even where emoji appear in isolation in a text, they are likely to be dependent on co-occurring language within the broader context of situation, for instance, a preceding linguistic move in an exchange, as suggested by research on the role of images as moves in social media interactions (Jovanovic & van Leeuwen, 2018). The idea that emoji serve a paralinguistic function is also supported by corpus-based studies that have observed their semantic coordination (Gawne & McCulloch, 2019) and syntagmatic alignment (McCulloch & Gawne, 2018) with language. Our approach is also compatible with experimental studies that have suggested that, while emoji have some capacity for very simple sequencing and tend to interact with the linguistic grammatical structure, they do not seem to have developed their own grammatical structural potential (Cohn, Engelen, & Schilperoord, 2019). Emoji's visually stylised under-specification is also one of the reasons that emoji tend to coordinate with more elaborated meanings construed in their written co-text.

However, while we consider emoji as a form of paralanguage, we do not follow the approach taken in some studies of directly equating emoji with gestures (Gawne & McCulloch, 2019; McCulloch & Gawne, 2018). This is because we view emoji as a distinct semiotic mode with its own particular affordances and meaning potential. These affordances are realised via the expression plane of the 'picture character'; a different expression plane to modes which realise their meaning via embodiment (e.g. gesture, posture, voice quality, etc.). As previously mentioned, emoji are a 'designed' resource with specific digital affordances, and it is crucial to isolate these affordances to understand their semiotic potential. In simple terms, rather the studying emoji as if they were images or gestures, we study them for their own distinct meaning potential, taking into account their unique design and digital functions. Studies which liken emoji to gesture appear to be motivated by the apparent iconicity of popular emoji that depict stylised facial expressions and body gestures (e.g. CRYING FACE 😢, ROLLING ON THE FLOOR LAUGHING 🤣, THUMBS UP[3] 👍, OK HAND 👌, CLAPPING HANDS 👏, etc.). However, a direct equivalence of emoji and gesture risks proscription of emoji's meaning potential – as Albert observes, 'the formal analogy between emoji faces in general and the corresponding facial expressions provokes the misleading inference that there must also be a functional analogy' (2020, p. 68). While it may be tempting to suggest that emoji 'share various properties and characteristics with other systems, they're actually adding something quite new to the resources we use to express ourselves' (Seargeant, 2019, pp. 35–6).

This is not to say that emoji are not agnate to other kinds of paralanguage. A dimension that gesture and emoji do share in common is their general dependency on their linguistic co-text. Employing McNeill's (1992) diagnostic criteria for determining the degree to which semiotic modes can function independently of language, Gawne and McCulloch (2019) observe that 'gestures and co-speech emoji are closely integrated into meaning with the accompanying speech/text'. This study suggests that emoji may be likened to gesture since they 'do not decompose into smaller morphological units, they do not show predictable syntax, their meaning is shaped by context-specific use, and there is accepted variation in form' (Gawne & McCulloch, 2019). According to this account, unlike language, emoji are global and synthetic, non-combinatoric, context-sensitive, and do not have standards of form.

1.5   A Social Semiotic Perspective on Emoji–Text Relations

The central goal of a social semiotic approach to communication is to understand how the different resources available to language users make meaning in the contexts in which they are used. In order to achieve this aim, not only do we need a theory of meaning and tools for analysing meaning-making, but we need a principled means for exploring how communicative modalities combine. In addition, we require ways of managing this complexity so that we achieve an elegant description of such semiotic coalescence. To systematically explore the meaning made in emoji–text relations, we will draw on social semiotics and its multimodal concern with understanding the semiotic systems that operate within and across modalities. We will approach these meanings methodically as 'bundles of oppositions' (Ngo et al., 2021, p. 8), adopting the relational theory of meaning that underlies work in Systemic Functional Linguistics (SFL). This kind of approach treats semiosis as a resource rather than a collection of rules

---

[3] Emoji glosses are sourced from https://emojipedia.org/ (accessed 11 November 2020), an emoji dictionary developed by professional lexicographers.

and treats the relations between choices in meaning as key to understanding how those choices function in real-world contexts.

Our functional approach manifests as a concern with three essential functions of language, termed 'metafunctions' by Halliday and Hasan (1985): the ideational (how experience is represented), interpersonal (how relationships are enacted), and textual (how text is organised). For instance, the oppositions in meaning we touched on when considering Text (1.1) at the beginning of this chapter can be seen to span what an SFL perspective on language views as *field* (the domain of experience), *tenor* (the interpersonal construction of relationships and stances), and *mode* (the organisation of the information flow of text) (Halliday & Matthiessen, 2004). In terms of field, the emoji in Text (1.1) contribute to co-construing the kinds of topics and experiences at stake: the MICROBE, AMBULANCE, and HOSPITAL converge with verbal meanings about a health emergency. In terms of tenor, the PENSIVE FACE and BROKEN HEART resonate with details about deaths in the written verbiage to suggest negative emotions about this emergency. In addition, in terms of mode, the emoji themselves act as visual bullet points, organising the text into a list, at the same time as thematising the key information elaborated in the co-text. It is this kind of combinatorial meaning-making that we will focus on in the chapters which follow.

Inspired by work attempting to model paralanguage using Systemic Functional Semiotics recently consolidated in Ngo et al. (2021), one of the major assumptions that we make in this book is that language and other modalities coordinate inter-semiotically to make meaning. As such, we view written language and emoji as complementary semiotic resources and are interested in how they are interwoven, or more technically '*converge*' to create meaning in social media texts. This assumption of complementarity is also in line with earlier research into how images and written language coordinate in picture books where three types of relations of convergence were described: *concurrence* in ideational meaning, *resonance* in interpersonal meaning, and *synchronicity* in textual meaning (Painter & Martin, 2012; Painter, Martin, & Unsworth, 2013). These types of relations were used by Ngo et al. (2021) to explore how gesture and co-speech interrelate in embodied semiosis, resulting in the social semiotic model of paralanguage which informs the analytical approach adopted in this book.

Parkwell's (2019) metafunctional analysis of the meaning-potential of the TOILET emoji aligns with our approach and serves as a noteworthy example of previous social semiotic work specifically focused on emoji. The TOILET was used by popular musical artist Cher to discuss former US President Donald Trump on Twitter without using his name. The study draws on the perspective of multimodality (as outlined by Kress and van Leeuwen, 2001; O'Halloran, 2004) and Zappavigna's (2018) metafunctional analysis of hashtags, to demonstrate how a single emoji can express experiential, interpersonal, and textual functions. The conclusion of the study highlights the highly contextual and flexible nature of emoji as a modality that is 'likely to continue to shift and morph with the changing needs and contexts of social media users' (Parkwell, 2019, p. 9). Another social semiotic study, conducted by He (2022), analysed the use of emoji in news story comments on the Chinese social media platform Weibo. This study adopted the 'intermodal coupling' of semiotic resources as its analytical unit, building upon the notion that meanings created through different modes can be complementary, as proposed by Painter et al. (2013). It found that emoji realise two distinct interpersonal functions: construing attitude targeting linguistic co-text and enacting social bonds with interactants around shared attitudes. These functions encompass emoji's capacity to 'not only directly reflect a commenter's attitude through the depiction of facial expression and gesture, but … to guide readers to detect the buried implications in a text' (He, 2022, p. 12). Other social semiotic studies of Weibo have also identified that emoji offer expanded pragmatic potential in relation to the co-text, serving as 'a multimodal layer of meaning in which emojis may not only substitute, reinforce, or complement text, but also perform speech acts, highlight subjective interpretations, and convey higher degrees of informality and/or casualness' (Yang & Liu, 2021, p. 166).

1.6   Using Corpora to Understand Emoji

The majority of corpus-based studies on emoji have been undertaken within the realm of computational science, utilising a corpus-driven methodology and incorporating machine learning techniques. These studies frequently aim to leverage emoji to enhance sentiment analysis (Kralj Novak et al., 2015; Shiha & Ayvaz, 2017) and typically view emoji as 'emotion tokens' for monitoring sentiment polarity (Wolny, 2016). Some studies aim to create emoji sentiment lexicons in an effort to surpass classification methods that are based on manual annotation or CLDR Short Names (Fernández-Gavilanes et al., 2018; Kimura & Katsurai, 2017; Kralj Novak et al., 2015), while others utilise the Unicode description as a means of classifying emoji (Eisner et al., 2016). A number of studies have centred on emoji sense prediction and disambiguation (Barbieri et al., 2018; Guibon, Ochs, & Bellot, 2018; Shardlow, Gerber, & Nawaz, 2022), and have monitored longitudinal changes in emoji semantics (Robertson et al., 2021).

This methodological context has proven fertile for research into how emoji have been used during the COVID-19 pandemic, primarily through the lens of quantitative studies using corpus-driven or sentiment analysis techniques to analyse emoji frequency and density in social media discourse (Das, 2021). This line of inquiry holds promise for yielding valuable insights that can benefit domains such as public health initiatives and finance. For example, some studies have proposed new methods for understanding the gender-based disparities in the effects of COVID-19 (Al-Rawi et al., 2020) and for charting the correlation between emotional uncertainty and market volatility (Lazzini et al., 2021). Especially germane to this book is the vein of research examining the role of emoji in discourse related to remote work, including studies that examine emoji usage in videoconferencing chat (Dürscheid & Haralambous, 2021) and closed captions (Oomori et al., 2020).

Quantitative studies across various domains have shown a general interest in determining the most commonly used emoji. Unicode releases up-to-date information on emoji usage patterns, including the Unicode Emoji Subcommittee Chair's report on the most frequently used emoji in 2021 (Daniel, 2021). Additionally, various tools such as 'Emoji Tracker' (Rothenberg, 2013) aim to monitor emoji uptake in real-time, offering a dynamic insight into emoji trends and usage patterns. The top ten emoji used worldwide in 2021, according to Unicode (Daniel, 2021), were the following.

1 FACE WITH TEARS OF JOY 😂
2 RED HEART ❤️
3 ROLLING ON THE FLOOR LAUGHING 🤣
4 THUMBS UP 👍
5 LOUDLY CRYING FACE 😭
6 FOLDED HANDS 🙏
7 FACE BLOWING A KISS 😘
8 SMILING FACE WITH HEARTS 🥰
9 SMILING FACE WITH HEART EYES 😍
10 SMILING FACE WITH SMILING EYES 😊

While this kind of frequency list cannot tell us the 'meaning' of these emoji, it does suggest that they are most likely involved with construing broadly positive meanings, depending on how they interact with their co-text.

Efforts within corpus linguistics to study emoji usage are relatively new, likely due to the technical challenges posed by the unique features of emoji that can complicate the use of traditional corpus analysis tools such as concordance software. Chapter 2 will delve into the specific challenges posed by emoji as special characters in corpus processing, exploring both their encoding and rendering. These issues require the analyst to pay close attention to what is actually being counted. While emoji might be roughly interpreted as a 'lexical unit', they are in fact often composed of Unicode character sequences. This means that corpus linguistic software will not necessarily be able to capture all emoji unless it has the capability for recognising these sequences as a single unit. Thus some kind of work-around for concatenating relevant emoji sequences will be required to meaningfully process emoji

(Zappavigna & Logi, 2021). Accordingly, this book relied on a custom script, along with a python library, to accurately count and inspect emoji concordance lines. This approach ensured that Unicode emoji sequences, which are not readily recognisable by standard concordance systems, were properly accounted for.

Corpus-based studies of emoji in linguistics have nevertheless attempted to draw on standard corpus methods such as analysis of frequency lists, concordance lines, and n-grams. Some corpus-based studies have combined pragmatics and corpus analysis methods (Li & Yang, 2018; Pérez-Sabater, 2019; Sampietro, 2019). For example, Kehoe and Gee (2019) undertook a large-scale data-driven corpus pragmatic analysis of emoji use on Twitter, using a corpus of 40 million English and German language tweets. Replicating the results of previous research, the FACE WITH TEARS OF JOY 😂 was the most frequent emoji in this dataset, followed by LOUDLY CRYING FACE 😭 (in English) and the RED HEART ❤ (in German). The study employed collocational analysis to disambiguate different emoji uses. For instance, it distinguished multiple meanings for FOLDED HANDS 🙏, including 'thanking, pleading, praying or giving a high five' (Kehoe & Gee, 2019, p. 2). The study noted that collocational span, as well as the frequent repetition of emoji within tweets, posed challenges for corpus analysis of emoji patterning.

Another relevant study adopting a corpus analytical approach is a multimodal analysis of Facebook posts incorporating emoji and annotated for images (Collins, 2020). This study also found FACE WITH TEARS OF JOY 😂 to be the most frequent emoji. Echoing the challenges noted by Kehoe and Gee (2019), the study suggested that the traditional concept of a collocational span, established as useful for work on written text, was problematic for exploring emoji and for relations of images to text. These issues were somewhat ameliorated when dealing with images in the corpus by employing a large collocational span of 365 tokens (which was determined from the longest text in the corpus), while keeping a keen eye on confidence measures. The author decided, drawing on Spina's (2019) work on emoticons, that emoji 'should also be investigated within a narrower collocational span (at the "type" unit level), since research has shown that there are conventions for the position of emoji, which interact with the syntax and punctuation of written material' (Collins, 2020, p. 190). In our own work we adopt a similar approach, drawing on collocational patterns and n-grams where possible to both motivate and buttress our more qualitative discourse semantic analysis.

1.7 Corpora Analysed in This Book

In this book we employ a corpus-based approach to understanding the use of emoji in social media posts, informed by a social semiotic orientation to discourse analysis. This kind of methodological position is sometimes termed 'corpus-based discourse analysis' (Baker, 2006; Bednarek, 2009) since the close textual analysis is informed by patterns detected in corpora. This means that we use evidence drawn from corpora created according to specific selection criteria. It also means that, while we ground our analysis in this evidence, we draw on theoretical tools for interpreting the patterns of meaning we observe: in this case, a combination of Systemic Functional Linguistics and Multimodal Discourse Analysis.

A significant limitation of the scope of the corpus data that we consider is that we only analyse emoji used in English language posts. This choice was largely a pragmatic one, based on the linguistic proficiency of the authors and their areas of expertise relative to the complexity of the multimodal meaning-making encountered in the social media texts collected. Future work will be needed to explore emoji used with a wider range of languages, each of which might involve different systems of meaning-making. Such studies are needed to address popular claims that emoji offer a kind of 'universal' language that bridges cultural contexts (Abel, 2019). Some corpus-based cross-cultural work is emerging in this area, often tracking how a particular emoji is used across multilingual contexts. For instance, kissing face emoji have been shown to exhibit cultural variation within Europe (Sampietro, Felder, & Siebenhaar, 2022), and predominantly Western users of Twitter associate different emoji to feelings of surprise and trust than users of Chinese social media platform Weibo do (Li et al., 2019).

Four corpora are used in this book. All posts are anonymised for identifying information such as names and locations. For instance, usernames are replaced with '@user'. The first is the Sydney Emoji Corpus, which was primarily used for exploratory analysis, drawing on work presented in Logi and Zappavigna (2021b) for mapping out emoji meaning potential. This is a relatively small corpus of approximately 1,000 social media posts and digital messages collected from undergraduate university students across a range of platforms and services.[4] Its constrained size made it suitable for close, explorative, and detailed discourse analysis. The general aim of this initial work was to identify the various ways in which emoji can coordinate with language in order to make meaning. The functions and patterns of meaning identified by this initial analysis were then explored in a larger corpus, the Hot Beverage Emoji Corpus, approximately 2.5 million tweets containing the HOT BEVERAGE ☕ emoji. This corpus was created by removing retweets and tweets by bots from a larger 12 million tweet corpus collected using the Twitter Application Programming Interface (API). It was also processed to include only English language tweets. The most frequent emoji in the Sydney Emoji Corpus and Hot Beverage Emoji Corpus are shown in Table 1.1.

[4] Demographic information was collected in this study but are not reported here since sociolinguistic variables are not our current focus.

Table 1.1 *Emoji frequency list for the Sydney Emoji Corpus and the Hot Beverage Emoji Corpus*

	Sydney Emoji Corpus			Hot Beverage Emoji Corpus		
N	CLDR Short Name	Emoji	Frequency	CLDR Short Name	Emoji	Frequency
1	RED HEART	♥	195	HOT BEVERAGE	☕	13,169
2	FACE WITH TEARS OF JOY	😂	118	RED HEART	♥	1,320
3	SMILING FACE WITH HEART-EYES	😍	114	SUN	☀	1,082
4	SMILING FACE WITH SMILING EYES	😊	91	SMILING FACE WITH SMILING EYES	😊	750
5	LOUDLY CRYING FACE	😭	88	HUGGING FACE	🤗	494
6	TWO HEARTS	💕	75	CHERRY BLOSSOM	🌸	490
7	FACE BLOWING A KISS	😘	71	SUNFLOWER	🌻	485
8	PARTY POPPER	🎉	65	COOKING	🍳	453
9	SPARKLES	✨	54	FACE BLOWING A KISS	😘	422
10	SLIGHTLY SMILING FACE	🙂	54	FACE WITH TEARS OF JOY	😂	389

The Sydney Emoji Corpus spanned posts across a range of social media platforms (e.g. Twitter, Facebook, Instagram, etc.); however, the Hot Beverage Emoji Corpus contained only tweets. While this poses a potential limitation for the work presented in this book, we did not notice a large variation in the functional potential of emoji across platforms. However, readers are advised that particular platform constraints and affordances may influence the ways in which emoji can be used. As we will explore in Chapter 2, in terms of the rendering of emoji as colourful glyphs (as opposed to their encoding as Unicode characters), emoji will have a different visual appearance that varies with platform, software, and operating system.

Two specialised corpora are used in this book to explore how emoji function to support ambient affiliation, in terms of both dialogic affiliation (where users interact with each other) and communing affiliation (where there is little direct interaction). The corpus used for the first scenario is the Quarantine Hotel Food Review TikTok Comment Corpus, employed in Chapter 7 to explore the role of emoji in negotiating affiliation in interactions between TikTok creators and commenters. This corpus was created by extracting TikTok comments from the comment feed of a TikTok video series about a Creator's experience of the food delivered to their room during a fourteen-day isolation in a quarantine

Table 1.2 *Emoji frequency list for the Hotel Quarantine TikTok Comment Corpus and the #Domicron Corpus*

	Quarantine Hotel Food Review TikTok Comment Corpus			#Domicron Corpus		
N	CLDR Short Name	Emoji	Frequency	CLDR Short Name	Emoji	Frequency
1	FACE WITH TEARS OF JOY	😂	700	FACE WITH SYMBOLS ON MOUTH	🤬	1,196
2	SMILING FACE WITH HEARTS	🥰	660	POUTING FACE	😡	477
3	PLEADING FACE	🥺	309	BACKHAND INDEX POINTING DOWN	👇	431
4	GRINNING FACE WITH SWEAT	😅	283	FACE WITH ROLLING EYES	🙄	350
5	ROLLING ON THE FLOOR LAUGHING	🤣	204	FACE WITH MEDICAL MASK	😷	247
6	FLUSHED FACE	😳	177	ROLLING ON THE FLOOR LAUGHING	🤣	234
7	HEART SUIT	♥	166	THINKING FACE	🤔	233
8	SMILING FACE WITH HEART-EYES	😍	133	FACE WITH TEARS OF JOY	😂	218
9	LOUDLY CRYING FACE	😭	128	CLAPPING HANDS	👏	205
10	RED HEART	❤	107	PILE OF POO	💩	184

hotel. This corpus included all exchanges between users in these comment feeds (5,386 posts, 60,496 words). The second corpus is the #Domicron Twemoji Corpus, collected during a period in which the Australian state of New South Wales was emerging from a COVID zero policy to an approach politicians termed 'living with COVID'. 'Domicron' was a pun amalgamating 'Dominic' and 'Omicron' (a COVID-19 variant), employed as a way of attacking the performance of the Australian state of NSW's Premier (head of government) Dominic Perrottet. This corpus contained 4,275 tweets containing one or more emoji together with the hashtags #Domicron or #LetItRipDon (117,666 words) and is used to explore how users commune around or contest social bonds tabled in tweets. The most frequently used emoji in the two specialised corpora are shown in Table 1.2.

1.8   Structure of This Book

This book is structured so as to consider the relationship of emoji to their written co-text in a systematic way. We will begin in Chapter 2 by addressing the difficult and interesting problems that emoji pose for corpus analysis.

This chapter will explore the technical dimensions of emoji, considering their affordances as 'picture characters' that are encoded as Unicode and visually rendered as glyphs. Chapter 3 then articulates the theoretical approach to emoji–text relations that undergirds the corpus-based discourse analysis undertaken in the rest of the book, focusing in particular on the logic underlying our position that emoji function as paralanguage. The chapter will then present our framework for analysing emoji–text convergence that incorporates three simultaneous dimensions: textual synchronicity, ideational concurrence, and interpersonal resonance (as flagged in the relations we discussed for Text (1.1) at the start of this chapter). The three chapters that follow pick up each of these types of relations in turn, considering emoji one metafunction at a time at the level of discourse semantics.

Following this metafunctional exploration, Chapters 7 and 8 consider how these kinds of relations can act in the service of affiliation in terms of how social media users commune around or negotiate social bonds. We then consider in Chapter 9 the impetus towards customisation and personalisation in visual glyphs, as social media users seek to make meanings beyond Unicode character constraints with the use of digital stickers, GIFs, memes, and other kinds of visual phenomena. The book concludes by reviewing the meaning potential of emoji and visual social media paralanguages in terms of what they tell us about the development of digital communication, intermodal semiosis, and society.

2   Technical Dimensions
The Encoding and Rendering of Emoji

2.1   Introduction

Emoji, along with other kinds of non-canonical tokens, present a set of interesting practical and conceptual challenges to text analysts wishing to avoid factoring out their non-trivial affordances as digital resources. This chapter delves into some of the key technical dimensions of emoji as Unicode characters. While these dimensions are often glossed over, they are critical to understanding how emoji make meaning. The details of how emoji are encoded and rendered are also important to their proper handling and processing in corpus-oriented studies. Emoji are semiotically slippery because their meaning potential is inflected both by their *encoding* as Unicode characters and by their dynamic *rendering* as small graphical icons in the form of coloured glyphs that vary in visual presentation across platforms, operating systems, and software versions. This means that, like other semiotic resources commonly used in social media such as hashtags (Zappavigna, 2018), emoji's range of potential semiotic functions are interwoven with their technological affordances.[1]

These affordances mean that, while emoji draw on the visual mode in their rendering as small icons, they are presented in line with other characters, and thus can enter into seamless syntagmatic relations with their co-text. In this way, as picture characters, they are 'a phenomenon *sui generis* somewhere between images and logograms' (Albert, 2020, p. 77). A stronger version of this characterisation is that emoji 'constitute a distinct modality from text or images' (Cappallo et al., 2018) and, as such, should be approached in terms of their own unique affordances. As we flagged in Chapter 1, the contiguous in-line coordination of emoji with the surrounding co-text is a technical affordance. Emoji and the other characters in, for instance, a tweet can

---

[1] The concept of 'affordance' refers to what a user can do with a technology. It was first introduced by Gibson (1979) in his theory of human perception and has since been applied to fields such as design (Norman, 1988) and human–computer interaction (McGrenere & Ho, 2000). When it comes to digital technologies, the term has been crucial in understanding how technology shapes social interactions (Hutchby, 2001) and how social interactions shape technology.

all be presented in formation since they are all technically glyphs representing standard Unicode characters, even though we tend to think of them as different kinds of phenomena. Where emoji and other characters differ is in what
the glyph displays: a small pictorial image (e.g. 💉) in contrast to a letter (e.g.
W), digit (e.g. 5), or symbol (e.g. $).[2] Recognition of this enigmatic distinction
informs our broader motivation for approaching emoji as a form of paralanguage, given the general orientation of images to realising more fuzzy, topological meaning and language's orientation to typological meanings (Lemke,
1998). It also undergirds prioritising the analysis of emoji–text relations in our
text analysis. It does not, however, constitute an argument that emoji's status as
paralanguage means that they cannot be systematically analysed with linguistic or multimodal tools. Rather, as a paralinguistic semiotic system, they are
highly dependent on language and their technical instantiation encourages this
dependency.

Because emoji are encoded as characters and rendered as graphics, they
enact affordances from both modalities. Approached as a visual resource and
from the perspective of their *rendering* as a glyph by a font, emoji might be
thought of as a kind of graphical icon or 'graphicon', as in studies such as
Herring and Dainas (2017). This kind of classification groups emoji with other
visual phenomena often embedded in social media texts, such as digital stickers, memes, and GIFs. Graphicons afford to digital communication a high
degree of '*communicative fluidity*, where communication can be smoother
and more seamless because of the multiple channels we can tap to express ourselves' (Lim, 2015, p. 2, emphasis in original). As we will see in Chapter 9,
these kinds of graphical resources have arisen with the 'demand for customizable glyphs', generated by a pressure to be able make meanings beyond what
is possible inside the constraints of any single encoding standard (Loomis,
Winstein, & Lee, 2016, p. 2).

For example, a variety of graphicons have become prevalent in discourse
about vaccination, a widely discussed and heavily debated issue during the
ongoing COVID-19 pandemic. In addition to the use of the SYRINGE 💉
emoji, social media posts contributing to this discourse often make use of
visual resources such as GIFs and digital stickers that represent vaccination
(Figure 2.1). These resources may coordinate with the written verbiage in a
post in a variety of ways in terms of its multimodal structural layout. However,
since they are not standardised characters, they cannot occupy the same special
seamless role as Unicode emoji within the written text. Instead, the particular
platform would need to offer a way of emulating this Unicode character

---

[2] While these are the main types, Unicode also includes other characters such as control characters
which control the flow of text and formatting, non-printing characters (e.g. spaces and line
breaks), diacritic marks, special characters, and historical scripts.

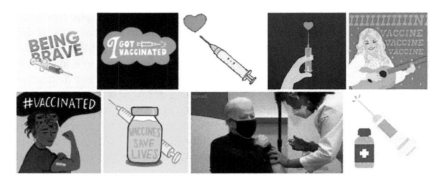

Figure 2.1 GIFs and digital stickers used to express ideas about vaccination in social media paralanguage

integration by presenting the embedded image with the same scale and leading as adjacent text (see, e.g. Figure 9.2 in Chapter 9). Most social media platforms offer particular layouts for incorporating multimedia that tend to foreground what they consider to be the primary aspect of a post. Another complicating factor, which we will return to in Chapter 9, is that graphicons do not necessarily incorporate only one semiotic modality. The examples in Figure 2.1 are multimodal ensembles, involving graphical icons (e.g. a love heart), motion (e.g. the action of syringe being pushed to release a love heart icon) and text (e.g. the phrase '*I got vaccinated*').

2.2   How Emoji Are Developed

Emoji are a special and expanding set of Unicode characters. For an emoji to be included in Unicode it must go through an approval process via the Unicode Consortium Emoji Subcommittee.[3] Emoji are selected on the basis that they have broad relevance and meet a number of criteria. The particular inclusion and exclusion factors that the committee consider when assessing an emoji proposal are summarised in Table 2.1. According to the selection process, emoji are expected to be distinctive but not so specific that they can only represent one idea. Instead they should have multiple potential senses beyond their literal or iconic meaning: for instance, an emoji might encompass metaphorical or symbolic meanings, and the most frequently used emoji tend to enable non-literal senses (Daniel, 2021). An example is the PRETZEL emoji 🥨, which was proposed as a Unicode character in 2016. The authors of the proposal

---

[3] The list of 'all emoji that have been requested of the Emoji Subcommittee' is available here: https://unicode.org/emoji/emoji-requests.html.

Table 2.1 *Selection factors for including a proposed emoji character in Unicode*

Selection Factor	Justification	Unicode Requirement
Inclusion	Compatibility	Compatible with frequently used emoji in popular existing systems, such as Snapchat, Twitter, or QQ
	Expected usage level - Frequency - Multiple usages - Use in sequences - Breaking new ground	High frequency of expected use, including multiple senses spanning notable metaphorical references or symbolism (not including puns). Capacity for use in sequences and representing novel concepts
	Distinctiveness	Represents a distinct, visually iconic entity
	Completeness	Fills a gap in existing types of emoji
Exclusion	Petitions/frequency of request	Not considered useful metrics
	Overly specific	Limited to a narrow or restricted usage
	Open ended	One of several possibilities, without any particular advantage or superiority over the other options in its category
	Already representable	Concept can be represented by another emoji or sequence, even if the image is not exactly the same
	Logos, brands, UI icons, signage, specific people, deities	Images unsuitable for encoding as characters
	Transient	Level of usage unlikely to continue into the future
	Faulty comparison	Justification based primarily on being similar to (or more important than) existing emoji
	Exact image	Image unable to be varied
	Region flags without code	Must have a valid Unicode Region Code or Subdivision Code
	Lack of required rights or licence for images	Lack of legal permissions
	Variations of direction	Merely varies orientation of existing emoji.
	Includes text	Incorporates text into the image

offered the following as a synopsis of their rationale for why the emoji should be included in Unicode:

The recognition of the pretzel, imbued with versatile symbolism, is widespread and cross-cultural, despite its long European tradition. The pretzel, a timeless and widely appreciated baked food, has emotional and cultural significance for a lot of people across the world, especially in Europe and America. The pretzel emoji has a potential for versatile usage due its unique looped shape which can be reinterpreted to stand for many things. (Dabkowski & Bai, 2016, p. 2)

Indeed, since the PRETZEL emoji entered Unicode, we can observe that it has been used to construe multiple types of meaning in conjunction with language. These include representing a baked good, suggesting an instance of miscommunication, construing a process of bodily contortion, and acting as a symbol of German identity, as suggested in Text (2.1) to Text (2.4).

Text (2.1)   I ate a pretzel for the first time in my life, very tasty will eat again! 🥨

Text (2.2)   You've contorted yourself into a 🥨 with that one

Text (2.3)   When I send a "🥨" I hope you know you got me twisted.

Text (2.4)   germans will understand 🥨

While the PRETZEL emoji may seem uncontroversial and these kinds of explicit inclusion and exclusion criteria might make it appear that emoji are selected in a relatively objective manner, the process is complex and fraught. Unicode's treatment of emoji proposals has been criticised in terms of the political and cultural factors that influence emoji acceptance. Determining emoji inclusion 'is a significant site of cultural power, as those who set the factors for inclusion and exclusion, and those who vote on individual proposals, are responsible for setting part of the contemporary digital visual lexicon' (Berard, 2018). This raises concerns about who acts as gatekeeper for a system that underlies mass public digital communication itself:

… [as] the content of emoji becomes more visible, publicly contested, and a basis for various social causes, they foster a discussion of who decides what emoji are made, who is making decisions about character standards, and who decides what kinds of symbols and what languages make up the digital cannon. (Berard, 2018)

A critical issue is whether we can trust corporate technology companies to act for the public good. Given that full membership with voting rights can be purchased for a high fee, it is one of the many examples of consolidation of corporate control. These forms of control give institutions power over governing the very parameters of digital communication itself in terms of what can and cannot be expressed. There have thus been calls to democratise the Unicode committee membership selection process to overcome such concentrations of power (Sutton & Lawson, 2017).

Another issue impacting which characters are in Unicode is the rules regarding the inheritance of existing characters. A fundamental premise of Unicode is that no character should be removed. This means that there is some ongoing bias toward Japanese-specific characters:

Beyond the meek listing of 10 national flags in the original sets (later remedied by the inclusion of most United Nation flags), the Unicode set of emoji remains highly biased toward Japanese culture up to this very day. Despite the famous addition of taco to the emoji syllabary and its 'diversification' through six skin tones (by 'diversification modifiers' in 2015), there persists a disproportional representation of Japanese cultural icons, such as sembei, 煎餅 (rice crackers); love hotels; tengu, 天狗 (mythological creatures); Japanese driving learners' permit emblems; and curry rice. (Abel, 2019, p. 34)

As we will explore in more detail in Section 2.3 when we deal with emoji sequences and modifiers, at the heart of Unicode is a deeply problematic conception of what counts as a 'default' or 'neutral' icon. This involves questions about how diversity of experience should be represented without creating emoji that are too specific to be flexibly applied. Debate over emoji diversity has generated a range of initiatives such as 'Emojination', who campaigned for the inclusion of emoji such as WOMAN WITH HEADSCARF 🧕 (enabling representation of women wearing a Hijab), DUMPLING 🥟, and PERSON IN A STEAMY ROOM 🧖 (enabling representation of people using a sauna). Successful campaigns by other organisations include the call for an emoji for representing menstruation (DROP OF BLOOD 🩸) and for a mosquito emoji to assist with public health messaging (MOSQUITO 🦟). Vendors have also changed their rendering of emoji to reflect social values or concerns, for instance, Apple replaced its WATER PISTOL (originally PISTOL in Unicode 6.0) emoji, which it depicted as a handgun in iOS 8.3 with a design resembling a water pistol toy in iOS 10.0. Microsoft's rendering of this emoji transitioned from a space ray gun to a handgun and finally to a water pistol. In 2021 many platforms changed their rendering of the SYRINGE emoji to remove depiction of blood (suggestive of drawing blood or blood donation) to an empty needle barrel to accommodate meanings related to vaccination relevant to the communicative context of mass vaccination during the COVID-19 pandemic.

2.3   Encoding Emoji

Encoding refers to the process of translating one representation of data into another. It is a fundamental aspect of how emoji are processed so that they can be understood by the technology underlying social media platforms. In general terms, encoding is a process that enables the software you use, for example, word processing software, to interpret the raw binary data of a file: the 0s and 1s that make up that file on the disk. Unicode code points are numerical values written in hexadecimals with U+ used to indicate their connection to Unicode. Unicode code points can be stored in a file or sent over a network in a number of different 'encodings'. Examples of these encodings are UTF8 and UTF16, each of which have a different representation when converted to bytes. For example, the code point for the HOT BEVERAGE emoji is U+2615, which is represented in UTF 8 as the hex sequence E2 98 95, which corresponds to the binary numbers shown in Figure 2.2. Decoding reads those bytes and converts

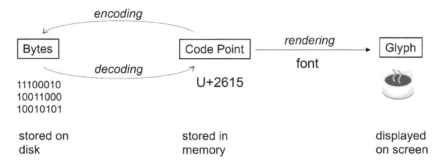

Figure 2.2 An overview of how an emoji code point becomes a picture character on a screen

them back to the code point when the software reads the file. Another process, that of rendering, is used to express the Unicode code point as a glyph, enabling the kind of visual typography that is presented to the user on the screen when using software, as further explained in Section 2.4. This process allows the HOT BEVERAGE emoji to be presented as ☕.

The details of emoji encoding and rendering are explained in the sections which follow. These technical details are important to understand as they impact not only how we process and count emoji in files for corpus-based and quantitative projects, but also how we consider issues relating to semiotic mode and visual representation in qualitative and multimodal studies.

2.3.1   Unicode Characters

While the concept of a digital character might seem rudimentary, an accurate definition is actually quite complex. Emoji, although they are presented to users in social media texts as small images (as we covered above), are characters defined by the Unicode Standard (hereon Unicode). This is an encoding standard produced by the Unicode Consortium which is used across software, platforms, and protocols worldwide in the processing, storing and interchanging of textual data for most languages (Unicode Consortium, 2021b). A character is usually defined as a letter or symbol in written communication, although in the context of digital encoding, a precise definition is quite difficult to encapsulate due to the many edge cases that have to be considered. Characters include graphemes and symbols, such as letters, punctuation marks, digits, whitespace, and control characters (e.g. carriage return). While Unicode provides a code point, name, and keywords for each emoji, it does not define how an emoji should be visually presented. As Section 2.4 will outline, this visual presentation is managed by the way platforms and software choose to render characters. We will refer to emoji throughout this book using their Common Locale Data Repository (CLDR) Short Name, e.g. HOT BEVERAGE for ☕. CLDR Short Names provide a standardised and human-readable identifier for each emoji, allowing them to be easily referenced and used in software and other forms of digital communication; however, they should not be confused with the 'meaning' of an emoji.

Unicode's provision of a unique code point for every character (e.g. U+2615 for ☕) was aimed at unifying the hundreds of different character encodings that it inherited from historical computer representations of different languages. It was a reaction to the fact that a single encoding that could accommodate all the letters, punctuation, and other kinds of symbols used in a single language, let alone all languages globally, did not exist. Unicode also aims for characters to be independent of software, platform, or language, and to allow more character sets than are accounted for by ASCII (American Standard Code for Information Interchange). This includes an attempt to overcome incompatibilities between different character encodings in processing multilingual scripts. Unicode can currently encode approximately 1.1 million characters as code points. However, problems and controversies remain, such as how Chinese characters are handled (Lu, 2019).

Code points are abstract representations that do not specify how they should be visually displayed. In the event that a software application does not support a particular Unicode code point, the result can be an incorrect display, such as a square box, a question mark, or a combination of junk characters. This can create problems when these code points are included in a corpus, as it can be difficult to identify the original code point and to correctly display the intended emoji (glyph) in concordance software if the issue is not addressed during corpus construction.

Since Unicode is so foundational to contemporary digital technology it needs to be a relatively stable standard. Thus applications for new characters pass through a long review process and are required to adhere to a set of guidelines (Unicode Consortium, 2022b). However, Unicode is also a system that has inherited the products of older practices and hence some emoji have been included simply to complete existing partial sets of characters or to integrate with widely used fonts or other existing corporate standards. A full history of emoji evolution and politics is beyond the scope of this book. It is nevertheless important to note that emoji are a 'designed' semiotic system, and that this design occurs within the institutionalised context of the Unicode consortium whose power structures and skewed representation impact the kinds of discourses of 'diversity, globality and neutrality' it projects (Katsumata, 2022, p. 21). Specific emoji cannot be customised, aside from some of the limited choices afforded by modifiers and sequences that we will cover in the next section.

2.3.2   *Emoji Code Points, Modifiers, and Sequences*

While emoji can be encoded as unique code points, this only enables simple emoji to be expressed. The way the Unicode consortium decided to develop emoji has meant that single code points are often inadequate for reflecting the complex experience of contemporary social life. The development of Unicode emoji is an example of technology producers failing to understand that technology is not neutral and that constructing a framework for expressing visual meanings is essentially an ontological task that is likely to embed the world-view of the people creating the framework. Unicode has been heavily criticised for drawing on a 'White Male'-centric perspective in this process. The consortium failed to adequately account for non-Western, non-White, non-binary, and inclusive worldviews, largely because Unicode initially did not recognise the social and political dimensions of the semiotic technology they were developing. The consortium claimed that the yellow colour used for body parts and people in the original emoji set was 'similar to that used for smiley faces', implying that this renders the visual choice benign. They also stated that the representation was 'intended to be generic and shown with a generic (non-human) appearance' (Davis & Edberg, 2018). However, it is questionable whether such a choice could ever bypass the complexity of issues inherent in representing humans and their experiences. Indeed the yellow emoji have been criticised as in fact solidifying a position of colourblind racism (Miltner, 2020).

In response to this criticism, Unicode attempted to express 'more human diversity' (Davis & Edberg, 2018) in emoji through the use of emoji modifiers and sequences. Modifiers that express skin tone and gender differences were implemented by a modifier character placed immediately after a 'base' emoji. For example, to represent the VULCAN SALUTE emoji in light skin tone , this would be encoded as the sequence, U+1F596 U+1F3FB, where U+1F596 is the VULCAN SALUTE base emoji and U+1F3FB is the skin modifier (Figure 2.3). These skin tone modification choices were based on dermatological Fitzpatrick skin phototypes, which classify human skin colour using a numerical classification schema based on skin pigment and photosensitivity (Fitzpatrick, 1988).

The Unicode skin tone modifiers remain problematic since they were themselves 'shaped by an institutionalized form of colorblind racism which insists that concerns regarding racial representation and identity are irrelevant to "neutral" technical systems and workplaces' (Miltner, 2020, p. 517). The entire model by which base emoji are altered through emoji sequences to represent racial diversity has been noted to re-centre and reinforce whiteness 'as the unmarked baseline from which human characters may be otherwise superficially racialized through the application of skin-tone' (Sweeney & Whaley, 2019). Behavioural experiments have shown that emoji are a salient indexer of

Skin tone		Light	Medium light	Medium	Medium dark	Dark
Code	U+1F596	U+1F596 U+1F3FB	U+1F596 U+1F3FC	U+1F596 U+1F3FD	U+1F596 U+1F3FE	U+1F596 U+1F3FF
Emoji						

Figure 2.3 Examples of the skin tone modifier acting on the Twitter rendering of the Vulcan salute base emoji

identity, with readers tending to ascribe ethnic identity to an author on the basis of emoji skin tone (Black for dark skin tone and white for light or no tone (yellow default)) (Robertson, Magdy, & Goldwater, 2021).

In order to represent other kinds of diversity beyond skin tone, it is necessary to use emoji 'Zero Width Joiner' (ZWJ) sequences. These incorporate the invisible ZWJ character to create sequences of emoji that are rendered as a single glyph. ZWJ is a Unicode character that concatenates two or more other characters together in sequence by telling the software that a single glyph should be presented if possible. For example, the symbol for MAN SINGER emoji 🧑 is encoded as U+1F468 U+200D U+1F3A4, where U+1F468 is the MAN emoji 👨, U+200D is the ZWJ, and U+1F3A4 is the MICROPHONE emoji 🎤. However, if the particular software rendering the emoji character does not recognise or support this sequence, the ZWJ character will be ignored and the separate emoji will be displayed as a 'fallback' (e.g. Figure 2.4).

Again, these kinds of emoji sequences are problematic in terms of how they implicitly construe what is 'default' and 'normal'. Other dimensions alongside 'default whiteness', such as 'default atheism' instead of religious adherence, have been noted in the choice to explicitly include particular 'religious' emoji (McIvor & Amesbury, 2017). In this way, what might be otherwise considered simply a technical choice in fact embeds assumptions about what counts as default and what is peripheral. Thus by 'including and prioritising certain resources for making meaning and excluding or backgrounding others, software developers define the semiotic potential of software tools' (Djonov & van Leeuwen, 2018, p. 248).

In addition to sequences enabling human attributes and identities to be expressed in emoji characters, other kinds of emoji sequences include the use of variation selector-16. This is an invisible code point for enabling a

CLDR short name	Code	Emoji	Fallback
office worker: medium-light skin tone	U+1F9D1 U+1F3FD U+200D U+1F4BC		
woman factory worker: medium-light skin tone	U+1F469 U+1F3FC U+200D U+1F3ED		
woman technologist: light skin tone	U+1F469 U+1F3FB U+200D U+1F4BB		
man: dark skin tone, curly hair	U+1F468 U+1F3FF U+200D U+1F9B1		
woman: medium-light skin tone, red hair	U+1F469 U+1F3FC U+200D U+1F9B0		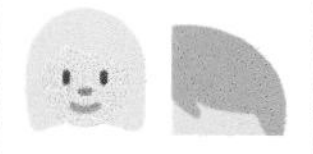

Figure 2.4 Examples of emoji sequences and their fall-back positions

preceding character to be displayed with emoji presentation if it defaults to text presentation (see Figure 2.6). Examples include flags (e.g. ⒜ Regional Indicator Symbol Letter A + ⒰ Regional Indicator Symbol Letter U = 🇦🇺) and keycap sequences that combine a keycap character with another character: (e.g. U+23 U+FE0F U+20E3 = #️⃣). As we will explore in Section 2.8, emoji sequencing creates sizeable problems for corpus analysis of emoji. Most concordance software does not have the capacity to deal with emoji sequences, potentially rendering frequency counts for particular emoji inaccurate. For instance, take the example given earlier regarding the presentation of MAN SINGER 🎤 in particular software environments. This also has implications for corpus processing since the 'fallback position' that occurs when software does not recognise an emoji sequence means that a single instance of this emoji will contribute to the counts for both MAN 👨 and a MICROPHONE 🎤 emoji (the base emoji for the sequence).

2.4   Rendering Emoji as Glyphs: Emoji Display across 'Vendors'

While Unicode defines the code point and CLDR short name for each emoji, it does not play a role in standardising how they should look in their graphical form. Instead, the visual appearance of an emoji is generated by software when it converts the emoji character into a glyph using a specific font. This is a process known as *rendering*. For example, the Twemoji font will present the HOT BEVERAGE emoji as ☕. Rendering is the purview of what Unicode refers to as 'vendors', entities spanning operating systems, devices, platforms, and software. Emoji are rendered differently depending on design choices vendors make, meaning that they do not each have a single, stable visual manifestation. In addition, as vendors update their technology, they may release new versions of their emoji with differences in their visual presentation. For example, the BRAIN emoji is shown from above in Twemoji 2.3 as ● but has changed orientation in Twemoji 2.4, where it is represented side-on as ●, retaining this depiction into Twemoji 14.0. If a particular emoji is not supported by a vendor (for instance, because it has not yet been implemented in a software update) it will be replaced by a symbol such as a question mark or box which signals to the user that an emoji should appear in this position but cannot be presented. This is particularly problematic for corpus studies and may occur when files are transposed from their original format (e.g. a format native to the social media platform from which they were collected) to the file format required by concordance software or other kinds of processing software.

Figure 2.5 presents different renderings of the HOT BEVERAGE emoji across vendors, providing an indication of the different kinds of visual possibilities. It also includes a sample of emoji versions by vendor to give a sense of how they may change over time. For instance, some versions include steam, latte art, and are more or less stylised, including more or less visual details such as shadows, depth, tone etc. In addition, the Skype versions, which the service refers to as Skype 'emoticons', incorporate simple animations of steam wafting above the cup.

This capacity for multiple renderings means that a text producer, and the recipient or audience of that text, may view different visual presentations of an

	Apple	Google	Facebook	Microsoft	Twitter	Samsung	Skype
Current version							
Older versions (abridged)							

Figure 2.5 Different renderings of the HOT BEVERAGE emoji, U+2615, across a selection of vendors[4]

---

[4] For the full Unicode Standard rendering list, see https://unicode.org/emoji/charts/full-emoji-list.html.

emoji depending on the software and/or device they use to read the text. Thus some studies have suggested that multiple renderings may be associated with miscommunication resulting from variation and ambiguity in how single emoji can be interpreted across platforms (Miller et al., 2016). Many users may be unaware that emoji they use have the potential to appear differently to their followers/interactants (Miller Hillberg et al., 2018). There is even some evidence that a proportion of users would not have published or sent messages containing emoji had they had this awareness (Miller Hillberg et al., 2018).

Some Unicode characters can be displayed both in emoji and text style (generally monochrome), in the same way that a typeface might be presented in italics or bold. For example, during the creation of the HOT BEVERAGE emoji corpus used in this book, instances of the HOT BEVERAGE emoji, when extracted from Twitter via its API in JSON file format, were present in both forms (Figure 2.6). While this may seem innocuous, it will impact correctly counting emoji as the two presentations will not register as the same type of token by corpus processing software and will instead be counted as separate types. Text presentation is influenced by factors such as the text colour setting chosen in a word processor via a font, whereas emoji will not change based on these settings. An operating system may choose the most appropriate style based on context. For example, a full colour emoji may be used for display on screen whereas the black and white text presentation emoji may be used in printing.

Alongside variation in how emoji are rendered across operating systems, software, and devices, some services offer non-Unicode emoji as digital stickers, effectively embedded images customised to reflect their branding. These forms of visual paralanguage will engender all the difficult problems for corpus processing that come with trying to account for multimodal artefacts in systems that have been designed with the assumption that texts are made only of words. We will return to these other kinds of visual paralanguage in Chapter 9.

2.5   Emoji Organisation

As a designed character set, emoji are impacted by the choices made by developers, not only in terms of their visual display but also in terms of their organisation as a character set. Emoji are organised as a kind of 'picture character'

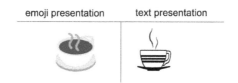

emoji presentation   text presentation

Figure 2.6 Two types of emoji presentation

lexicon by Unicode through its categorisation of emoji into blocks (e.g. 'Miscellaneous Symbols'), categories (e.g. 'Food & Drink'), and subcategories (e.g. Drink), and its allocation of CLDR short names and keywords to emoji. The Unicode CLDR Project notes that rather than generating formal taxonomies, the 'goal of keywords is to define what people might search for in addition to the defined name' (Unicode Consortium, 2022a). Thus emoji organisation and labelling has a potential impact on the way that users select or search for the emoji which they include in their posts. Emoji are organised within Unicode into the following high-level groups: *Smileys & Emotion*; *People & Body*; *Component*; *Animals & Nature*; *Food & Drink*; *Travel & Places*; *Activities*; *Objects*; *Symbols*; *Flags*. This classification for grouping 'related characters together' is presumably based on their purported iconic resemblance to material things, as suggested by their CLDR Short Names and keywords. It also seems to assume both degrees of resemblance and degrees of absoluteness, with the caveat provided by Unicode that the grouping is intended to be 'broad and not exclusive: and any character will match multiple categories' (Unicode Consortium, 2020). For instance, '*Drink*' is a subcategory within '*Food & Drink*' and includes the emoji shown in Table 2.2, which span

Table 2.2 *The Unicode 'Drink' subcategory*

Code	Emoji	CLDR Short Name	Keywords	Code	Emoji	CLDR Short Name	Keywords
U+1F37C		Baby bottle	baby | bottle | drink | milk	U+1F37C		Beer mug	bar| beer |drink |mug
U+1F95B		Glass of milk	drink | glass | glass of milk | milk	U+1F37B		Clinking beer mugs	bar | beer | clink | clinking beer mugs | drink | mug
U+2615		Hot beverage	beverage | coffee | drink | hot | steaming | tea	U+1F942		Clinking glasses	celebrate | clink | clinking glasses | drink | glass
U+1FAD6		Teapot	drink | pot | tea | teapot	U+1F943		Tumbler glass	glass | liquor | shot | tumbler | whisky
U+1F375		Teacup without handle	beverage | cup | drink | tea | teacup | teacup without handle	U+1FAD7		Pouring liquid	drink | empty | glass | spill
U+1F376		Sake	bar | beverage | bottle | cup | drink | sake	U+1F964		Cup with straw	cup with straw | juice | soda | malt | soft drink | water

Table 2.2 (*cont.*)

Code	Emoji	CLDR Short Name	Keywords	Code	Emoji	CLDR Short Name	Keywords
U+1F37E		Bottle with popping cork	bar | beverage | bottle | cup | drink | sake	U+1F9CB		Bubble tea	bubble | milk | pearl | tea
U+1F377		Wine glass	bar | beverage | drink | glass | wine	U+1F9C3		Beverage box	beverage | box | juice | straw | sweet
U+1F378		Cocktail glass	bar | cocktail | drink | glass	U+1F9C9		Mate	drink | mate
U+1F379		Tropical drink	bar | drink | tropical	U+1F9CA		Ice	cold | ice | ice cube | iceberg

milk, hot beverages, alcoholic beverages, various sweet drinks, the action of pouring a liquid, and the state of being hot, cold, sweet, etc.

Most of the emoji in the drink subcategory are depicted as static objects. Exceptions include the POURING LIQUID, CLINKING GLASSES/BEER MUGS, and BOTTLE WITH POPPING CORK emoji, which all include some indication of movement, for instance, through the impact lines in the CLINKING BEER MUGS emoji, used to visually suggest the collision of the mugs together in the process of clinking: . The bubbles and the position of the cork above the bottle are used in the BOTTLE WITH POPPING CORK emoji to suggest the explosion of sparkling liquid (presumably champagne or sparkling wine). Of course, all of these design elements vary by vendor, and as already mentioned, Skype emoji incorporate simple animation.

From a linguistic perspective, emoji involve 'semiotic metaphor' (O'Halloran, 1999, p. 321) since, aside from the minimal implications afforded by motion lines to suggest movement, they must illustrate processes and states as objects. In language this is a form of grammatical metaphor, with activities or properties 'reworded metaphorically as nouns; instead of functioning in the clause, as Process or Attribute, they function as Thing in the nominal group' (Halliday & Matthiessen, 2004, p. 729). This kind of shift has the advantage that complex meanings can be packed into discourse, hence its extensive use in registers such as science and technology discourses (Halliday & Martin, 2003). In a similar way, the ability of emoji to encapsulate complex ideas and cultural meanings as stylised objects means that, in conjunction with language, they can make a multitude of meanings. This can be seen in how the stylised depiction of a smiling face typically indexes positive emotions, rather than a facial expression attributed to an interactant or referent in a text. Thus, while in isolation emoji will generally depict a static tableau of objects, in conjunction with linguistic co-text they can index a great variety of related meanings that eclipse their monomodal meaning potential.

2.6   Semiotic Technologies

The issues in encoding and rendering emoji that have been explored so far are related to larger concerns about how the affordances and constraints of semiotic technologies impact meaning-making:

> The notion of semiotic technology thus signals an interest in technology as integral to multimodal meaning making and as an integrated part of social practices. Digital technologies, including social media, are therefore treated not merely as 'tools', or as technological 'carriers' of semiotic displays, but as social and semiotic artefacts in themselves. A combined interest for multimodal texts, digital technology, and social practices is thus at the core of a semiotic technology perspective. (Zhao et al., 2014, p. 596)

An important variable to consider is the extent to which the platform and device through which an emoji is chosen and shared enables or restricts meaning-making. Users do not typically type emoji directly on a keyboard; rather they pick the emoji they want to use from a searchable palette determined by the application (e.g. Figure 2.7). The CLDR Short Names and keywords associated with emoji via Unicode are relevant here as they will determine, depending on the platform's backend functions, which emoji are presented in response to the user's search term.

Platforms will also suggest emoji to users during the process of text production. This may occur as a list of options based on frequently typed emoji (or some other parameter) before the user has begun to compose the message (left image, Figure 2.8), or as a prediction during typing (right image, Figure 2.8). In this way, the platform technology, and the way it interacts with the Unicode emoji character organisation and keywords, may be deeply involved in the text creation process In terms of the syntagmatic organisation of the text, since emoji predictions are generated after a linguistic item has been entered via the platform interface, this makes emoji more likely to occur directly after related lexis. The kinds of emoji or emoji-like stickers (e.g. Facebook reactions) that platforms prefabricate are another example of the kinds of semiotic influence platforms have over how communication unfolds. Most social media platforms offer selective emotive responses such as liking or favouriting something by clicking an icon. These 'off the shelf' reactions are examples of the ways semiotic technologies direct communicative interactions towards particular repertoires that they then mine for corporate profit (Jovanovic & van Leeuwen, 2018, p. 693).

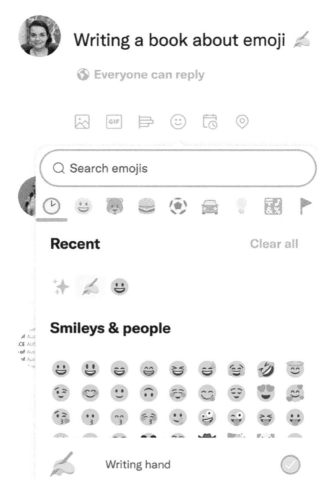

Figure 2.7 Adding an emoji to a tweet through a searchable palette

Further to language-based emoji prediction, it is worth noting here how emoji themselves have become resources in search queries on some platforms. Cappallo et al. (2018) has investigated how emoji might function as search queries for retrieving and exploring visual data on Bing and Instagram, observing how their independence from any specific language and high degree of cultural penetration means that 'emoji can be deployed as a query language in situations where a spoken language might fail' (Cappallo et al., 2018, p. 406). This function echoes the use of emoji in graphicon palettes as symbolic representations of categories of graphicons, as discussed above.

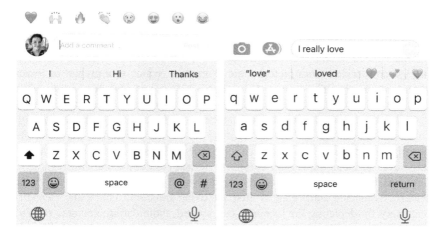

Figure 2.8 Instagram emoji suggestion (left) and iMessage emoji prediction (right) in the Apple iMessage application

2.7 Emoji Aesthetics

Emoji are regularly described as assuming a cartoon-like aesthetic. However, pinning down what this means requires engaging with the concept of 'provenance' in order to trace some of the key visual meanings that may be at stake in emoji design:

The idea here is that we constantly 'import' signs from other contexts (another era, social group, culture) into the context in which we are now making a new sign, in order to signify ideas and values which are associated with that other context by those who import the sign. To take a musical example, in the 1960s the Beatles introduced the sound of the sitar into their music to signify values which, in the 'psychedelic' youth culture of that time, were associated with the sitar's country of origin: meditation, drugs as expansion of consciousness, and so on. The idea of 'provenance' is closely related to the ideas of 'myth' and 'connotation' as introduced into semiotics by Roland Barthes (1972, 1977). (Kress & van Leeuwen, 2001, p. 10)

In terms of provenance, the general aesthetics of emoji design across vendor renderings appear to be influenced by the Japanese traditions of manga, kanji and street signs (Moschini, 2016). For instance, the depiction of a drop of liquid (as found in the CRYING FACE emoji 😢) is borrowed from manga art where it serves as a 'metaphorical figure symbol called *keiyu*' (Wallestad, 2013, p. 5), which can be applied to different parts of the face so as to represent sweat, tears, saliva or nasal discharge, with the meaning of the ensuing composite image adjusting accordingly (Wallestad, 2013). Another prevalent manga convention found in emoji is the exaggeration of size and articulation of the eyes, which in manga are considered 'the locus of facial expressivity' (Katsuno & Yano, 2002, p. 214). This convention was adopted from Disney comics by seminal manga author Osamu Tezuka (Pellitteri, 2018). In turn, manga reflects many conventions of kanji, the Japanese logographic writing system derived from pictographic characters, which to a greater or lesser extent index physical entities (Moschini, 2016). For instance, emoji have inherited a vertical orientation and squared form from kanji via manga.

The influence of manga has also contributed to the cute (in Japanese, *kawaii*), cartoon-like aesthetic of both the original set of emoji and new emoji subsequently introduced by Unicode. This is evident in the endurance of exaggeratedly large eyes in facial expression emoji. As Gn (2018) comments with regards to CAT FACE emoji (😺, 😸, 😻, etc.), rendered glyphs typically include three stylistic features associated with cuteness: first, the emoji are iconic, containing elements necessary for depicting the face of a cat; second, intimidating elements such as sharp teeth are omitted; and third, the face is anthropomorphised, with features rounded. Gn (2018) observes that 'these similarities adequately show how the cuteness of emoji modulates the foreign and unapproachable, by modifying the actual physicality of the object being denoted'. This concords with the connotations of *kawaii* cuteness in Japanese culture, which include 'cute', 'sweet', 'tender', 'childish', 'innocent', 'gentle', 'honest', 'soft', 'small', and 'lovely' (Lieber Milo, 2017, p. 3). In turn, emoji's cuteness contributes to their appeal among users, while the rich catalogue of emoji that index affective states skews their use towards interpersonal meaning. Gn (2018) concludes that 'as a systematic form of cuteness, emoji are rigid instruments of information capital; as compositional pictograms, they turn cuteness into an alternative linguistic tool'.

As far as accounting for the impact of cuteness on emoji semiosis, however, while it may be tempting to link cultural conventions of cuteness to the meaning made by emoji, we must be wary not to privilege the interpretive lens of any particular culture. Thus, while the aesthetic conventions of *kawaii* or cuteness have informed, and continue to influence, the design of rendered emoji glyphs, their adoption across a myriad of cultural communities requires that we analyse their semiosis in each context. We also need to temper the extent to which we privilege the visual representation of any emoji over its interaction with the language it accompanies. As we explored earlier, a key part of emoji's semiotic potential derives from its ability to be ambiguous and flexible, and to make underspecified and layered meanings that are highly sensitive to the co-text. Of course, it is difficult to know just where to draw the line in this respect. For instance, the shift in rendering of the BRAIN emoji from 🧠 to 🧠 in Twemoji versions would seem to result in less of an impact on the emoji's meaning potential compared to the shift of PISTOL/WATER PISTOL from 🔫 to 🔫. Consider, for instance:

Text (2.5)   Go drink ur coffee🔫

Text (2.6)   Go drink ur coffee🔫

In this case the second rendering is more realistic, resembling an actual pistol. Consequently, the meaning realised by the emoji in this text changes substantially depending on which glyph is rendered.

Nevertheless, in interpreting such emoji that may be used in threatening ways, the semiotic technology perspective (outlined in the previous section) should remind us to consider the inherent constraints of the platform. Twemoji are a predefined resource made available by the platform. As such they have become the palette through which all emoji articulation on this platform is filtered. Thus, it is unsurprising that threatening discourse is indeed possible with emoji, and hate speech, a colossal problem in online communication, finds articulation in emoji–language coordination. Hate speech research has shown the extent to which emoji can be weaponised in the service of attacks on groups such as Muslims. For instance, Al-Rawi (2022) has explored the coordination of emoji with anti-Islam hashtags, finding the MIDDLE FINGER 🖕 to be the most frequent emoji employed to direct Twitter hate at Islam, often used in association with the MOSQUE 🕌 and KAABA 🕋. The study also noted that death threats were associated with CROSSED SWORDS ⚔ and the SKULL 💀 emoji, and that apparently positive emoji such as CLAPPING HANDS 👏, THUMBS UP 👍, FACE WITH TEARS OF JOY 😂 and ROLLING ON THE FLOOR LAUGHING 🤣 were used to mock Islam and Muslims, as well as to support and encourage insults and hate speech. Returning to the worries expressed earlier in the chapter regarding how Unicode has chosen to represent diversity, skin tone emoji have been shown to be used in hateful ways as 'a vehicle for *othering*: light=we, dark=you (foreigners)' (Bick, 2020, p. 10). In addition to these obvious uses of emoji to directly express hate, emoji can function within antilanguages as coded expression designed to avoid scrutiny outside a particular community (Halliday, 1976). Alternatively, some groups capitalise on emoji that appear sufficiently innocuous that they are likely to be inadvertently spread by those who do not share the particular values of the host community. An example is ecofascist use of 'harmless-looking environmentally themed emojis – a pine tree, an earth and a mountain – often supported with a Norse/ Proto-Germanic rune Algiz, "ᚱ"' that are unwittingly spread by eco-conscious social media users who do not detect the darker meanings (Allison, 2020, p. 4). We will return to the emblematic use of emoji in Chapter 5.

2.8   Emoji Corpus Construction and Concordancing

Because emoji are Unicode characters, they have the advantage that they can be explored using corpus analysis techniques that work for standard characters. This is not the case for other kinds of visual resources that instead would require the analyst to annotate each instance so that it is readable by a machine. However, incorporating emoji into corpus analysis is not as simple as using the Unicode code points uniquely assigned to each emoji as identifiers in a corpus. This is due to the kinds of emoji modification and sequencing explained in Section 2.3.2. Generally, concordance software does not understand emoji sequences and thus will not handle emoji correctly. In addition, older systems may not support Unicode at all.

To identify all the emoji sequences in the corpora used in this book, the python library, 'demoji 1.1.0' (Solomon, 2021) was used. A python script was written that used this library to create the corresponding emoji frequency lists. The python script was designed to identify, extract, and tally the emoji sequences from the corpus. It was a 'greedy' algorithm in that it looked for the longest matching emoji sequence in order to ensure that the matching was done on the most specific emoji as opposed to the 'base' emoji. A frequent example from the HOT BEVERAGE emoji corpus was the WOMAN RAISING HAND: MEDIUM LIGHT SKIN TONE 🙋 emoji. This emoji is a ZWJ sequence combining:

- PERSON RAISING HAND🙋
- MEDIUM SKIN TONE
- ZERO WIDTH JOINER
- FEMALE SIGN♀

The python script recognised this sequence so that it would be counted as a single token in the word frequency list, rather than multiple tokens. Without this grouping, the emoji would contribute to the count of multiple tokens in the frequency list such as the PERSON RAISING HAND (without skin tone modification) and the FEMALE SIGN. Another issue that may be encountered is that some of the modifying emoji, for instance, the skin modifiers, may be counted as unique tokens.

An additional issue pertinent to corpus processing is that emoji sequences are progressively being created and added to Unicode as more emoji are approved. This means that processing software must always have the most recently provided set of sequences, because if the corpus contains a sequence that is not recognised, this will generate anomalies that may impact the counts of multiple tokens.

Emoji modification and sequencing also means that the researcher building a corpus needs to adopt a consistent and principled strategy about when to collapse or expand categories. This will be dependent on the kinds of questions that the corpus is being used to answer. Nevertheless, issues raised earlier relating to the identities and subject positions that are factored out when diversity is minimised should be taken into account when collapsing categories. An example of choice that a corpus analyst might need to make is whether they want to consider all of the skin tone and gender choices for particular emoji, e.g. for PERSON RAISING HAND ✋ emoji:

- PERSON RAISING HAND: LIGHT SKIN TONE✋
- PERSON RAISING HAND: MEDIUM-LIGHT SKIN TONE✋
- PERSON RAISING HAND: MEDIUM DARK SKIN TONE✋
- PERSON RAISING HAND: DARK SKIN TONE✋
- MAN RAISING HAND✋
- MAN RAISING HAND: LIGHT SKIN TONE✋
- MAN RAISING HAND: MEDIUM-LIGHT SKIN TONE✋
- MAN RAISING HAND: MEDIUM SKIN TONE✋
- MAN RAISING HAND: MEDIUM-DARK SKIN TONE✋
- MAN RAISING HAND: DARK SKIN TONE✋
- WOMAN RAISING HAND✋
- WOMAN RAISING HAND: LIGHT SKIN TONE✋
- WOMAN RAISING HAND: MEDIUM-LIGHT SKIN TONE✋
- WOMAN RAISING HAND: MEDIUM SKIN TONE✋
- WOMAN RAISING HAND: MEDIUM-DARK SKIN TONE✋
- WOMAN RAISING HAND: DARK SKIN TONE✋

Grouping all of these together can be difficult because as modified emoji must be replaced with base emoji. This involves designing the mapping of the modified emoji to the base emoji and then implementing the software to do the mapping.

An example of a study that chose to conflate certain emoji dimensions is an investigation of the most frequent emoji used in 2021 reported by the Unicode Subcommittee Chair, Jennifer Daniel. In this case, the decision was made to contract rather expand gender and skin tone variants:

Please note that gender and skin tone variants are combined into one representative item, to give a clearer picture of how frequently the overall concept of each emoji is used. For example, the frequencies of 👆 👆 👆 👆 👆 👆 and 👆 👆 👆 👆 👆 👆 are combined and represented using 👆. (Daniel, 2021, original emoji replaced with Twemoji rendering)

As this study also notes, when considering emoji usage diachronically, analysts should take care when drawing conclusions about frequency since Unicode is continually evolving. This development means that newer emoji will be reported as having a lower usage since time is needed for them to be distributed across vendors and for users to begin to recognise and use them. In addition, the analyst will need to keep track of how and when each social media post was created so as to preserve the relevant emoji rendering when displaying the output of the corpus analysis. These renderings may become obsolete over time so a mechanism for mapping between historical renderings and Unicode code points may be needed.

2.9   Emoji Corpus Annotation

As we have seen, emoji are more complex technical artefacts than 'words', involving sequencing and modifiers. They are thus more difficult to automatically identify, count, and annotate. Depending on the kind of linguistic analysis to be undertaken, some manual cleaning and tagging of the dataset may be needed. Since in this book we were interested in systematising how emoji make meanings with their co-text, in order to develop our model of emoji–text relations we needed to manually annotate our exploratory dataset (the Sydney Emoji Corpus). This was not only because of the difficulty of accurately processing emoji but because of the complexity of the discourse semantics involved in the emoji–text relations we were exploring, which could not be automatically analysed.

The software used to annotate our exploratory data was WebAnno (Yimam et al., 2013). WebAnno is a Java-based, web-hosted annotation programme that accommodates Unicode characters such as emoji and has a flexible, customisable interface for designing coding rubrics. While many text annotation systems exist, WebAnno was chosen since it offered the functionality to not only annotate particular textual features but also relations between features. This made it amenable to annotating emoji–text relations. The particular discourse semantic features and relations systematised through iterative text annotation using this software are explained in Chapter 3. The aim here is to sketch out our analytical process in a way that may be useful for future studies but is not constrained to the specificities of this particular software, which are likely to rapidly become obsolete as the software evolves.

The dataset of multi-platform social media and text messages was collected using Qualtrics, an online survey instrument, and was converted into .csv file format. It was then uploaded into a new WebAnno project, formatted for one entry per line. The software enabled two kinds of annotation: features in discrete layers and relations between features. Discourse semantic systems (explained in the next chapter) formed the annotation 'Layers' within WebAnno, with subsystems constituting the 'tags' applied with 'tagsets'. Finally, three sets of relations were defined to link coded features.

An example of how these layer features and couplings are shown when coded in the WebAnno interface is found in Figure 2.9. We can see that each individual feature and coupling (explained in Chapter 7) is labelled in the interface and, while it cannot be shown in a static image such as this one, each label is highlighted in bold font when the mouse pointer is held over it. The programme abbreviates the features in the visualisation: Att = Attitude; Ide = Ideation; Pos = Position (relating to the location in the text where an emoji occurs); Pol = Polarity (specifying whether instances of attitude are positive or negative). Coding of emoji resources for these features was conducted by

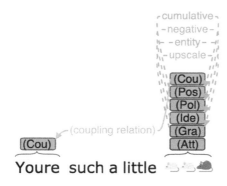

Figure 2.9 An example of a text annotated using WebAnno

interpreting emoji intramodally (within a single mode) and then intermodally in batches of forty to fifty texts. After each batch, the researchers would confer to discuss any issues in the coding rubric or points of interest. In light of revisions to the coding rubric or how it should be applied to particular cases, coding was repeated or updated where necessary.

As reported in Logi and Zappavigna (2021b) in considering the importance of the context of communication for interpreting the meaning of emoji, the authors of texts were interviewed and asked about the tenor of the text (the relationship between the author and recipient or audience), the field of the text (the topic or domain), and the mode (the platform through which the text was produced and disseminated). Annotation results were compared to these descriptions. The degree of convergence (agreement) between the annotation and the authors' descriptions were coded as either 'fully agree', 'partially agree', or 'disagree'. The annotation fully agreed with the author descriptions in 81 per cent of cases, and if including partial agreement, accorded in 93 per cent of instances.

This exploratory coding process gave us a rich understanding of the kinds of relations that emoji can hold with the discourse semantic meanings for which linguistic technicality has already been developed. This enabled us to create system networks for systematising and generalising these relations, as will be presented over subsequent chapters in this book.

2.10   Conclusion

This chapter has introduced the key concepts that are needed to understand both the technical affordances of emoji as picture characters and how these may impact how an analyst interprets the meanings that emoji can make together with written language. As a designed semiotic technology, the affordances of emoji are both enabled and constrained by the technical parameters of the software and hardware involved in their creation and display. These parameters thus may have an impact on the repertoire of possible meanings that might be made with emoji when they are ultimately put to use in social media texts. This makes emoji semiosis highly sensitive to its technological context.

Given the linguistic creativity of social media users and the huge number of potential semiotic permutations and combinations that emoji can enact together with language, this is likely a relation of expansion in meaning potential, or what Lemke has termed a multiplication of meaning:

In multimedia genres, meanings made with each functional resources in each semiotic modality can modulate meanings of each kind in each other semiotic modality, thus *multiplying* the set of possible meanings that can be made (and so also the specificity of any particular meaning made against the background of this larger set of possibilities). (Lemke, 1998, p. 92)

It is to these multiplied meanings that we turn our attention for the remainder of this book.

In the domain of corpus linguistics, emoji present a number of challenges that must be overcome if they are to be successfully processed and analysed in corpora. In particular, an understanding of how emoji are encoded, decoded, and sequenced is especially important for them to be successfully counted. Moreover, analysis of corpora composed of data from multiple vendors may need to account for how emoji are varyingly rendered. In sum, the most important advice this chapter can offer the corpus analyst is to inspect carefully how emoji are incorporated into any corpus that they design, remembering to account for emoji modifiers and sequences, and to factor in how original emoji renderings will be tracked and preserved.

With an understanding of the substantial variation in emoji affordances arising from differences between the vendors, platforms, and devices that encode, decode, and render them, we can proceed in the next chapter to introducing our framework for analysing how emoji make meaning in coordination with language. As we will see, the youth, ubiquity, and ongoing evolution of emoji, coupled with the wide variation in their technical realisation, renders emoji meaning potential richly articulated and affords kaleidoscopic possibilities for intermodal semiosis.

3   Modelling Emoji–Text Relations

3.1   Introduction

This chapter introduces the framework for exploring emoji–text relations used in this book. When attempting to account for how modes combine there are several key theoretical challenges that require the analyst to address important assumptions. These include how systems of meaning across modes 'end up seamlessly instantiated as coherent text', how much of this coordination should be attributed to a single mode or to a higher order semiotic such as a rhetorical pattern, and to what extent modes other than language can be explained using 'hierarchies developed for language' (Ngo et al., 2021, p. 207). In order to manage this complexity, Ngo et al. (2021, p. 208) advise approaching 'models of intermodal relations one metafunction or stratum at a time – taking care to specify which strata or which metafunctions are in focus and, where relevant, which ranks'. Taking this advice, in this book we will focus on the stratum of discourse semantics and explore emoji–text relations by metafunction. Thus, we are concerned with mapping out the resources required to analyse three kinds of convergence relations:

- *concurrence* with ideational meaning
- *resonance* with interpersonal meaning
- *synchronicity* with textual meaning

The chapter begins with an overview of the model of language that we use to undertake our discourse semantic analysis of the written language in our data. Introducing this technicality is important since we are arguing that emoji are highly dependent on accompanying linguistic meaning. To this end we provide a summary of the key discourse semantics systems (experiential, ideational, and textual) developed within SFL for work on language. These systems offer a systematic description of the kinds of meanings with which emoji can coordinate at the discourse semantic stratum. Each of the three chapters which follow will draw on the linguistic framework described in this chapter.

Having outlined the architecture of our linguistic theory, we then introduce the notion of a 'semiotic mode' as developed within research into multimodality. This is necessary for understanding the distinct affordances of both written text and emoji in social media posts. We also consider how relations across modes, in particular between written text and images, have been theorised in multimodal research. Our next step is to explain the kinds of relations we posit are possible between emoji and their co-text as distinct modes, with emoji acting as paralanguage dependent on the comparatively elaborate affordances of written co-text. This enables us to introduce our model of emoji–text relations as the system network in Figure 3.16. This network offers a high-level overview of the types of relations possible and was developed in our exploratory work using the Sydney Emoji corpus (Logi & Zappavigna, 2021b). Chapters 4, 5, and 6 will each elaborate one of the three systems of convergence (concurrence, resonance, and synchronicity) to greater levels of delicacy using the corpus evidence from the Hot Beverage Emoji Corpus, with each chapter exploring a different metafunction in order to manage the significant complexity involved.

3.2   Discourse Semantics Systems for Analysing Linguistic Meanings

This section introduces the approach adopted for exploring the linguistic meanings with which emoji coordinate. In order to explore these meanings, we will conduct our text analysis at the level of discourse semantics, drawing on the linguistic stratification modelled within Systemic Functional Linguistics (Figure 3.1). The discourse semantic stratum describes meaning made at the scale of entire texts and their unfolding. Discourse semantics is a term used to account for two key insights into meaning: that a text is a *semantic* whole rather than simply 'a big sentence', and that *discourse* involves 'text relations beyond the sentence'[1] (Martin, 2014, pp. 6–7). Thus, analysis at the level of discourse semantics aims to account for meanings made beyond the clauses and clause complexes that are the focus of the lexicogrammatical stratum. In turn, patterns in the meaning-making resources at the discourse semantic stratum realise the higher stratum of register, which describes the social situation within which a text is occurring. As such, and reflecting the core principle that language is 'a metaphor for society' (Halliday, 1978, p. 186), applying a discourse semantic lens to the analysis of meaning implies consideration of how texts enact and reflect the social reality they occur in and what role a text is playing in social life (Martin & Rose, 2007).

As mentioned earlier, the SFL model of language also explores semiosis through three metafunctional lenses: interpersonal, ideational, and textual (as suggested in Figure 3.1 by the lines dividing the co-tangential circles into

---

[1] A central idea in Stratificational linguistics.

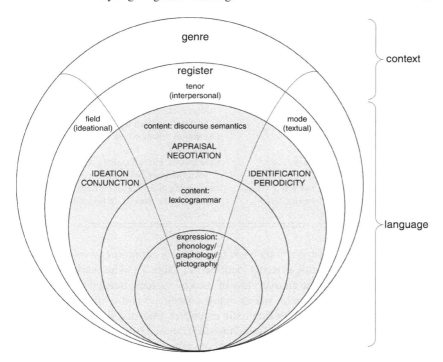

Figure 3.1 The SFL model of language[2]

three). These correspond with the three register variables of tenor, field, and mode, respectively, which we drew on in explaining the meanings made in the tweets used in the opening of this book. The tenor of a text refers to the social relationships it enacts, including the relative status of participants, and the degree of contact and solidarity among them. Field encompasses experiential meaning – the activities and processes in which participants engage. Mode describes the role language is playing; how language is used to achieve the purpose of a text (Halliday & Hasan, 1985). In turn, register variables are realised at the discourse semantic stratum by six semiotic systems: IDEATION, CONNEXION, APPRAISAL, NEGOTIATION, IDENTIFICATION, and PERIODICITY. The relationship between metafunction, register variable, and discourse semantic system is shown in Table 3.1.

---

[2] This illustration of the SFL model of language has been adapted from Martin and Rose (2007, p. 309) to show the names of discourse semantic systems and the resources of the expression plane; at this plane, 'pictography' has been added to 'phonology' and 'graphology' to capture the role of pictorial resources such as emoji in expressing meaning.

Table 3.1 *Metafunction, register, discourse semantics*

Metafunction	Register Variable	Discourse Semantic System	Description of Resources
Ideational	Field	IDEATION	Sequences, figures, and elements representing experience as activities and states
		CONNEXION	Additive, comparative, temporal, and causal relations between figures
Interpersonal	Tenor	NEGOTIATION	Exchanges organised into moves with speech functions
		APPRAISAL	Evaluations, intensifications, and acknowledgement of other voices
Textual	Mode	IDENTIFICATION	Introducing and tracking participants
		PERIODICITY	Organising the flow of information in a message

It is beyond the scope of this book to provide a comprehensive description of the discourse semantic systems identified in Table 3.1. The sections that follow will instead provide an overview of the key systems needed to understand the linguistic meanings with which emoji coordinate and which are explored in this book, illustrated with linguistic examples from the data. The reader is directed to Martin (1992) for a foundational account, later condensed as Martin and Rose (2003). Work on interpersonal meaning in the Appraisal framework is detailed in Martin and White (2005) and systems of ideational meaning have been developed in Hao (2020).

3.2.1   Ideational Meaning

According to a social semiotic perspective on meaning, language, in the way that it construes experience, can act 'as a theory of reality, as a resource for reflecting on the world' (Halliday & Matthiessen, 1999/2006, p. 7). Ideational meaning thus involves resources for construing 'what kinds of activities are undertaken, and how participants undertaking these activities are described and classified' (Martin & Rose, 2007, p. 17). Ideational meaning is described via the discourse semantic systems of IDEATION and CONNEXION, which realise the field register variable. Our exploration of ideational meaning will focus on IDEATION as emoji appear to have only limited capacity to coordinate with CONNEXION (concerned with logical, conjunctive relations between stretches of discourse). Similarly limited convergence has been identified for other paralinguistic resources such as gesture (Ngo et al., 2021).

IDEATION encompasses resources for construing experiential meaning. As such, it focuses on activities, the participants involved in them, and their qualities and relationships (Martin & Rose, 2007). IDEATION models this potential

Table 3.2 *Ideational elements*

ideational [element]	[entity]	[occurrence]	[entity]	[quality]
language from data	I	drink	tea	like it's going out of fashion

construal by describing experiential meaning as [sequences], [figures], and [elements]. In turn, [elements] can be either [entities], which name or taxonomise items, e.g. as objects such as 'tea', [occurrences], which construe events or activities, e.g. as happenings such as '(to) drink', or [qualities] that fashion descriptions or assessments, e.g. as attributes such as 'like it's going out of fashion'. Table 3.2 identifies these [elements] in Text (3.1):

Text (3.1)   … I drink tea like it's going out of fashion☻

[Figures], comprise one or more [elements], and [sequences] comprise one or more [figures]. Accordingly, ideational meaning is built up in texts as [sequences] of [figures] made up of [elements] ([entities], [occurrences], and [qualities]). This is summarised in Figure 3.2 where the crowfoot symbol, not conventionally used in Systemic Functional Linguistics and borrowed from Information Engineering, is used to indicate a 'one or more' relationship between [sequences], [figures], and [elements].

As Figure 3.2 illustrates, elements combine to form [figures]. IDEATION allows for two types of [figures]: [occurrence figures] and [state figures] (Hao, 2015, 2020). [Occurrence figures] include [occurrences] such as material or behavioural processes, for example 'I **drink** tea' in the example above. [state figures] do not include [occurrences] and instead feature relational or existential processes about a state of affairs, for example descriptions such as 'The coffee **is** really hot'.

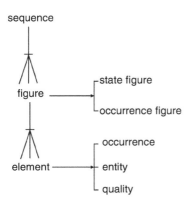

Figure 3.2 Fundamental organisation of IDEATION

In turn, [figures] combine to form activity [sequences]. For example, Text (3.2) contains seven [figures] organised into a [sequence]:

Text (3.2)   1   This weekend we will be opening our Grange Location only for three days
             2   to serve you some coffee and beans☕
             3   We will only be open for this weekend,
             4   then we will fully open
             5   when the stay-at-home order is over!
             6   See you this weekend
             7   and stay tuned for a giveaway coming on Friday✦✦

Ideational [elements] can be further subcategorised, with more delicate options for [entities] especially relevant to the description of emoji semiosis. Hao (2020) differentiates between six [entity] types: [source], [thing], [activity], [semiotic], [place], and [time] (p. 64). [Source entities] include the [entities] to which projected speech and thought are attributed, and those that are the agents in material processes. [Thing entities] are non-conscious, often material participants. [Activity entities] are typically processes that have been nominalised. [Semiotic entities] encompass participants related to facts, locutions, or ideas. [Place] and [time entities] include spatial and temporal localisations, respectively. These subcategorisations of [entities] are illustrated with examples from the data in Figure 3.3.

In summary, with this repertoire of descriptors for different types of experiential meaning, IDEATION describes the field of a text, illustrating the activities, participants and qualities being construed.

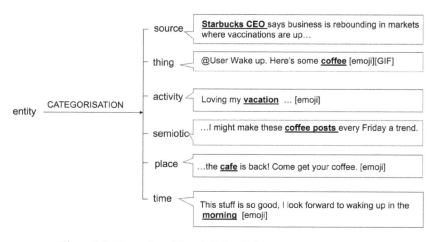

Figure 3.3 Examples of linguistic [entity] types

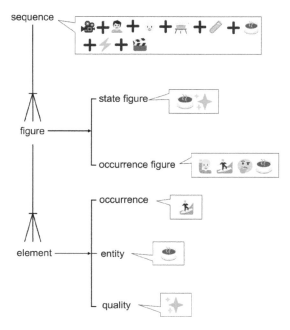

Figure 3.4 Emoji realising ideational discourse semantic choices (factoring out language)

Turning now to how these ideational features can be realised by emoji, if we artificially factor out co-occurring language and approach emoji in semiotic isolation, emoji can be seen to notionally realise all of the ideational discourse semantic systems possible for language (Figure 3.4). However, a review of the examples shown in Figure 3.3 attests to the fuzziness with which this realisation occurs. Due to the reduced affordances emoji have for committing ideational meaning potential, all of these examples are highly underspecified and ambiguous. Perhaps the least debatable example is the realisation of a [thing entity] by the HOT BEVERAGE ☕ emoji. However, as we look to the examples of emoji realising other kinds of [elements] and then to [figures] and [sequences], the potential for alternative, divergent interpretations increases. For instance, while the MAN SURFING 🏄 emoji can conceivably realise the [occurrence] corresponding to the process, 'to surf', it might equally also realise the [entity] 'person on a surfboard', the [occurrence figure], 'person surfing', or even the [state figure] 'a person is on a surfboard'. At the level of [sequence], this indeterminacy undermines any attempt to argue for a particular interpretation of the sequence of emoji in isolation from linguistic co-text.

As such, we argue that emoji typically make ideational meanings in coordination with language. Emoji also only really make sense in relation to the particular context of situation in which they arise, for instance, with reference to a previous linguistic move in a conversation or through other kinds of connection with linguistic semiosis. An emoji occurring in isolation is the marked choice, and emoji almost always accompany language or are used in close proximity to language in an interaction or response to a social media post. It also highlights the problem with mapping emoji to a single 'object' as might be suggested by their CLDR Short Names and by the rudimentary classification of emoji into types seen in Unicode. The Unicode Consortium itself acknowledges this point: 'Because emoji characters are treated as pictographs, they are encoded in Unicode based primarily on their general appearance, not on an intended semantic' (Unicode Consortium, 2022b). For these reasons, we do not attempt to create separate networks defining the choices possible for realising each of the discourse semantic features in emoji alone and instead focus on modelling emoji–text relations. In this way our approach differs to Ngo et al.'s (2021) method for modelling how gestures function as paralanguage where they develop separate networks for 'paralinguistic entities' (etc.), even though we employ the same theoretical underpinnings.

3.2.2   Interpersonal Meaning

The interpersonal metafunction offers a lens on meanings relating to the relationships among participants in a text. For instance, it considers their relative status and their roles in the text's production, thereby enacting the tenor variable of a text's register (Halliday, 1989). The systems that realise interpersonal meaning are APPRAISAL and NEGOTIATION. Previous work has shown that other forms of paralanguage such as gesture do 'not involve resources for explicitly distinguishing moves in dialogue' (Ngo et al., 2021, p. 38). This has been confirmed by our own analysis of emoji data; consequently, we focus here only on realisations of APPRAISAL.

APPRAISAL describes resources for evaluating experience, intensifying and de-intensifying evaluations, and introducing and positioning external perspectives. Evaluative language is described by the system of ATTITUDE, resources for up-scaling and down-scaling language are described by the system of GRADUATION, and those for expanding the heteroglossic space of a text are described by ENGAGEMENT (Figure 3.5). As the primary discourse semantic system responsible for realising a persona's alignment with or disalignment from particular value positions, APPRAISAL is central to the dynamics of affiliation, discussed in Chapters 7 and 8.

ATTITUDE comprises resources for construing feelings, opinions, and judgements of various types of experiential entities, and is in turn

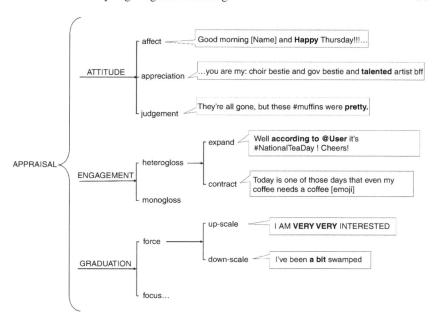

Figure 3.5 The APPRAISAL system

subcategorised into [affect], [judgement], and [appreciation]. [Affect] encompasses emotional responses and states, e.g. '*happy*' in Text (3.3).

Text (3.3)   Good morning {name} and **Happy** Thursday!!! …

[Judgement] is concerned with evaluations of character, e.g. '*talented*' in Text (3.4).

Text (3.4)   … you are my: choir bestie and gov bestie and **talented** artist bff

and [appreciation] relates to aesthetic evaluations, e.g. '*pretty*' in Text (3.5).

Text (3.5)   They're all gone, but these #muffins were **pretty**.

The above examples illustrate how ATTITUDE can be explicitly inscribed by lexical items that index specific emotions, opinions, and evaluations. ATTITUDE can also be invoked through more implicit resources such as metaphor.

GRADUATION describes resources for intensifying (up-scaling) and weakening (down-scaling) attitudinal meaning. Linguistically, this can be realised through the modification of an attitudinal lexical item, such as '*very*', which up-scales '*interested*' in Text (3.6):

Text (3.6)   I AM **VERY VERY** INTERESTED

This example also illustrates how repetition and typographic features such as ALL CAPS can realise up-scaling of ATTITUDE. An example of down-scaled ATTITUDE is the modification of the attitudinal resource 'swamped' by 'a bit' in Text (3.7):

Text (3.7)   I've been **a bit** swamped

Further to modification, up-scaling and down-scaling can be realised by infusing a lexical item with attitudinal meaning. For instance, across Text (3.8) to Text (3.11), we can see how a baseline positive evaluation such as 'good' in Text (3.8) can be up-scaled with comparatively more intensified positive evaluation such as 'great' in Text (3.9), 'wonderful', 'magical', 'amazing' in Text (3.10), and 'perfect' in Text (3.11).

Text (3.8)   Have a **good** day! …

Text (3.9)   … Here's a **great** read …

Text (3.10)   Wishing you the most **wonderful magical** and **amazing** day

Text (3.11)   The canal walk is **perfect** this Sunday.

ENGAGEMENT encompasses resources for referencing and positioning external perspectives in a text. Instances where no external perspectives are present constitute [monoglossia] and are realised linguistically by the absence of grammatical features such as modalisation and projected speech. An example is Text (3.12), which presents an observation without modalisation or projection.

Text (3.12)   Today is one of those days that even my coffee needs a coffee☕

Conversely, instances where alternative perspectives are construed constitute [heteroglossia]. Where these voices are acknowledged and endorsed, this constitutes heteroglossic [expansion], such as when a source is cited as an authority on a subject as in Text (3.13).

Text (3.13)   Well **according to** @{User} it's #NationalTeaDay ☕! Cheers!

Instances where external perspectives are dismissed or negated constitute heteroglossic [contraction], for instance, 'claiming they are trans' in Text (3.14):

Text (3.14)   Unbelievable is the FACT that @DHSgov and @ODNIgov may have been told by @SecDef and @SecVetAffairs to STAND DOWN because the two in question walk on the wild side and are **claiming** they're Trans?????????🤢

In terms of emoji realisations of APPRAISAL resources, similarly to the discussion of ideational meaning above, emoji alone can only be confidently coded as realising a small range of more generalised interpersonal meanings. Perhaps most widely familiar will be the use of various facial expression or gestural emoji to realise positive or negative ATTITUDE, such as the SMILING FACE WITH SMILING EYES ☺, THUMBS UP gesture 👍, and CRYING FACE 😢 emoji. While these were found to have relatively stable patterns of correspondence with positive or negative ATTITUDE in the dataset, even these emoji are sensitive to coordinated co-text and can have their attitudinal polarity reversed in instances of sarcasm and irony. With regards to GRADUATION resources, the most widely observed emoji realisation is the repetition of attitudinal emoji, such as in Text (3.15):

Text (3.15)   … Have a stupendous one! 😊 😊 😊 😊

A further common realisation of GRADUATION is the use of emoji that constitute infused up-scaling; as with attitudinal resources realised by language, emoji resources can be organised on a cline from 'baseline' attitudinal realisations, such as the simple smiley face 🙂, through more intensified expressions including ☺, 😊, 😍, 😆. We will explore these kinds of meanings in more detail in Chapter 6.

3.2.3 Textual Meaning

The textual metafunction describes the role language plays in organising texts into meaningful wholes. It comprises resources for creating cohesion and continuity, binding texts internally, signposting them to predict what is about to be communicated, and synthesising what has been communicated prior (Halliday & Matthiessen, 2014). The textual metafunction enacts the register variable of mode, which is realised in discourse semantics by the systems of IDENTIFICATION and PERIODICITY.

IDENTIFICATION describes resources for tracking participants in texts, for presenting them to readers when first introduced, and for referencing them, both within the text and in relation to the situational context of a text. A primary distinction made among linguistic resources for identification is whether a participant is being presented as unknown to the reader or presumed as in some way recoverable. Presented participants are often signalled with the indefinite article 'a' or unspecific amounts 'some', which construe the participant as unknown to the reader (as opposed to a participant referenced with the definite article 'the', which would imply the reader is able to recover the reference from their prior knowledge). For instance, in Text (3.16), the [entity] 'a rabbit' is presented as unknown to the reader:

Text (3.16)   Either teacups or maybe a white rabbit 🐰 🍵

Table 3.3 *Examples of types of phoricity*

Phoricity	Example
Anaphora	Good morning Bettina, I wish you a fantastic Thursday. Make the most of **this** day
Cataphora	**It** sounds like a small pleasure but one of my BIG JOYS on weekend mornings lately is taking time to make myself NICE coffee, lately my jam is cafe cubano style espresso with LOTS of espuma! ☕ ✦ ☕□
Exophora	Who else is loving **this** weather? ☂ …
Homophora	bro just listened to you for the first time fascinating **the Burpo story** in Heaven at age 3

In terms of presuming IDENTIFICATION, there are a number of options for phoricity that describe whether a participant is recoverable from earlier within the text (anaphoric), from later in the text (cataphoric), from the situational context of a text (exophoric), or from shared general knowledge (homophoric). Realisations of these features found in the data are shown in Table 3.3, with referents underlined and in bold.

Compared with language, emoji demonstrate limited potential for realising IDENTIFICATION resources in the dataset analysed here, which may reflect the reduced grammaticality of the mode. Instances where emoji did realise IDENTI-FICATION tend to be generic or exophoric, with some endophoric phoricity (reference to other referents within the co-text) also realised by emoji containing deictic vectors. Generic references typically occur in accompaniment to linguistic co-text referencing the same generic participants, as can be seen in Text (3.17), where the HOT BEVERAGE ☕ emoji cataphorically points ahead to 'coffee' and the CHOCOLATE BAR ✦ emoji anaphorically points backwards to 'chocolate'. As references to generic participants, however, the phoricity of these resources is less tightly bound to the context of the specific text.

Text (3.17)   Afternoon tweets ☕ ☾ ☾ what a hectic morning -all i need now is plenty coffee and chocolate✦ 😋 😋

Instances where emoji realised exophoric reference were often characterised by emoji indexing homophoric referents specified by the cultural context established in the co-text. For instance, in Text (3.18), the OWL emoji 🦉 homophorically references the owls commonly found in the town of Twin Peaks from the eponymous 1990s television series.

Text (3.18)   Very #TwinPeaks feel.🦉 ☕

As this example shows, while emoji can realise IDENTIFICATION resources, these instances rely heavily on convergence with linguistic co-text. In these cases, emoji that might in other circumstances only realise ideational meaning are loaded with textual meaning when the linguistic co-text specifies a particular context within which to interpret them. So for this example, rather than realising a generic 'owl' participant (which would not constitute an IDENTIFICATION resource), the linguistic co-text establishes a particular cultural context (the universe of *Twin Peaks*), within which a reference to an owl is no longer generic. A similar relationship between the ideational meaning of an emoji and the co-textually established context is found in Text (3.19), where the BEAR emoji 🐻 realises homophoric reference to the Birmingham Bears cricket team (which can be deduced by references to cricket terms 'over' and 'bowler'). In this example, because the team is mentioned explicitly in the first line of text ('The Bears'), the emoji technically can also be analysed as realising anaphoric reference; in any case, the referent recovered by the emoji reference remains the same.

Text (3.19) The Bears return to the field after reaching 291 at Tea. 🐻
30 more overs for the bowlers this evening.
Watch the live stream and view the highlights in the match centre.
📁 https://t.co/M1IBW0XrkT
🐻 #YouBears

Another potential dimension of emoji phoricity is that emoji which iconically represent embodied paralanguage (such as facial expressions and hand gestures) could be interpreted as exophorically referencing the paralanguage of the author of a text. The canonical example of this kind of phoricity is the use of the SMILEY FACE emoji 😊 to convey positive ATTITUDE, as in Text (3.20); in these instances, the emoji could also be interpreted as indexing the author's expression at the time of creating the text.

Text (3.20) Morning Chris!!🐻 😊

Finally, local endophoric phoricity can be realised by emoji that contain deictic vectors, such as the BACKHAND INDEX POINTING UP/DOWN/LEFT/RIGHT emoji 👆/👇/👈/👉 . For instance, in Text (3.21), the BACKHAND INDEX POINTING RIGHT emoji 👉 realises cataphoric reference to the following URL code.

Text (3.21) 20% Off Coffee Break Room Supplies 👉 [URL]
Your office coffee problems solved. 🐻 Save 20% on cups, stirrers, cream, sugar, & more. Order coffee supplies to complete your break room & ensure increased productivity!
#distillata #coffeesupplies

PERIODICITY describes how texts are organised into cohesive waves of information; how information is previewed in advance and synthesised in retrospect, and how this functions to divide a text into stages and phases. The two primary units of analysis for describing PERIODICITY are Theme and New. These are 'two overlapping waves … : a thematic wave with a crest at the beginning of the clause, and a news wave with a crest at the end (where the main pitch movement would be if the clause were read aloud)' (Martin & Rose, 2007, p. 192). In clause grammar, the Theme is the point of departure of a clause; the New is the information elaborated. In discourse semantics, the unit of analysis expands to scope over longer stretches of discourse, with hyper-Themes/hyperNews previewing and synthesising whole phases and stages of discourse, and macroThemes/macroNews previewing and synthesising stages or whole texts. Given the constraints on text size imposed by Twitter, posts in our corpus show limited higher level (macro) PERIODICITY, but an example of hyperTheme can be seen in Text (3.22), where the first clause '*{Name} sent me the most beautiful little package I just can't* 😫' establishes the participants of the text ({name}, package and its contents), and dominant attitudinal resources (positive [affect], positive [appreciation]) of the remainder the text.

Text (3.22) {Name} sent me the most beautiful little package I just can't 😫
The art is 😍
🫖 🕊 🎶 💜 🧺 😌 💮 🐚 🕯
The playlist 🎶
The cookies and tea🫖 💮 🍵
The marigolds🪴
I love you so much😍 💕 @{User} I've been feeling sick and you made me smile so so much! Tea tasting today🫖 💕

An example of a hyperNew is found in Text (3.22), where the final sentence '*Devise a coffeehouse name, protect your identity*' synthesises the point made in the text prior.

Text (3.23) Over Sharing is giving the Starbucks barista your government name, they announce + write it on your cup, now you're walking around displaying your name to all. Seemingly innocent but …
Devise a coffeehouse name, protect your identity☕

Emoji realisations of PERIODICITY resources were rare in the corpora analysed, with the only clear examples occurring when emoji were used as bullet points in social media posts, such as in Text (3.24).

Text (3.24) 🐦 The Orangery Lawn is the perfect place for some #summer fun!

🧺Bring a #picnic
🏏Take a wicket
🥾 Try one of our #Trails
🌳 Nestle in amongst #nature
🐝 Enjoy the #wildlife

We're open daily, 10am-5pm, along with Stables Kitchen☕ 🍴

In this example, the emoji both serve to separate the ideational [figures] of the text, and to preview one [element] in each of the [figures].

3.3 Tenor Relations and Bi-stratal Semiosis⊡ ⊡

Before turning to a more systematic description of how emoji realise discourse semantic features in the following chapters, we will note here a particular semiotic affordance of emoji: their simultaneous construal of lexicogrammatical and registerial meaning. By this we mean that emoji at once converge with meaning made in linguistic co-text and serve to enact the registerial variables of a text. These situational factors can be mapped as combinations of specific resources across field (ideational), tenor (interpersonal), and mode (textual), thus meaning realised in the lexicogrammar of a text will both reflect and enact particular registers (see Figure 3.1). To illustrate this point, we will focus on how emoji simultaneously converge with interpersonal meaning realised by linguistic co-text and enact specific features of the tenor of a text.

Within the social semiotic model of language, tenor is described via two continua: status, which is concerned with the relative dominance and deferral among participants in text, and solidarity, which is concerned with the degree of social contact and alignment among interactants. The relative equality or inequality of status among interactants in a text can be determined by whether they have reciprocity in acts of meaning; in other words, the more interactants have symmetrical options for meaning-making, the more equal their status (consider the contrast in reciprocity between a teacher speaking with students and a teacher speaking with other teachers). Solidarity is determined by the degree of contraction and proliferation of meaning among interactants; the more succinctly or indirectly interactants can refer to shared knowledge (for instance, via acronyms in a technical community or slang in a friendship group), the greater their social contact, and the wider the breadth of meaning they can share (such as potentially transgressive evaluations), the greater their alignment.

In terms of how emoji realise the tenor proliferation variable, consider the posts in Exchange 3.1, that begins with a TikTok user's comment on a hotel quarantine food review video (which we will explore further in Chapter 7 on DIALOGIC AFFILIATION).

Exchange 3.1

Text (3.25)   **User 1:** better life there than normal life of some of us😂

Text (3.26)   **Creator:** I'm super aware of this 😊 I don't want to come off ungrateful but I'm still a person having real life experiences that I want to share.

In Text (3.25), the FACE WITH TEARS OF JOY 😂 emoji indexes some degree of non-seriousness in the linguistic co-text, which serves to limit conflict arising from potentially transgressive meaning. We can fairly confidently interpret this non-serious meaning as relating to the potential reading of the linguistic co-text as accusatory, as if User 1 were recriminating the original Creator for perceived insensitivity to the hardships faced by others. In this regard, the emoji is serving to temper or soften the intensity of the interpersonal meaning realised in the co-text. Simultaneously, the emoji indexes the affective state of the author of the post, which, as an expression of potentially transgressive playfulness, suggests User 1 is comfortable sharing more private or intimate meanings, and thus that there is a certain degree of proliferation and solidarity among the interactants.

As a further example, Text (3.27) illustrates how emoji can enact contraction while simultaneously RESONATING with interpersonal resources in the co-text. Here, the FIRE 🔥 emoji is used to indicate positive ATTITUDE, as per contemporary internet slang. As such, the emoji converge with the positive ATTITUDE realised linguistically but also serve to signal that the author of the post assumes its addressee is sufficiently socially close to them to understand this vernacular dimension of the 🔥 emoji's meaning.

Text (3.27)   That all looks yummy, especially that fettuccine … 🔥 🔥

Examples that illustrate how emoji enact status were not found in the dataset, presumably because in the communicative context of comments on TikTok videos all commenters have equal access to emoji use, and thus reciprocity is symmetrical. Indeed, as a semiotic resource predominantly used in more casual, informal communicative contexts, it is hard to imagine a setting where the use of emoji would be restricted to only one or some interactants. While that limits their use as a diagnostic for instances where status is unequal, it does suggest that when emoji are found in texts, the status among interactants is likely to be equal.

3.4   Intermodal Convergence

Thus far we have explained the model we draw upon for analysing linguistic meaning. However, our interest in understanding emoji necessarily pushes us to explore non-linguistic meaning-making. Mode is central to the question of how both linguistic and non-linguistic resources realise meaning. It refers to the role that language and other semiotic systems can play in a particular context and is a central idea in the field of multimodal discourse analysis, as developed by Kress and van Leeuwen (2001). Kress (2010, p. 79) defines a mode as 'a socially shaped and culturally given semiotic resource for making meaning' which offers different meaning potential based on its particular affordances. In this approach, individual modes are seen as parallel but potentially overlapping resources for meaning-making. We model emoji as a semiotic mode in this tradition and adopt an 'instantial integration' perspective whereby texts are forged through 'a coupling process weaving together meanings from different modalities' (Martin, 2011, p. 254).

Social media discourse is inherently multimodal. It incorporates both optional and obligatory elements from visual modalities, such as static images and video, and graphic choices in typography and layout, as well as problematising a sharp distinction between modes as in emoji picture characters. As we saw in Chapter 2, multiple modalities are involved both in social media text production and publication, and these processes are inflected by the affordances of the user interfaces of the digital platform used. For instance, when a user posts a tweet, they make choices across written and visual modes. Some choices are obligatory (non-editable) such as the font and layout imposed by the platform, the visual appearance of how emoji are rendered as glyphs, and the number of characters that can occur in a post. These can be seen as part of the constraints of 'new writing' where forms of technological control are built into visual technologies (van Leeuwen, 2008, p. 134) of the kind we explored in Chapter 2.

However, the complexity of the semiotic phenomena we deal with in exploring emoji–text semiosis means that we also need to think carefully about which modes are at stake. As the semiotic technologies of digital communication have expanded and developed, so have the complex modal relations in which they are involved. The expansion in meaning potential offered by digital technologies means that there is an ever-increasing range of options for expressing meaning, supported (and at times thwarted) by the parameters of the technology. This development has been so extensive that in some situations modes are 'so utterly intertwined with one another that they no longer make sense on their own' (van Leeuwen, 2011, p. 176). Emoji are a case that would appear to illustrate this point. As picture characters they are inserted into a post as if they were a textual character and are presented in-line with other text as small, coloured glyphs. Thus, as we explored in Chapter 2, they have some of the affordances of both text and images. This kind of shift in use is important to theorise as it has significant implication for how digital texts make meanings:

Today, however, in the age of digitisation, the different modes have technically become the same at some level of representation, and they can be operated by one multi-skilled person, using one interface, one mode of physical manipulation, so that he or she can ask, at every point: 'Shall I express this with sound or music?', 'Shall I say this visually or verbally?', and so on. Our approach takes its point of departure from this new development, and seeks to provide the element that has so far been missing from the equation: the semiotic rather than the technical element, the question of how this technical possibility can be made to work semiotically, of how we might have, not only a unified and unifying technology, but also a unified and unifying semiotics. (Kress & van Leeuwen, 2001, p. 2)

A key tool for mapping how the meaning potentials of different modes is the concept of affordance, as it illuminates 'the inherent potentialities and limitations of a semiotic mode' (Kress et al., 2006, p. 46). Accordingly, the mode of written language possesses different affordances to the mode of spoken language: the former can make meaning through resources relating to the written medium such as font, size, bolding and punctuation, whereas the latter can make meaning through phonological resources such as stress, intonation, volume, and speed. While both are commonly considered linguistic modes, their affordances across different media make possible substantially different realisations of meaning. More different still are the affordances of images. Images do not symbolise words or particular sounds, nor are they organised by the syntactical or grammatical rules of speech or written language. Consequently, they bring to bear a suite of affordances unavailable in linguistic modes, such as size, colour, shape, composition, framing and so forth. Yet despite these differences images and language can realise similar kinds of meaning:

On the one hand, language has extensive resources for inscribing affect, judgement and appreciation, whereas image arguably inscribes a narrower range of typological affectual distinctions and can only invoke, not inscribe, judgement and appreciation; at the same time, images arguably afford a visceral somatic attitudinal punch … that can only be approximated in language through verbal imagery (i.e. lexical metaphor). (Martin, 2011)

When extrapolating these principles to the relationship between emoji and written language, we are first confronted by the differences between emoji and images. While emoji share the depictive affordance of images, many of their affordances are more closely aligned with those of written language.[3] From their production via keyboards, to their congruence with font size and line spacing, and their shared canvas with graphology, it is clear that the affordances of emoji are closely entwined with those of written language. As such, it follows that interpretation of emoji semiosis should be closely informed by the semiosis of this co-text. That said, the depictive properties of emoji mean that they make meaning in different ways to the language with which they co-occur, so the framework for identifying relationships between emoji and language semiosis must be flexible enough to allow for these contrasting affordances. To this end, we cast a wide net when describing the potential meanings of each mode, but then narrow the range of instantiated meanings to those shared across both.

Within social semiotics the concept of intermodal convergence has been used to consider how modes coordinate to make meaning. This notion has its

---

[3] Consequently, and in line with our conceptualisation of emoji as a mode that straddles imagic and graphological affordances, we adopt Siever's (2019) definition of texts that combine emoji and language as examples of 'iconographetic communication'.

origins in the idea of intersemiotic complementarity, that is, the 'proposition that both the verbal and visual modes of communication, within the boundaries of a single text, complement each other in the ways that they project meaning … through various linguistic and visual means peculiar to the respective modes' (Royce & Bowcher, 2007, p. 63). For instance, the notion of complementarity has been used to explore how images and text work together in picture books (Painter & Martin, 2012; Painter et al., 2013; Unsworth, 2006). It has also been used in work on paralanguage to consider embodied meaning and co-speech gesture (Martin & Zappavigna, 2019; Ngo et al., 2021; Zappavigna et al., 2010) (for a history of this work, see Logi, Zappavigna, and Martin (2022)).

Drawing on the metaphor of light converging through a lens (Figure 3.6), in exploring emoji–text relations in this book we seek to model how the three kinds of intermodal convergence relations introduced in Chapter 1 apply to emoji–language semiosis: 'degrees of concurrence for ideational meaning, degrees of resonance for interpersonal meaning and degrees of synchronicity for textual meaning' (Ngo et al., 2021, p. 21). In other words, instead of reductively classifying meaning by 'type', convergence acts as a lens on different and complementary facets of meaning. Looking through each of these three metafunctional lenses will illuminate a different dimension in how emoji and their written co-text work together.

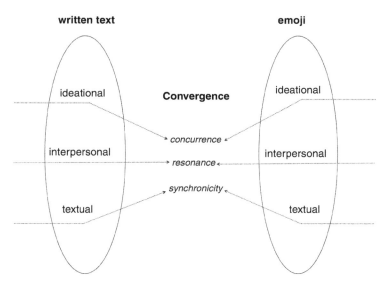

Figure 3.6 Intermodal convergence in relations between written verbiage and emoji

It should be noted that by convergence we do not intend that the meaning-potential contributed by language and emoji are 'the same' (so we do not mean convergence in the sense of matching), but rather that we can look at how these meanings operate together by approaching them through the same lens, in other words be considering that same dimension for each. It is for this reason that we do not correspondingly investigate 'divergence' since this would simply mean everything that is outside the current lens. This is not to say that the meanings cannot be contrasting, as is most obviously the case when we look at the inversion and subversion of evaluative meaning occurring within examples of humour and sarcasm in Chapter 6.

However, before we can jump into analysing this convergence it is necessary to explain the principles that we apply for determining how we locate the shared regions of meaning (Section 3.5) and introduce the network that we use for describing these areas of meaning-potential so that they can be systematically examined (Section 3.6).

3.5   Principles for Determining Emoji–Language Convergence

This section explains the principles guiding our interpretation regarding which emoji interact with which stretches of language in a social media post. Because emoji lack syntagmatic resources to link them explicitly to other semiotic resources, they evade traditional linguistic description. Their limited sustained syntagmatic meaning potential, in contrast to linguistic resources such as word order or conjugation, mean there is typically very little grammatical basis for determining the linguistic meaning with which an emoji is coordinating. In response we employ the following diagnostic questions to aid our discourse semantic reasoning for asserting instances of emoji–text convergence:

- *Proximity* – is the emoji adjacent to particular language features in the unfolding text?
- *Minimum mapping* – can the emoji and the language be said to co-construe a cohesive dimension of field or tenor?
- *Prosodic correspondence* – Do the language and emoji coordinate together prosodically, for instance, shifting together with changes in attitudinal meaning across the text?

In essence, these three questions suggest that the scope of a particular emoji's interaction with accompanying co-text extends as far as it remains the emoji most closely committed to the linguistically construed tenor and field. We explain each of these principles in more detail with examples in the sections that follow.

3.5.1 Proximity

Where an emoji is located in the text with respect to other linguistic resources such as [elements] and [figures] is an important dimension in unravelling emoji–language semiosis. This is best explained with an example. In Text (3.28) there are four emoji contributing to the text's meaning.

Text (3.28)   Love starting my mornings with a cup of cafecito ☕, hearing the birds chirping & reading a good book. I love to read on my free time. 📚🐛 Had been wanting to read 'The Four Agreements' for the longest time. Heard it's a good book for journalists. Chapter one here we go!🤓

The first of these, HOT BEVERAGE ☕, we interpret as coordinating with the [thing entity] '*a cup of cafecito*' (*cafecito* is Spanish for 'small coffee'), both because it is adjacent and because the two resources share a direct overlap in their meaning potentials. The intermodal semiosis occurring in this instance is shown in Figure 3.7, with linguistic semiotic resources outlined in long dashes, emoji in short dashes, intermodal semiosis in alternating long and short dashes, and the shared region of meaning intermodally realised outlined in a solid box. This interpretation is rendered relatively common-sense by the adjacence of the interacting emoji and language, and by the absence of any other potentially interacting meanings realised by the language.

The second two emoji in Text (3.28), BOOKS 📚 and BUG 🐛, are interpreted as interacting primarily with the ideational [state figure]: '*I love to read on my free time*' (Figure 3.8). Our interpretation of this interaction is guided by adjacency as well as minimum mapping (explained in Section 3.5.2): here the emoji sequence 📚🐛 occurs after the [state figure]. As readers of the text we are thus prompted to consider what regions of each mode's meaning potential

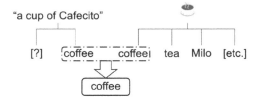

Love starting my mornings with a cup of cafecito ☕ hearing the birds chirping & reading a good book. I love to read on my free time. 📚🐛 Had been wanting to read "The Four Agreements" for the longest time. Heard it's a good book for journalists. Chapter one here we go!🤓

"a cup of Cafecito"   ☕

[?]   coffee   coffee   tea   Milo   [etc.]

coffee

Figure 3.7 Emoji coordinating with a [thing entity]

Love starting my mornings with a cup of cafecito ☕, hearing the birds chirping & reading a good book. I love to read on my free time. 📖 🐛 Had been wanting to read "The Four Agreements" for the longest time. Heard it's a good book for journalists. Chapter one here we go! 🙃

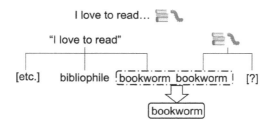

Figure 3.8 Emoji interacting with a [state figure]

might overlap; in this case, we make the semantic connection between a person who likes to read and the idiomatic expression '*bookworm*', which is then realised by the emoji depiction of 📖 for '*book*' and 🐛 for '*worm*'. We might also interpret 📖 as loosely interacting with the repeated references to '*books*', '*reading*' and '*chapter*' in the text, but again, given its direct coordination with an adjacent figure, these interactions would appear to be secondary.

If, however, there were multiple linguistic meanings the emoji could be interacting with, but there were also other emoji that could be interacting with these, again, location within the text would impact the interpretation of which emoji are interacting with which stretches of language. For instance, if a text contained a reference to a second hot beverage such as 'tea', our interpretation of whether the emoji is interacting with only one or both of these linguistically construed [thing entities] would be guided by the location of the emoji relative to the linguistic co-text. For instance, in Text (3.29) the [figure] realised in the first clause contains both the [thing entity] '*a cup of tea*' and '*coffee*'.

Text (3.29)   Sit back and grab a cup of tea or coffee while our skilled technicians repair your vehicle ☕ 🚗
Whether your vehicle requires a clutch replacement, exhaust, cambelt, or any other repair, we are confident that our prices will always be competitive and our service unrivaled 🔧

Given its location at the end of the clause complex containing this [figure] and the absence of any other emoji that could be interacting with these linguistic meanings, in this case the HOT BEVERAGE ☕ emoji is interpreted as interacting with both [thing entities] (Figure 3.9). Also noteworthy here is that as the emoji coordinates with more linguistic resources, its meaning becomes less committed so as to encompass the more expansive linguistic meaning.

Sit back and grab a cup of tea or coffee while our skilled technicians repair your vehicle
Whether your vehicle requires a clutch replacement, exhaust, cambelt, or any other repair, we are confident that our prices will always be competitive and our service unrivaled

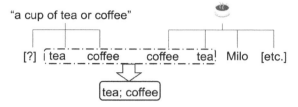

Figure 3.9 A single emoji interacting with two linguistic thing entities

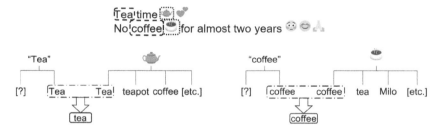

Figure 3.10 Two field-related emoji interacting with different linguistic [entities]

Another example involving two [thing entities] is Text (3.30).

Text (3.30)   Tea time 🫖 🍃
No coffee☕for almost two years😊 ☺ 🙏

Here the HOT BEVERAGE ☕ emoji could theoretically interact with both *'coffee'* and *'Tea'*; however, the presence of the TEAPOT 🫖 emoji adjacent to *'tea'* suggests that *'tea'* is coordinating with TEAPOT 🫖, while *'coffee'* is interacting with HOT BEVERAGE ☕. Of course, *'tea'*, *'coffee'*, ☕ and 🫖 are closely clustered in terms of their ideational field, so they are all interacting to some extent in terms of register. However, when interpreting the discourse semantics of ☕ and 🫖 in this text, their coordination with distinct, linguistically realised entities within this field means we are more likely to minimally map these as indexing the [thing entities] *'coffee'* and *'tea'* respectively (Figure 3.10), as opposed to a more generalised hot beverage meaning as in Text (3.29).

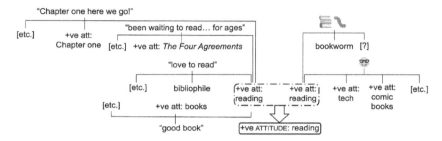

Figure 3.11 An emoji interacting with multiple linguistic resources in a text

Returning to Text (3.28), the last emoji in this post is the NERD FACE 🤓, which occurs at the end of the post after multiple ideational [sequences]. Our interpretation of which parts of the text this emoji interacts with are informed by the most salient interpersonal and ideational meanings realised in the text, which in this case centre around positive evaluation of books/reading (Figure 3.11). Thus, the nerd face, with its (smiling) depiction of a cultural cliché associated with interest and aptitude for technical and academic pursuits, encapsulates both the general interpersonal ATTITUDE (positive) and the general ideational field construed in the text.

3.5.2   Minimum Mapping

The Minimum Mapping hypothesis was developed by Zhao (2011) for understanding how modes combine in digital multimedia to make ideational meanings. The hypothesis states that 'if verbiage and image can co-construe one aspect of a social action, e.g. process (what is going on), participant (the participants that engage in the process), etc., they form a verbiage-image coupling' (Zhao, 2011, p. 171). Thus, while individual resources might potentially construe generalised or multiplied meanings, when they co-occur in a text their meaning potential is constrained to the region of meaning shared between them. An example explained in Logi and Zappavigna (2021b) from the Sydney Emoji Corpus is the case where a [thing entity] in the written verbiage converges with the BABY BOTTLE emoji:

Text (3.31)   Thoroughly disappointed with the lack of milk🍼

This follows a pattern of hypo/hypernymy as visually represented in Figure 3.12. In this example the written co-text '*milk*' might realise a number of

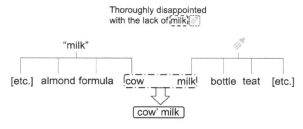

Figure 3.12 Emoji interacting with a [thing entity]

linguistic [thing entities] – 'cow's milk', 'formula milk', or 'almond milk' (other potential interpretations are possible, as '[etc.]' in Figure 3.12 allows for). Similarly, the BABY BOTTLE 🍼 emoji can be divided into the visual components that constitute the glyph: 'bottle', 'milk', 'teat', and so forth. Applying the minimum mapping hypothesis, we propose that the intermodal meaning jointly construed by the emoji and the co-textual [thing entity] is the region of meaning shared between them: 'cow's milk'. 'Formula milk' also seems like a possible candidate, but, given the less typical association with the lexical item 'milk' and the absence of contextual indicators foregrounding it, this region of meaning is considered secondary in this instance. The intermodal semiosis of this text is summarised in Figure 3.12. In turn, the intermodally converged entity '*milk* 🍼' is nested within a linguistically realised [state figure], '*lack of milk*'. This kind of reasoning will be explored more fully in Chapter 5, where we draw on the system of IDEATION to show how emoji converge with language through concurrence relations with ideational discourse semantic meanings made in the co-text.

3.5.3   Prosodic Correspondence

In instances where the emoji in a text are primarily realising interpersonal meaning, the scope of emoji–language interaction is governed by the prosodic correspondence of attitudinal and affiliative meaning. These are realised prosodically 'since the meaning is distributed like a prosody throughout a continuous stretch of discourse' as a 'motif or colouring' (Halliday, 1979). For instance, in Text (3.32) the attitudinal prosody reverses across both language and emoji.

Text (3.32)   @{User 1} @{User 2} @{User 3} @{User 4} @{User 5} @{User 6} @{User 7} @{User 8} @{User 9} @{User 10} @{User 11} Good morning 😍 ☕#BrewCrew ☕ 😍 😩I ran out of #coffee 😵 😵 😊 😩 😩 😩 having😩 Tea instead 😖 😖 😖 😖 😖 but if this is worst thing … I'm good 😊 & #grateful I have everything else I need 😊 have a blessed day! 👊 💜 😊

..[Good morning] 😋 ☕ [#BrewCrew] ☕😋😂 [I ran out of #coffee] 😕😟😖😔😔😔 having
Tea 😫 instead 😩😫😩😩😩 but if this is worst thing. [I'm good] 😊 & #grateful I have
everything else I need 😌 have a blessed day 🙌💜😊

Prosody	Interpersonal meaning
Good morning 😋 ☕ #BrewCrew ☕😋😂	solidarity / positive affect
I ran out of #coffee 😕😟😖😔😔😔 having Tea 😫 instead 😩😫😩😩😩 but if this is worst thing	negative affect / appreciation
...I'm good 😊 & #grateful I have everything else I need 😌 have a blessed day! 🙌💜😊	positive affect

Figure 3.13 An example of emoji interacting with positive and negative interpersonal prosodies

Thus, for each segment of emoji–language interaction, we can identify a minimally mapped interpersonal meaning feature that is shared across both language and emoji (Figure 3.13).

Importantly, prosodic regions reflect both interpersonal and ideational meaning. For instance, in Text (3.33), we can identify a linguistically construed interpersonally positive prosody spanning '*Morning. Thank you for all my Birthday tweets yesterday!!*', followed by an interpersonally negative prosodic segment spanning the remainder of the post.

Text (3.33)   Morning. Thank you for all my Birthday tweets yesterday!! I'm proper suffering this morning!! Incoming anxiety ridden hangover !!!! 🐝..☕☕ ☕☕☕😵😷😫

The boundary between these informs the interpretation of the emoji that conclude the post; this is relatively uncomplicated for the negative ATTITUDE facial expressions that resonate with the negative [affect] (e.g. '*suffering*', '*anxiety ridden*'). However, it has a more nuanced effect on the potential ideational CONCURRENCE of the repeated HOT BEVERAGE ☕ emoji. Here, due to their position within a prosody of negative [affect], the emoji are interpreted as minimally mapping with '*anxiety*' rather than with the first instance of '*Morning*', as '*Morning*' occurs within the prosody of positive ATTITUDE where the author is expressing thanks for birthday greetings (Figure 3.14).

While proximity, minimum mapping, and prosodic correspondence are relatively robust principles for justifying interpretation of emoji–language interaction, they should not be taken as absolute requirements for emoji and language to coordinate. Rather, these are tendencies of interaction we have noted over the course of conducting analysis for this book. A more universal observation is that precisely because of their semiotic flexibility, emoji can coordinate with language in novel, at times surprising ways. Moreover, the constraints on text length imposed by Twitter preclude exploration of how

Morning. Thank you for all my Birthday tweets yesterday!! I'm proper suffering this
morning!! Incoming anxiety ridden hangover !!!! 😨 .. 😐 😐 😐 😐 😐 😵 ☹ 😡

Prosody	Interpersonal meaning
Morning. Thank you for all my Birthday tweets yesterday!!	Solidarity / positive affect
I'm proper suffering this morning!! Incoming anxiety ridden hangover !!!! 😨 .. 😐 😐 😐 😐 😐 😵 ☹ 😡	Negative affect

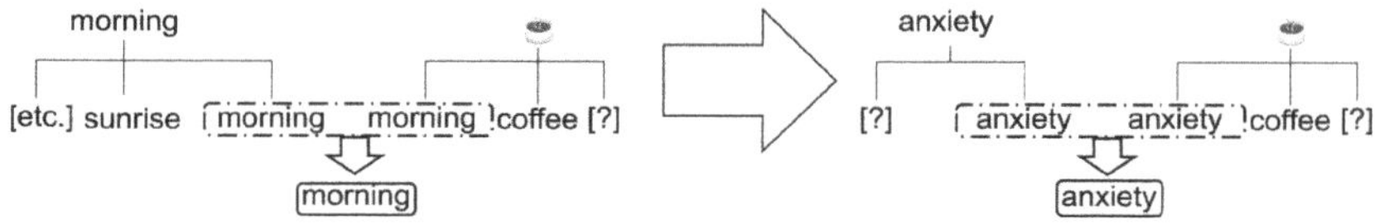

morning   anxiety

[etc.] sunrise [morning   morning] coffee [?]   [?]   [anxiety   anxiety] coffee [?]

[morning]   [anxiety]

Figure 3.14 Attitudinal prosody and emoji–language interaction

emoji might be used over longer texts, where intermodal coordination might
span longer stretches of discourse.

3.6   The System of Emoji–Text CONVERGENCE

Having articulated the principles that we use to establish which emoji may
be interacting with which linguistic resources in a social media post, we now
explain how we describe the nature of this interaction. The general parameters
we use to describe CONVERGENCE – ideational CONCURRENCE, interpersonal
RESONANCE, and textual SYNCHRONICITY – were drawn, as explained earlier,
from current social semiotic work concerned with modelling paralanguage
spanning paralinguistic modes such as gesture, facial expression, and voice
quality.

To implement our text analysis of CONVERGENCE relations we will use system networks as means of encapsulating the significant semiotic complexity involved in these relations. System networks are a formalism developed
within Systemic Functional Linguistics that take the form of a graphical notation format. A 'system' in this graphical representation is a particular region
of meaning realised through particular linguistic choices. A choice between
two options, termed 'features', is represented with square brackets, indicating
a logical 'or' relation. For example, in SYSTEM 3 the square bracket indicates
that a choice must be made between [feature E] and [feature F] (Figure 3.15).
One feature must be chosen, and both cannot be chosen together. By way of
contrast, a logical 'and' relation is represented with a brace. This is used for
choices which can occur simultaneously, where two systems share an entry
condition. For instance, a choice can be made from both SYSTEM 2 and SYSTEM
3 (Figure 3.15). The progression from system to subsystem, left to right across
a network, is referred to as the degree of delicacy. For an overview of system

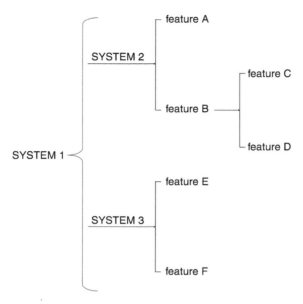

Figure 3.15 An example of a system network

networks and further explanation of more complex conventions, see Martin (2013), and for a comparison of this notation strategy with other formalisms such as tree diagrams used to represent knowledge in linguistics and other disciplines, see Doran (2019).

The benefit of using a system network to express the kinds of relations that emoji can have with their co-text is the ability to leverage both paradigmatic and syntagmatic perspectives, in other words to gain insight into both system (what are the possible sets of choices?) and structure (how are choices sequenced in a text?).[4] The system we have developed for analysing emoji–text CONVERGENCE is shown in Figure 3.16. This network is presented at the first level of delicacy for the purposes of providing a general overview. It is possible to specify subsystems, which we will do in the next three chapters where we consider more delicate relations that emoji can have with their co-text in terms of SYNCHRONICITY, CONCURRENCE, and RESONANCE, respectively.

Each system in the network has two features that encapsulate the main distinctions in meaning realised through different types of emoji–text relations. The main choice in ideational CONCURRENCE is between an emoji congruently

---

[4] The complementarity perspective into system and structure afforded by system network is referred to as 'axis'.

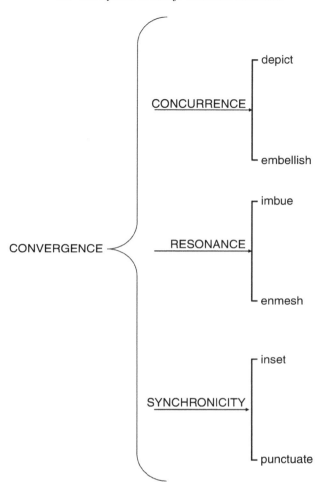

Figure 3.16 The system of emoji–language CONVERGENCE

depicting the IDEATION expressed in the co-text or metaphorically embellishing it. This contrast can be seen in Text (3.34) and Text (3.35).

Text (3.34)   Update: I can't drink the coffee fast enough☕

Text (3.35)   Can't wait to hear what she says☕

In Text (3.34) the linguistic [thing entity] '*the coffee*' is depicted by the HOT BEVERAGE ☕ emoji, whereas in Text (3.35) the HOT BEVERAGE ☕ emoji does not appear to directly represent any of the [elements] in the [figure].

Instead, it embellishes the meaning made in the [figure], adding the additional meaning of encouraging the sharing of gossip or secrets (i.e. 'spilling the tea') where, as we will see in further examples in Chapter 5, the HOT BEVERAGE ☕ emoji acts as an emblem that activates this idiomatic meaning potential.

In terms of the interpersonal system of RESONANCE, the main distinction in meaning is between the cases where emoji enmesh with an interpersonal meaning realised in linguistic co-text, and instances where emoji realise interpersonal meaning that imbues linguistically realised ideational meaning in the co-text. For instance, in Text (3.36), the emoji sequence TULIP 🌷, HIBISCUS 🌺, and SPARKLING HEART 💖 enmeshes with the positive appreciation '*beautiful*'.

Text (3.36)   You're so beautiful🌷 🌺 💖

Alternatively, if the linguistic co-text does not include resources realising interpersonal meaning then emoji can imbue linguistic ideational meaning. This can be seen in Text (3.37), where the SMILING FACE WITH SMILING EYES 😊 emoji washes positive ATTITUDE over the linguistically construed [thing entity]: '*that first sip of coffee in the morning*'.

Text (3.37)   That first sip of coffee in the morning☕ 😊

Turning finally to the system of textual SYNCHRONICITY, the main choice is between insetting the emoji into the discourse semantic structure of a [figure] or [sequence] or punctuating the co-text.

Text (3.38)   I'd love some🍰

Text (3.39)   🍰 🍰 This is the best Victoria Sponge ever!!🍰 🍰

In Text (3.38) the SHORTCAKE 🍰 emoji functions as if it is a linguistic [thing entity] such as 'cake' or 'dessert', thus completing the [figure]. On the other hand, the two instances of emoji sequences at the beginning and end of Text (3.39) do not form part of the structure of the language that they bookend as this language is a well-formed [state figure] in its own right.

It is these distinctions of meaning that we will investigate in the chapters which follow, elaborating the CONVERGENCE network to greater levels of delicacy as we explore the patterns of meaning we observe in the HOT BEVERAGE emoji corpus.

3.7   Conclusion

This chapter has introduced the framework used for exploring emoji–text relations in this book. It has explained how emoji are analysed as a unique semiotic mode with particular affordances, and how these affordances interact with

those of other modes such as written language through intermodal CONVER-
GENCE and minimum mapping. The possibility for sequences of emoji to make
meaning in the absence of language was also touched on, although this was
noted as less relevant to the focus of this book. We have introduced a system
network for systematically describing the kinds of relations that emoji enact
with their written co-text along three dimensions of CONVERGENCE: ideational CONCURRENCE, interpersonal RESONANCE, and textual SYNCHRONY. The
chapter has also explained the model of discourse semantics used to describe
the linguistic component of emoji–text relations, or in other words, the linguistic meanings with which emoji coordinate to make multimodal meanings. Having thus established the analytical framework that will be employed
to investigate emoji–language semiosis, we can proceed in the following
chapter to analysing the first of the three dimensions of CONVERGENCE: textual
SYNCHRONICITY.

4   Emoji Synchronising with Textual Meaning

4.1   Introduction

This chapter considers how emoji and language synchronise in terms of the information flow of a social media post. In other words, we are concerned with the textual metafunction: how ideational and interpersonal meanings are woven together to form a coherent and cohesive text (Halliday, 1978). While emoji's role in emotional discourse and negotiating social relationships is perhaps more recognisable, we have chosen textual SYNCHRONICITY as our point of departure for investigating CONVERGENCE. This is because textual relations inform and reflect which emoji interact with which stretches of language. Thus, an understanding of these textual relations will be useful to draw upon in subsequent chapters dealing with ideational and interpersonal meaning.

In terms of the linguistic discourse semantics with which emoji can synchronise, the key systems at stake are IDENTIFICATION (resources for tracking participants in texts) and PERIODICITY (organising texts into waves of information), as summarised in the previous chapter. It is worth noting here how, in terms of SFL's model of textual meaning as realised by a hierarchy of larger waves comprising smaller waves, emoji appear to be realising a wavelength that sits between the clause and higher-level PERIODICITY – not quite a hyper-Theme, perhaps, but something more than simply a Theme. Moreover, the unique affordances of emojis create fresh opportunities for conveying textual meaning by expanding their functionality to resemble that of punctuation and discourse markers.

Most of the previous research into emoji concerned with dimensions of textual meaning has been undertaken at the level of clause/sentence grammar. One of the first ways in which emoji were recognised to coordinate with language was through performing roles in the grammatical structure of a text akin to punctuation. Many studies have noted emoji's capacity to function either as punctuation (Parkwell, 2019; Sampietro, 2016) or as discourse markers (Wiese & Labrenz, 2021). Danesi (2016) distinguishes adjunctive emoji, that make meaning alongside language, and substitutive emoji, that replace language, observing that an emoji's intelligibility declines in correlation to its independence from language. Other studies have foregrounded emoji's capacity to substitute for written language in various ways; for instance, emoji 'can substitute for words, and emoji sequences can resemble complete utterances with subject, verb, and object' (Ge & Herring, 2018). Sampietro (2016, p. 109) refines the comparison between emoji and punctuation, noting that while emoji might seem to be replacing punctuation, this function only extends to social contexts where language is marked by positive interpersonal affect.

Many studies refer to functions that might fit into the social semiotic perspective on textual meaning (organising experiential and interpersonal meanings to form a coherent text) adopted in this book, without explicit framing. For instance, the pointing function of some emoji such as hand emoji (Gawne & Daniel, 2021, p. 2) might relate to textual deixis, and the use of emoji to index the facial expressions or activities being performed by the author of a text might correspond to a phoric function (cf. 'Physical Expression' in Dainas & Herring, 2021). Other studies have adapted existing linguistic frameworks such as rhetorical structure theory to analyse how emoji sequences relate to their accompanying co-text, rhetorically and logically (Ge & Herring, 2018). Focusing on the phoric function of emoji from a psycholinguistic perspective, Kaiser and Grosz (2021) divide emoji–text relationships into those linking facial expression emoji with emoters (the participant experiencing the ATTITUDE) construed in the linguistic co-text and those linking action emoji with third-person pronouns. They state that 'face emoji and activity emoji differ in their linguistic properties, with face emoji incorporating first-person indexicality and activity emoji incorporating anaphoricity via an open argument slot' (2021, p. 1019).

4.2   Systematising Emoji–Text Synchronicity

The system network for emoji–text SYNCHRONICITY is shown in Figure 4.1. The main distinction is between whether an emoji is inset into the discourse semantic structure, or whether the emoji punctuates the structure, functioning in a manner similar to punctuation or discourse markers. This is a similar distinction to that made by Danesi (2016), who distinguishes adjunctive emoji, which make meaning alongside language, from substitutive emoji, which replace language. Other studies have posited similar relations, for instance, Ai et al. (2017) contrast complementary (co-occurring with words) and supplementary relations (replacing words) along similar lines, that is, the extent to which they impact the meaning of the message if they are removed.

The section will illustrate the features in this network using frequent patterns found in the Hot Beverage Emoji corpus.

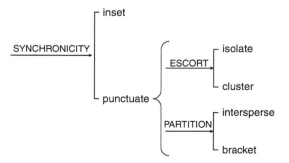

Figure 4.1 The system of emoji–text SYNCHRONICITY

4.3   Inset

Where emoji are inset, they can adopt particular functional roles within the discourse semantic structure of the text wherein they occur in terms of how they interact with the linguistic co-text in the post. These roles can span both ideational and interpersonal functions. In terms of the ideational meaning that we explore in Chapter 5, [inset] supports the [integrate] choice where the emoji adopt various kinds of roles within the system of IDEATION. For example, in Text (4.1) the PILE OF POO 💩 emoji functions as part of the exclamation *'oh* _____ *'* in the first [occurrence figure], likely standing in for the expletive 'shit'. Similarly, the HOT BEVERAGE ☕ emoji likely substitutes for a [thing entity] in the second [figure].

Text (4.1)   @{User} Oh 💩 I forgot the litter boxes yesterday.
              I know what's first after ☕ of course.

Text (4.2)   @{User} I 💜 Morning Joe #morningjoe EVERYDAY ☕ [GIF]

However, there is often both a degree of ambiguity when emoji are inset into the functional structure of a post, both in terms of the lexis which might substitute for the emoji if we were to read the post aloud and their functional role. For instance, as we will explore in Chapter 5, the HOT BEVERAGE ☕ emoji is relatively under-committed, so disambiguating the exact type of hot drink (tea, coffee, hot chocolate?) in Text (4.1) requires additional information from the context of situation. The RED HEART 💜 in Text (4.2) might be read as 'love' but could also express different degrees of [affect] or could refer to the idiomatic expression 'I heart X', from the social media practice of favouriting/liking material with a heart or thumbs up graphicon.

This practice of reading emoji aloud as their CLDR Short Name occurs in text-to-speech translation contexts such as when a text message is read aloud by a smartphone assistant. It often results in humorously incoherent expression since these Short Names do not adequately encapsulate emoji meaning, being unattuned to co-textual relations. A particular, though infrequent, type of emoji use that would seem to invoke the aural mode is rebus uses. This is a word-form based strategy drawing on phonetic pronunciation where the emojis, when read aloud (possibly as their CLDR Short Name depending on user knowledge), sound like the target word. An example is the sequence of a BOOKS and HOTEL emoji (📖🏨) or a PLANE emoji (📖✈️) to stand for 'book a hotel/flight'. However, cognitive studies have suggested that this is an uncommon communicative choice among emoji users (Wicke & Bolognesi, 2020).

Other examples of emoji inset into [figures] that would be incomplete without them include Text (4.3) to Text (4.5).

Text (4.3)   @{User} take some ☕ and 🥐 in return!

Text (4.4)   … I'll make you a ☕ and find you a hobnob …

Text (4.5)   @{User} I literally have no clue what's going on but this ☕ is good regardless

In Text (4.3) and Text (4.4), the HOT BEVERAGE ☕ emoji behaves as a [thing entity] within [occurrence figures]. However, while we could also make a similar argument for this emoji functioning as a [thing entity] within the [state figure] in Text (4.5), there is some ambiguity here. In this instance the HOT BEVERAGE ☕ emoji may instead be functioning as a [semiotic entity], if we interpret the emoji as an emblem indexing the sharing of gossip (see Section 6.2 of Chapter 6 for more on this emblematic function). By way of contrast the CROISSANT 🥐 emoji in Text (4.1) relatively clearly construes a croissant, although it could perhaps index sweet pastries more generally.

All of these are examples of synchronous substitution that Siever (2019) describes as having referential function, where emoji replace words or parts thereof, and can even be hyphenated (or otherwise adjusted) so as to concord syntactically with the linguistic text they are replacing. They are instances where removing the emoji would break the coherence of the text, and the reader must actively transduce emoji into language in order to complete the texts. However, depending on the rank at which analysis is conducted there can be more or less functional ambiguity. For instance, at the level of the nominal group, the entity in Text (4.6) realised by the emoji sequence, HOT BEVERAGE and SHORTCAKE ☕🍰, may be interpreted in more than one way.

Text (4.6)   … Maybe more ☕🍰 is needed? …

The sequence may imply the conjunction 'and' creating the complex nominal group 'coffee and cake'. However, the HOT BEVERAGE emoji could also be functioning as a Classifier, modifying the meaning of the second emoji, as in 'coffee cake' or 'tea cake'.

While these examples illustrate how inset emoji can function as somewhat ambiguous substitutes for written language, in practise a post can oscillate between the inset and punctuate choices as in Text (4.7).

> Text (4.7)   @{User} Good Morning {name} 🤗 ☕ Happy FRIYAY, dear friend! The Weekend is Here 🌅 I Hope FRIYAY ends on a good note to slide right into the weekend! Hope your ⛽gets back to normal! Overindulged yesterday 🍸 🍸 Gin & Tonic! OY! 😵 😵 Make it a SUPER Day💜 🔋❇ ☕ 💜Namaste🙏

Here, most of the emoji punctuate between [figures], with the exception of the FUEL PUMP ⛽ emoji in the underlined [figure]. In light of the vocative *'dear friend'* and the @mention which both direct the post to a particular user, and the reference to the end of the working week via the celebratory portmanteau *'FRIYAY'* (Friday + yay), the FUEL PUMP ⛽ emoji most likely means 'human energy' rather than the more literal interpretation of 'vehicular fuel'. This is not to say that punctuated and inset emoji do not interact textually. The punctuating emoji such as MAN RAISING HAND 🙋, PARTYING FACE 🥳, COCKTAIL GLASS 🍸 etc. help to organise an ongoing field of personal weekend celebration that cues us in to the metaphorical use of the FUEL PUMP.

4.4   Punctuate

In contrast to emoji which are inset into the discourse semantic structure, emoji can interact with that structure in a manner analogous to punctuation. For instance, in Text (4.8) the emoji sit outside the [figures], all of which would remain coherent even if the emoji were removed.

> Text (4.8)   Ya just plain boring😔 😔 I can't wait to catch-up man, sorry I couldn't make it to falls😔 Missing you heaps can't wait until you finally come to the mainland💜 💜

The emoji in this example organise the ideational and interpersonal meanings that are made by the linguistic discourse semantics. They punctuate the [sequence] in the post by marking some, but not all, of the [figures] in positions where we might otherwise expect a sentence boundary marker such as a full stop. The emoji also act as a kind of affectual punctuation by delimiting the boundaries of the attitudinal prosodies which resonate interpersonal meaning across the scope of each preceding [figure]. For instance, we might segment the text as follows on the basis of emoji or actual punctuation as boundary markers that signal attitudinal shifts.

1   Ya just plain boring😴 😴
2   I can't wait to catch-up man,
3   sorry I couldn't make it to falls😌
4   Missing you heaps can't wait until you finally come to the mainland😍 😍

By this logic, we might expect a full stop in 4 between '*heaps*' and '*can't wait*'. However, this might act as an attitudinal prosody blocker, impacting the scope of the two SMILING FACE WITH HEART EYE 😍 😍 emoji. Without this punctuation, the meaning of this emoji is free to resonate across the two [figures] in 4, connecting them as we might expect of a discourse marker and washing positive ATTITUDE across both the expressed longing ('*missing you*') and impatience ('*can't wait*') that is realised in these two [figures]. Numbers 2 and 3 are an example where the comma does block the flow of ATTITUDE, preventing the negative ATTITUDE of SAD BUT RELIEVED FACE 😌 from spanning across the expressed desire to meet '*can't wait to catch-up*'. In this way emoji have accrued structural potential that seems to take on the affordance of both punctuation and discourse markers.

The main choices within the punctuate system are escorting or partitioning (Figure 4.2). These are simultaneous systems since emoji, due to their graphical articulation, can break the text into parts, at the same time as referring to particular linguistic features in the co-text.

An example of this dual capacity is the emoji–text coordination in Text (4.9).

Text (4.9)   I'm ready for <u>fall weather</u> 🍂, watching <u>scary movies</u> 🦇, wearing sweaters and <u>ugg boots</u> 👢 going to <u>the fair</u> 🎡 drinking <u>hot chocolate</u>☕ and eating s'mores, trick or treating on <u>Halloween</u> 🎃, <u>Thanksgiving dinner with family</u>❤ and all that.

In this example emoji coordinate with the underlined [entities] while simultaneously segmenting the information flow of the text into a list of activities. Each of the emoji also has an ideational correspondence with these [entities] that we will explore further in Chapter 5 when we consider how emoji can depict ideational meanings.

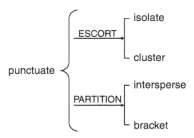

Figure 4.2 The punctuate system

4.4.1   ESCORT: Isolate

When escorting the language in a post emoji coordinate with the discourse semantics by isolating particular meanings as salient. A common example is where emoji appear adjacent to an [element] in a [figure], for instance, emoji are positioned adjacent to the linguistic [entities] (underlined) and [occurrences] (**bold**) in Text (4.10) to Text (4.13).

Text (4.10) Sometimes self care is a movie 🍫 chocolate 🍫 and latte ☕ that is all☕

Text (4.11) Tea☕ or Coffee☕

Text (4.12) One of iraq traditions is drinking boiling tea ☕ in summer even though it was 55 centigrade

Text (4.13) Done **baking** 🍞 plus it's **raining** ☔ I'm going to make a ☕ [2 images]

Escorting can organise not only ideational but interpersonal meanings. For instance, in Text (4.14) the RED HEART 💜 coordinates with the [affect] (happiness) '*love*'. The MUSICAL NOTE 🎵 together with the SMILING FACE WITH SUNGLASSES 😎 isolates '*Blondie*' (an American rock band) in terms of field (that it is related to music) and tenor (that it is positively [appreciated]).

Text (4.14) @{User} Good Morning {name}!! ☕
Yes I love 💜 Blondie🎵 😎

Emoji can refer both anophorically and cataphorically simultaneously in terms of how they escort the co-text. In other words emoji can refer both forwards and backwards to discourse semantic features in a post. For example, in Text (4.15) there is a cataphoric relation between '*tea*' and the TEAPOT 🫖 and TEACUP WITHOUT HANDLE 🍵 as well as an anaphoric relation between '*tea*' and the HOT BEVERAGE ☕

Text (4.15) @{User 1} @{User 2} @{User 3} 🫖 🍵Thanks! **tea** and cake were consumed☕ 🍵

In addition, it should be noted that emoji can isolate a range of different discourse semantic features all within the one post:

Text (4.16) @{User} Hello dearest friend #{name} 💜[1] yummy 😋[2] and delicious my favourite please save me some 😋[3] hope you enjoy! much love and peaceful blessings to everyone in India 🇮🇳[4] with their chai ☕[5] and bhajiya kinda day 😋[6]

For instance, the emoji in Text (4.16) isolate both [elements] (bold in 1, 2, 4) and [figures] (underlined in 3).

1 @{User} Hello dearest friend #{name}💜
2 **yummy** 😋 and delicious my favourite

3   please save me some☺

4   hope you enjoy! much love and peaceful blessings to everyone in India 🇮🇳
    with their chai ☕ and bhajiya kinda day😋

As mentioned earlier, all of these examples are well-formed grammatically
without the emoji, and the emoji serve to augment the posts by making textually salient key ideational and interpersonal dimensions. What would seem
to distinguish emoji from other kinds of punctuation is the extent to which
meaning is double articulated across emoji and written verbiage. For instance,
in the case of adjacency relations of the kind favoured by isolating, emoji tend
to enact a kind of redundancy[1] in how they map to the ideational and interpersonal meanings in the co-text, with the exception of where the emoji target the
ideational meaning in the co-text (as in 3 in Text (4.16)) as often occurs with
longer stretches of text at the [figure] and [sequence] level. We will return to
examples of these in Chapter 6.

4.4.2   ESCORT: *Cluster*

Emoji can also cluster interpersonal and ideational meanings, compounding
and consolidating their meaning, typically at the end of a post. This affords
these meanings textual prominence, in part due to their increased visual
salience as a collection of colourful graphicons, compared with the uniform-
ity of the monochrome co-text. For example, Text (4.17) is responding to a
post which mentions that it has been a year since the COVID-19 lockdown
began.

Text (4.17)   @{User} Can't believe it's been a year Got quite teary when I was
              watching the news & listening to people's stories Mighty thankful to
              still be here 🕯😊🥺🥺🥺😭😭😭💜💜💜🐾🐾🧸💜🧸

The collection of emoji increases the salience of the author's expression of
gratitude and aids in positioning this as the news in the information flow of the
post. The blend of object, face, and symbol emoji is typical of the collections
of emoji which are brought together to express a generalised positivity, skewed
towards a particular field. In this case the field is suggested via the BOUQUET
💐 and TEDDY BEAR 🧸, which are related to illness (e.g. gifts when visiting
a patient in hospital). The PAW PRINTS 🐾 emoji appears to be related to an
interest of the author, who also includes a dog as their profile picture. We will
not delve too deeply into these ideational correspondences since they will be
taken up in more detail in Chapter 5.

---

[1] A similar kind of 'redundant addition' has been noted by Panckhurst and Frontini (2020, p. 86)
in the use of emoji in SMS messages, whereby 'an emoji is used as well as written text, but it is
not required in order to understand the SMS (within the context of the exchange)'.

A frequent pattern in the corpus, which we will explore further in the coming chapters, is expression of morning greetings with a cluster of emoji in culminative position as a 'burst' of positivity, as seen in Text (4.18) to Text (4.23).

Text (4.18)   Good morning delightful friends. We had pouring rain ⛅ all day yesterday and there is no end in sight for today, Saturday. I hope you're having a fine day.😎🌷😊

Text (4.19)   @{User} Good morning {name}, I wish you a fantastic Thursday. Make the most of this day. May your time be filled with joy, laugh and fun. Enjoy every moment. #TakeCare #BeSafe #StayHealthy😎☕😊🌺 🌹🍎🐞☀🌼🌾

Text (4.20)   @{User} Good Morning Lee ☕😎😎🎵 [image]

Text (4.21)   @{User} Good morning {name}!! My congratulations. England won (I red newspapers)!!! Have a good Thursday🇬🇧⚽📺😎🍵😋😋😊

Text (4.22)   @{User} Good morning my dear Irish☺🐎😊😎🌸😎🌸

Text (4.23)   @{User} Good morning cutie pie🍪😘🐎💗🐕😎✨

These emoji not only coordinate with the expression of positive ATTITUDE, they also mix this with relevant IDEATION. For instance, Text (4.21) appears to be about a televised Soccer game involving the English team, and the emoji pick up these field-related meanings through the SOCCER BALL ⚽, FLAG: UNITED KINGDOM 🇬🇧, and TELEVISION 📺 emoji.

Clustering can also occur at wavelengths smaller than a whole post. For example, in Text (4.24) the groups of emoji consolidating interpersonal meaning are positioned at the end of two [figures].

Text (4.24)   Good morning beautiful lovelies😎🌸✨ Let's do this👊 😘😘

What distinguishes them from isolate is not just that they are a sequence of emoji, but that they are not directly 'pointing out' particular linguistic items and are instead consolidating a range of meanings into one. For instance, the ONCOMING FIST 👊 and the two FACE BLOWING A KISS 😘 😘 emoji bring together meanings of solidarity in 'doing things together' (possibly facing the day together) and affection.

4.4.3   PARTITION: Intersperse

The most frequent choice in partitioning a post is intersperse, where emoji interrupt the post at the points most commonly associated with traditional punctuation, as we saw in Text (4.8). Text (4.25) is a similar example.

Text (4.25)   @{User} Good morning sweetheart 😎 😘 Thank you 🙏 Have a gorgeous day lovely, be happy and look after yourself💜 💜 💜

We could break this post up into segments as follows:

1   @{User} Good morning sweetheart 🖤 🥺
2   Thank you 🙏
3   Have a gorgeous day lovely, be happy and look after yourself 💜 💜 💜

Again, the emoji divide the post by speech function. Here, in contrast to the case in Text (4.8), we interpret the comma as listing the two commands, rather than blocking the prosodic ATTITUDE, hence the three RED HEART 💜 💜 💜 emoji would appear to scope backwards across this entire segment.

Since we have already covered a number of examples of interspersing in the section about isolating, we will instead here focus on a marked choice. With the exception of emoji bracketing the hyperTheme that we will explore in the next section, they rarely functioned in the corpus to initiate a post, making this kind of interspersal a marked choice. Some examples include Text (4.26), Text (4.26), and Text (4.27) where the emoji can either be interpreted as thematising a particular meaning that synchronises with a more elaborated linguistic Theme in the written verbiage. Because of the brevity of tweets, the Theme is often wholly or partially elided.

Text (4.26)   ☕ 0 cups of coffee were drank this afternoon, making it 0 cups today.

Text (4.27)   🤮 🤮 🤮 I almost spat my ☕ out of my mouth. 💀

The HOT BEVERAGE emoji in Text (4.26) is relatively straightforward in how it realises textual meaning in previewing the IDEATION about coffee which follows. The sequence of FACE WITH OPEN MOUTH VOMITING 🤮 emoji in Text (4.27) previews both the ideational elements of the occurrence figure in the following clause (the emoji iconically represents a person 'I', vomiting 'spat' and a mouth 'mouth'), as well as the interpersonal negative [affect] it invokes. Text (4.28) is similar to the post which we used in the opening of the book at the beginning of Chapter 1 where the emoji act as visual bullet points.

Text (4.28)   ☕ had coffee from {coffee shop}
              🪴 shopped at Zen Succulent
              🍲 & lunch at [restaurant]

The emoji both organise the tweet as a list, and also thematise the key actions in the activity sequence: the HOT BEVERAGE ☕ for having coffee, the POTTED PLANT 🪴 for shopping at a plant shop and the SHALLOW PAN OF FOOD 🍲 for eating at a restaurant. This kind of choice is more commonly used in posts that appeared to be advertising or marketing. When functioning as visual bullet points the modal continuity among the vertically arranged emoji allows a vector for reading the text that runs perpendicular to the typical left-to-right reading direction of Latin alphabet-based languages. This might be likened to the traditional 'bullet point'; however, since emoji are graphical icons that can encapsulate underspecified meanings about the content of each point, a reader can at a glance gain a generalised sense of how ideational meaning is distributed across a text, before further specifying it by reading the linguistic co-text.

4.4.4   *Partition: Bracket*

Bracketing occurs when emoji begin and end a segment of the post, thereby interacting with the ideational and interpersonal meaning of the bracketed segment. Such is the case in Text (4.29).

> Text (4.29)   🌱 🌿 Good morning, lovelies.🌿 🌱
> I hope this beautiful Sunday is filled w laughter and hugs. May it also bring hope and peace in order to recharge mind & body for this upcoming week.

The emoji in Text (4.29) surround the greeting that begins the post, bracketing it from the rest of the post in conjunction with the carriage return which places the rest of the material on a new line. This serves as a form of visual marking of the morning greeting which positions it as a hyperTheme that scopes over the rest of the text. This type of textual meaning is related to two types of bracketing identified by Kaiser and Grosz (2021, p. 1), which they term 'focus marking', that affords both informational and affective emphasis, noting that the BACKHAND INDEX POINTING LEFT/RIGHT 👈 👉 and SPARKLES ✨ emoji frequently have this function. An example of the latter found in our dataset are Text (4.30) and Text (4.31) where the emoji bracket the theme of the post.

> Text (4.30)   ✨N E W V I D E O✨
> WEEKEND READING VLOG
> A long overdue weekend reading vlog as promised
>   - Lockdown blues
>   - Shit talking with mum
>   - Italian hot chocolate
>   - Bodybuilders looking like croissants
>   📖🐌☕
> Up on my channel: [link]

> Text (4.31)   🌸 Happy Sunday🌸
> Daily Comment Threads
> 🌷RT and follow me
> 🌷Share your blog post link
> 🌷Engage with others ☺
> Returning comment on my latest✨ 👈

Similarly, the emoji could be used to emphasise new information at the end of a post, as in Text (4.32).

Text (4.32) @{User} Happy Sunday Choc☕
I'm looking forward to seeing a picture of those new dice all shiny
& polished. They are gorgeous! ✦ could you pop a link to your shop
here pls

Within the corpus, the HOT BEVERAGE ☕ emoji itself was often used for
bracketing. Text (4.33) to Text (4.36) are instances where emoji bracket a
figure, for example.

Text (4.33) @{User} ☕ I'll bring the coffee☕

Text (4.34) @{User} ☕☕ morning back at ya, gorgeous!!☕☕

Text (4.35) ☕ coffee & running late☕

In addition, other emoji which incorporate into their visual appearance objects
or emblems associated with attracting attention were also used in bracketing. For instance, this included the PARTY POPPER 🎉 in Text (4.36) and the
ALARM ⏰ in Text (4.37).

Text (4.36) 🎉 Today's NEW blog post!🎉
Did you catch the news? I'm excited to partner with the team at @
TraferaOfficial for a FREE spring webinar!
☕ P.S. They're giving out a cup of coffee to attendees – make sure to
grab a spot!
🕐 May 25th @ 3PM

Text (4.37) Looking forward to our ☕ & 🎉 sesh this morning at Washington!
Our one word agenda is … KEEP.
I'm curious to hear what colleagues will KEEP doing for the remainder
of the year and into next school year.
⏰ Spoiler alert. ⏰ Next week the one word agenda is … CHANGE.🌍

As these examples suggest, this kind of pattern is more likely to occur in pro-
motional discourse where attracting attention is part of what is at stake.

Text (4.38) ☕Save the date ☕
9th April at 10am is our next Zoom Coffee Morning. New carers of
autistic adults in Lothian welcome 😊 {email} for details. [image]

In these cases, the bracketing functions to make the entire bracketed component
more salient, in accord with Kaiser and Grosz's (2021) focus marking function.

4.5 Intertextual Cohesion

Further to resources for realising intratextual cohesion described above, emoji
in initial position can also serve to link individual posts into sequences oriented
towards a particular field or function (cf. Parkwell's (2019) description of how

Cher's posts ridiculing US President Donald Trump were linked by placing the TOILET 🚽 emoji in culminating position and Zappavigna's (2018) discussion of how hashtags organise discourse across posts). Examples of this kind of intertextual cohesion in the dataset analysed here were often authored by businesses such as coffee shops who use social media to announce when orders are ready, as in examples Text (4.39) and Text (4.40).

Text (4.39)   ☕ 🌸 ☕ 🌸 ☕ 🌸 ☕ 🌸 ☕ 🌸 ☕ 🌸
Order Ready ☕
For: {User}
Coffee from: {User}
Message: 'Remember we're always together anywhere I'll always console your life So just lean on me and rest sometimes'

Text (4.40)   ☕ 🌸 ☕ 🌸 ☕ 🌸 ☕ 🌸 ☕ 🌸 ☕ 🌸
Order Ready ☕
For: {User}
Coffee from: {User}
Message: happy birthday soulmate!! i wudnt know what to do w my life without you lol thank you for bringing equal amounts of chaos and calm into my life

The sequence of HOT BEVERAGE ☕ and CHERRY BLOSSOM 🌸 emoji in initial position is found in all posts announcing an order is ready by this social media user, and presumably assist waiting customers in noticing when an order-ready post has been made. This kind of cohesion among texts is made possible by the technological context within which emoji typically occur: device screens showing social media platform feeds of posts. As such, the nature and degree of intertextual cohesion possible will vary significantly depending on the particular device and social media platform in question.

4.6   Conclusion

This chapter has described the differing ways in which emoji and language interact to realise textual meaning and organised these as features of a system network. These descriptions build on earlier work noting how emoji can punctuate texts and realise phoric functions with context and linguistic co-text. Before stepping through the description of features, the question of how interactions between particular emoji and linguistic meaning were isolated was addressed, with the analytical approach employed here underpinned by the principles of proximity, minimum mapping, and prosodic correspondence.

In terms of the features of the emoji–text SYNCHRONICITY system network, a primary distinction is made between instances where emoji replace linguistic co-text ([inset]) and instances where emoji accompany the linguistic co-text ([punctuate]). Within the [punctuate] branch of the system network, emoji can either escort linguistic co-text in the ideational [elements] adjacent to them or partition linguistic meaning within a longer stretch of discourse at whose boundary they sit. Further to these features describing interaction between language and emoji within texts, the potential for emoji to realise intertextual cohesion was observed as a particular affordance made possible by the technological context within which emoji occur.

In practice, posts can draw on a range of textual resources in order to construct a coherent and cohesive text. For example, with emoji inset into the discourse semantic structure (2) at the same times as punctuating a post via adjacency relations (1, 4, 5, 6, 7, 8), as in Text (4.41):

Text (4.41)   {name} sent me the most beautiful little package I just can't😭[1]
              The art is 🙄[2]
              🍵🥄🎶💚🏠💮☕🍮🎠[3]
              The playlist 🎶[4]
              The cookies and tea🍵💮🍵[5]
              The marigolds🌼[6]
              I love you so much😭💕[7] @{User} I've been feeling sick and you made me smile so so much! Tea tasting today🍵💕[8]

In a post like this, we also begin to see how intertwined textual meaning is with interpersonal and ideational meaning. For instance, when reading '*The art is* 🙄', our interpretation of FACE WITH ROLLING EYES 🙄 as indexing generalised, possibly down-scaled negative ATTITUDE (interpersonal meaning) is informed by our understanding that the emoji is inset into the linguistic co-text, thus it must serve to grammatically complete the ideational [figure]. As such, alternative interpretations of the FACE WITH ROLLING EYES 🙄 such as depicting a facial expression of a participant in the text (ideational meaning) are backgrounded by its textual relationship with the linguistic co-text: 'the art is ok' is grammatically more coherent than 'the art is frown/frowning/person frowning [etc.]'. In summary, an understanding of how emoji and language interact to realise coherent texts equips us to proceed in the following chapters to describing how these interactions also realise interpersonal and ideational meaning.

5   Emoji CONCURRING with Ideational Meaning

5.1   Introduction: Representing Experience

This chapter is concerned with the region of meaning where emoji and language converge to construe ideational meanings. From the perspective of the SFL register variable of field, these meanings are concerned with how texts make meanings about the 'content' of the communication. In other words, these meanings are about representing experience as items and activities. When applying an ideational lens to how emoji and their co-text make these meanings together, we are concerned with understanding relations of concurrence. In order to explore the role of language in this coordination, we will draw on the discourse semantic system, IDEATION, that was introduced in Chapter 3. Our focus will thus be on how emoji coordinate with linguistic [sequences], [figures], and [elements]. Unless otherwise mentioned, all examples in this chapter are taken from the Hot Beverage Emoji Corpus.

The consensus in research on emoji is that they can make meanings about objects, events, and happenings, although this is formulated in different ways depending on theoretical orientation. Most studies suggest that emoji are in some way iconic with the function of reiterating 'the object or event being referred to', a usage more common than outright substitution, where an emoji replaces a lexical item entirely (Miyake, 2020, p. 6). Opinions vary on the degree of isomorphism between language or emoji and the material world, with some studies suggesting that emoji have greater iconicity: 'For example, the iconic nature of the relationship between an actual dog and 🐶 is not preserved in the sign dog' (Wicke & Bolognesi, 2020, p. 619). However, rather than cataloguing emoji based on their purported resemblance to material objects and activities, the approach we adopt in this book is to consider how they concur with selections in ideational discourse semantics. Thus in the case of the aforementioned example of the DOG FACE 🐶, rather than classifying this as an inherently iconic emoji indexing real life dogs, we consider the relation of this emoji to meanings made about relevant dimensions of field relating to dogs. For instance, Text (5.1) is a post from the Hot Beverage Emoji corpus, where such a relation occurs.

Text (5.1)   @{User} Good morning {name} .. my pups are so spoiled for sure, have a great day. 🐶 🌷

Here, we consider the relation of the DOG FACE 🐶 to '*my pups*' as the relevant [thing entity] in the co-text. This kind of ideational concurrence relation is the focus of this chapter.

Relations that might correspond or partially overlap with this kind of ideational concurrence include Gawne and McCulloch's (2019) ascription of an 'illustrative' function to emoji. This study characterises emoji's capacity to 'refer to concrete objects' by analogising with McNeill's (1992) conceptualisation of iconic co-speech gesture (Gawne & McCulloch, 2019). Most directly relevant to the approach taken in this book are emerging social semiotic studies that draw on Halliday's (1978) linguistic metafunctions. This includes work on how emoji 'can create experiential meaning by acting as or forming part of a participant, process, or circumstance within a text' at the level of lexicogrammar (Parkwell, 2019, p. 4). Also relevant are studies that consider how emoji can target interpersonal meaning at particular ideational meanings in its co-text (He, 2022), a notion that we will return to in Chapter 6.

5.2   Not Just a Catalogue of Types 🍵 🍵 🍸 🧋

It may seem tempting to adopt the emoji 'types' described in Unicode as a way of defining emoji's ideational classificatory potential. However, without considering the co-text this potential is somewhat blunted. As we explored in Chapter 2, Unicode embeds some assumptions about how experience might be organised in terms of how it notionally arranges emoji into categories such as 'Objects', 'People and Body', and 'Animals and Nature' (see, e.g. the 'Drink' category in Table 2.2 of Chapter 2). Each entry in a category also specifies keywords, based on likely terms a user might employ to search for a particular emoji, for instance, when using a messaging app. This organisation is relevant to understanding some of the minimal bracketing of semantic types that emoji, as designed resources, have 'hard-coded' into their design. The 'drink' subcategory for objects, for example, offers a restricted (though evolving) set of options for expressing beverage type. Within this category there is an obvious distinction in meaning between the HOT BEVERAGE ☕ and the WINE GLASS 🍷 emoji that does not necessarily require co-occurring verbiage to unpack. Text (5.2) is an example where this distinction in meaning at the level of emoji organisation is used in a post through emoji that are inserted into the discursive structure acting as [entities].

Text (5.2)   the biggest decision in my life right now …
              ☕ or 🍷
              i'd say things are pretty okay. 🧋

The semantic distinction also underlies the humour in Text (5.3).

Text (5.3)   I need a drink 🥃 No not that☕

However, while some minimal distinction in meaning can be adduced from these examples, this does not substitute for close textual analysis.

Some degree of emoji–internal subclassification can occur through emoji which appear next to each other (e.g. ☕ 🍵 in Text (5.4)); however, this too usually relies on coordinating verbiage and is highly underspecified. For example, the Hot Beverage Emoji corpus included many instances of object emoji in L1 and/or R1 position in relation to the HOT BEVERAGE ☕ emoji. These were usually also co-specified in the accompanying written text and would otherwise be too underspecified to understand what kind of [entity] was being expressed. For instance, the HOT BEVERAGE ☕ is used together with emoji such as the CHOCOLATE BAR 🍫 or CUSTARD 🍮, and is co-specified in the bolded co-text, in Text (5.5).

Text (5.4)   Afternoon delight #**CaramelMacchiato** ☕ 🍵 @{User}

Text (5.5)   I hope everyone is having a restful #Easter weekend so far. ☕ Taking a
              well-earned siesta rn that involves spring cleaning, fanfiction, and **hot
              chocolate**! ! ✔ ☕ 🍫 📖#WritingCommunity

However, without the linguistic [thing entities], '*CaramelMacchiato*' and '*hot chocolate*', the items being construed remain ambiguous.

More generally, emoji tend to remain relatively underspecified or ambiguous without a co-occurring linguistic [element], [figure], or [sequence], as the examples explored throughout this chapter will show. It would appear that the classificatory potential of emoji is limited. In some ways this is unsurprising as a requirement for an emoji to enter Unicode is that it is broad in its semantic scope. Thus, rather than simply approaching 'object' emoji as a catalogue of types, we explore the function that all emoji, as semiotic resources, can have in the orchestration of ideational meanings in texts.

5.3   Frequent Ideational Patterns in the Corpus

Before embarking on a detailed exploration of the ideational functions that emoji can enact, it is interesting as a starting point to consider some of the most frequent ideational meanings that are made in the corpus. The top ten most frequent collocates of the HOT BEVERAGE emoji (Table 5.1) provide a snapshot of the concurrence relations in ideational meaning that we will explore in this chapter. This frequency list was generated with a tight window (span = 1) so privileges local convergence (where an emoji is adjacent to the target lexis) as a starting point. This kind of coordination is a common scenario, where

Table 5.1 *Frequency list for collocates of HOT BEVERAGE emoji (window span = 1)*

Rank	Collocate	Freq(Scaled)	FreqLR	FreqL	FreqR	Example
1	☕	18,944	2,220	1,110	1,110	@{User} I've had 3 strong cups☕ ☕ ☕ I'm had a good reving up!
2	coffee	4,204	850	783	67	I finished my day with a cup of coffee☕
3	morning	7,344	799	753	46	@{User} Good morning Mike.☕
4	day	2,972	330	324	6	Good morning. Show Monday who is boss. Have a great day.☕
5	tea	934	190	178	12	On Sundays we have tea.☕
6	friend	650	134	133	1	@{User} Cheers my friend☕
8	you	5,328	139	110	29	@{User} Good morning to you.☕
9	too	564	64	63	1	@{User} You too☕
10	sweetheart	136	53	53	0	@{User} Good morning sweetheart ☕ Have a gorgeous day lovely and take care

emoji optionally coordinate, here and there, with localised ideational meaning. However, emoji can also co-construe IDEATION across broader spans, as later examples will demonstrate.

The most frequent collocate of the HOT BEVERAGE emoji in the corpus was the emoji itself. This was typically in instances expressing plurality (as shown in example 1 in Table 5.1) or up-scaled evaluation through GRADUATION (see Chapter 6). Other frequent collocates were the linguistic [thing entities] '*coffee*' and '*tea*', involved in congruently [illustrating] ideational meaning, as we will explore in Section 5. Collocates such as '*morning*', '*day*', '*friend*', and '*you*' enacted less congruent relations embellishing ideational meanings, as we explore in Section 6. These collocates were involved in greetings, the most frequent of which was '*good morning*', incorporating the metonymic association of coffee with morning. Similarly, collocates such as '*too*' and '*sweetheart*' were part of expressions of thanks in response greetings. These collocational patterns are reflected in the most common 3-grams involving the HOT BEVERAGE emoji shown in Table 5.2 (focusing on relations with language rather than with other emoji).

Table 5.2 *Most frequent 3-grams incorporating the HOT BEVERAGE emoji*

Rank	Type	Freq	Example
1	☕ ☕ ☕	676	@{User} Morning {name}☕ ☕ ☕
2	good morning☕	501	@{User} Good Morning☕
3	a coffee☕	237	@{User 1} @{User 2} Imma go make a coffee☕
4	my friend☕	87	@{User} Your Awesome Kate!!! Good mornin my friend☺ ☕
5	great day☕	86	@{User} A good strong cuppa definitely gets the day going right! Cheers, {name}, have a great day☕ ☕

5.4   A System Network for Emoji–Text CONCURRENCE

In order to systematically analyse the ideational concurrence relations between emoji and verbiage in this chapter we will use the system network shown in Figure 5.1. This network has as its basis a distinction between emoji which depict and which embellish ideational meanings in the co-text. Depiction involves congruent relations, where emoji directly co-represent experience by accompanying [elements], [figures], or [sequences]. The emoji in Text (5.6), for example, depict linguistic [thing entities] within a [sequence] of [figures]. From the perspective of field, together the emoji and the [thing entities] form multimodal items (underlined).

Text (5.6)   Good morning so far, got some dividend love, bought some future freedom, walked the dog 🐕 and having a cup of coffee ☕. Good way to start the day

On the other hand, emoji that embellish IDEATION enact an incongruent relation with the co-text. In these cases the emoji function to symbolise meanings from the context or in the co-text. For example, emoji might metaphorically represent experience via metonymic relations or through the use of emblems. An example is Text (5.7) where the HOT BEVERAGE ☕ and SUN ☀ emoji are associated with the [time entity] '*morning*' through metonymy.

Text (5.7)   Good morning!☕ ☀

The metonymy derives from the association of the sun rising with '*morning*' and coffee being a common breakfast beverage in many cultures.

In this way, the two systems of meaning are distinguished on the basis of whether the relations between the emoji and its co-text are congruent or incongruent; that is, whether they directly or indirectly express ideational meaning. The complete system network for modelling these kinds of distinctions in meaning is show in Figure 5.1. Each of the subsections which follow explores features of this network.

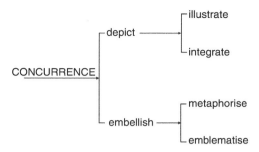

Figure 5.1 The system of emoji–text CONCURRENCE

While this network aims to model the relation of emoji to their co-text, since emoji are our primary concern in this book the network is skewed toward emoji. Just as Zhao (2011) has noted for classification-exemplification relations between language and images, some relations can be bidirectional and look different when viewed from the perspective of image than from the perspective of language. For instance, from the perspective of the emoji, in Text (5.8) the linguistic [thing entities] '*black coffee*' and '*vanilla latte*' classify the type of beverage; from the perspective of language, the emoji exemplifies some of the characteristics of this type of beverage (e.g. brown liquid with steam).

Text (5.8)   what's your choice of caffeine this morning? started off with a <u>black coffee</u> and now onto a <u>vanilla latte</u>. ☕

As noted in the previous chapter, these characteristics vary with the choices in visual representation made when particular vendors render the Unicode encoding as a glyph.

The sections which follow explain each of the more delicate sub-choices in the emoji–text CONCURRENCE network that are possible, drawing on examples of patterns in ideational meaning observed in the corpus.

5.5 Depict

Depiction is concerned with how emoji concur with the co-text to express multimodal items and activities within a field of experience by either illustrating ideational meaning made in the co-text or standing-in for ideational meanings by integrating themselves into the ideational discourse semantic structure. This latter option is supported by the textual resource [inset] that we explored in the previous chapter. As shown in Figure 5.2, the main choice is thus between emoji which integrate into [figures] and [sequences] by taking on a role such as an [entity] in place of language, and emoji which co-construe

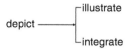

Figure 5.2 The system of depiction

ideational meaning alongside language. For example, consider the distinction between Text (5.9) and Text (5.10).

Text (5.9)   Give me some ☕ since im bored

Text (5.10)   I need a coffee☕

In Text (5.9) the HOT BEVERAGE ☕ emoji occupies the role that might be expected of a linguistic [thing entity] in the [figure] '*Give me some* ___ ... '. The emoji serves to complete the [figure] so that it is coherent by integrating it into the text. However, Text (5.10) already contains the complete [figure], '*I need a coffee*', so instead the emoji illustrates the linguistic [thing entity] '*coffee*' and together they form a multimodal item. This kind of illustration varies according to principles of generalisation-specification, where emoji and text can each deploy more or less of their meaning potential in order to realise multimodal IDEATION.

Since emoji and written verbiage are different modes with different affordances, they will contribute different degrees of meaning when involved in a relation of depiction. For instance, they may vary across parameters such as generalisation, with the visual perhaps more oriented toward topological meaning (Zhao, 2011, p. 240). This constitutes a variation in the deployment of meaning potential in terms of how 'a bimodal text has the potential to commit greater or lesser amounts of any kind of meaning from either semiotic system', in other words to share the semiotic load across modalities at the same time as expanding the range of meanings that can be made (Painter & Martin, 2012, p. 135). For instance, Text (5.11) is an example where in a depiction relation more ideational meaning about the beverage is committed through the use of linguistic Classifiers in the co-text than is in the emoji as a picture character.

Text (5.11)   @{User 1} @{User 2} I can't do anything without having **a cup of Yorkshire Tea** first☕

Commitment is a semiotic variable which will also vary depending on the design choices made by each vendor. For instance, the Samsung HOT BEVERAGE emoji does not include steam and the OpenMoji is black and white but does not show the liquid in the cup. Other emoji include animation (e.g. moving steam) which again inflects the degree of commitment.

5.5.1 Depict: Illustrate

Emoji which illustrate IDEATION can coordinate with a range of ideational discourse semantic features, from different types of [elements] to [figures] and [sequences]. The most common case in the Hot Beverage Emoji corpus was unsurprisingly the illustration of linguistic [thing entities] such as tea and coffee. While language is resplendent with resources for classification and qualification along typological parameters, emoji have less capacity for taxonomic organisation and, when depicting IDEATION, will tend to realise these meanings through close coordination with verbiage. Language has many resources for expressing type, for instance, through the Classifier ^ Thing structure of the nominal group, as can be seen in the linguistic co-text of Text (5.12) to Text (5.15) (Classifiers in bold; nominal group underlined).

Text (5.12)   **Sunday morning** coffee☕

Text (5.13)   **black** coffee☕

Text (5.14)   My mornings start with **iced** coffee☕

Text (5.15)   queen of **herbal** tea☕

In the corpus, the emoji tended to depict more linguistically committed [elements]. For instance, as indicated earlier, while the HOT BEVERAGE ☕ emoji has the potential to represent a range of heated drinks, such as coffee, tea, hot chocolate, etc., this typological differentiation most commonly occurred via coordination with the verbiage. The most common choice in the corpus was for the emoji and co-text to co-construe a [thing entity], as we saw in the most frequent collocate in the corpus (Table 5.1). For instance, the most frequent linguistic LR1 collocates of the HOT BEVERAGE emoji that were [thing entities] were '*coffee*' (FreqLR = 850) and '*tea*'3 (FreqLR = 190) (excluding intervening emoji), as shown in Text (5.16) to Text (5.25).

Text (5.16)   @{User} Time For **coffee**☕

Text (5.17)   Thank goodness for **coffee**☕

Text (5.18)   but first **coffee**☕

Text (5.19)   @{User} **Coffee** ☕?

Text (5.20)   starting the ordinary day with **coffee**☕

Text (5.21)   @{User} buy me a **coffee**☕

Text (5.22)   Dinner, then **coffee**☕

Text (5.23)   @{User 1} @{User 2} @{User 3} @{User 4} **Coffee** ☕ sounds lovely

Text (5.24)   Waking up to a **Tea** ☕ made by my bf is the best ✨

Text (5.25)   @{User 1} I've always bean a coffee girl ☕ Never could Aquire a taste for **tea**☕

In these examples, a more linguistically committed [thing entity] '*coffee/tea*' in L1 position specifies the beverage by type and is accompanied by the HOT BEVERAGE ☕ emoji. As we saw in Chapter 4, in terms of textual meaning the position adjacent to the linguistic [thing entity] assists in coordinating the mapping of meaning.

Text (5.26)   @{User 1} @{User 2} @{User 3} @{User 4} Coffee ☕ sounds lovely

When emoji accompany language in this way, they can follow a pattern of hypo/hypernymy. In these instances, meaning construed by one mode will be superordinate or subordinate to meaning construed by the other (Logi & Zappavigna, 2021b). For instance, in the examples Text (5.27) to Text (5.32), the HOT BEVERAGE emoji depicts a more committed linguistic [thing entity] (underlined), which, in these cases, is the type of coffee.

Text (5.27)   It's a grand day for a 'Grande'☕

Text (5.28)   today's drink: white mocha latte ☕7/10 …

Text (5.29)   Home & having a little cappuccino ☕ …

Text (5.30)   @{User} {name} dat not real coffee. Puertoricans we drink Yaucono☕ 🍵☕

Text (5.31)   @{User} Really appreciate the boost Raye, hope you enjoy the show and your next cuppa☕ ☕

Text (5.32)   Top of the morning a little coffee ☕ and rum 🥃 to start my day ☺ #JamaicaMon✉ [image]

If we position the interacting linguistic and emoji resources from Text (5.28) in a classification taxonomy as in Figure 5.3, we can see that the emoji sits at the more generalised end of the taxonomy, whereas the linguistic verbiage sits at the more specific. While the two modes co-instantiate a single ideational taxonomy, in this instance the emoji realises a more generalised, superordinate class of Things, while the linguistic resource realises a hyponym several layers more specific. In coordination, the linguistic co-text acts to specify the emoji.

The examples covered so far are relatively straightforward instances where emoji depict concrete [thing entities]. However, many examples are more complex and what is depicted is a facet of or association to an [entity] or a set of related components. For instance, Text (5.33) includes emoji that depict

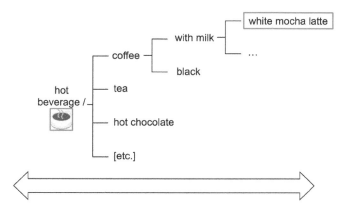

Figure 5.3 Classification taxonomy for emoji and language resources in Text (5.28)

[thing entities] (bold) within [figures] in the co-text as visual bullet points (see Chapter 4 re: textual meaning of this kind).

Text (5.33)   @{User 1} @{User 2} @{User 3}
               ☕ Up with **the sun**
               🐕 With **my dog**
               ☕ Drinking **a cup of coffee**
               🥐 And eating **a croissant**
               🌊 By **the river**
               🦦 🦆 🐢 Watching **wildlife**

The final line includes an OTTER 🦦, DUCK 🦆, and TURTLE 🐢 emoji that concur with '*wildlife*'. If we interpret this as a concrete depiction, then these three types of animals are the wildlife observed. However, they might also be interpreted as 'the idea of wildlife' in a general sense, in keeping with the general tendency of emoji towards stylising experience so as not to be too specific to be able to be used in multiple kinds of relations with language. In this case we might interpret the relation instead as metonymic.

While emoji tend to be attracted to linguistic [entities] in terms of co-construing ideational meaning, they can also coordinate with grammatical choices through which [entities] are realised. For instance, this might include meanings about the type or quality of [thing entity], realised linguistically as Classifiers or Epithets in the nominal group at the lexicogrammatical stratum. In these cases emoji sequences (e.g. 🍫 🥛 ☕) might be used to create more committed ideational meaning, for instance, to make meanings about the flavour or type of a beverage or foodstuff. Wicke and Bolognesi (2020, p. 622) categorise emoji sequence types into those involving polysemy (e.g. BREAD used with CLINKING GLASSES 🍞 🥂 to mean a celebratory 'toast' or cheers), similarity (e.g. the HIBISCUS, CHERRY BLOSSOM and SUNFLOWER 🌺 🌸 🌻 to mean flower), temporality (e.g. NOTEBOOK, PASSPORT CONTROL and PLANE 📔 🛂 ✈ to represent an activity sequence) and spatiality (e.g. AUTOMOBILE and HOUSE 🚗 🏠 to mean garage). However, the combinatorial meaning potential of emoji remains limited. For instance, the last example realising 'garage' may equally be interpreted as 'going home'.

Text (5.34) to Text (5.36) are examples where the HOT BEVERAGE emoji coordinates with linguistic Classifiers (shown underlined), concurring with '*mocha*', '*expresso*', and '*iced*' (in bold), both Classifiers in the linguistic nominal groups.

Text (5.34)   3 layered **mocha** chiffon + **mocha** icing numbered cake!!!🍫🫧🍩☕

Text (5.35)   Need a pick me up chocolate **espresso** martini 😋🫧☕ 🍸 @User

Text (5.36)   **iced** coffeeee 🥤☕. what are you sippin on?

This kind of co-occurrence is optional, and often the emoji will co-instantiate only one of multiple classifiers in the verbiage. For example, in Text (5.37) there is no direct coordination of emoji with '*caramel*' or '*mocha*' and only '*iced*' is co-classified, and in Text (5.38) there is no direct coordination with '*vanilla*':

Text (5.37)   **Iced** mocha **latte** and **Iced** caramel **macchiato** are absolutely my fav coffee drinks 🥤☕

Text (5.38)   **hibiscus** and vanilla **latte** with **coconut milk.**🌺🥥☕

As mentioned in the introduction to this chapter, emoji can employ the loose categorical distinctions embedded in the Unicode groupings. These categories may be mapped onto distinctions construed in the co-text. For instance, in Text (5.39) the multimodal [thing entity] forged through the concurrence of the HOT BEVERAGE emoji and '*coffee*' is contrasted with that realised by the concurrence of the TEACUP WITHOUT HANDLE emoji and '*African tea*'.

Text (5.39)   Coffee ☕ is not for all people😄 😄 😄
              Take your African tea 🍵 in peace

Alternatively, the HOT BEVERAGE emoji could concur with multiple [thing entities]. In these cases the emoji appears to act as a generalising hypernym in relation to co-occurring verbiage (shown in bold in Text (5.40)).

Text (5.40)   @{User} Agree on the **tea one** but **coffee** is good lots of **different ones** to try☕

Emoji can also illustrate [figures]. For example, in Text (5.41) to Text (5.45), while the emoji do in some sense coordinate with the '*coffee*' throughout, they are positioned at the end of [figures] such that they appear to encapsulate the overall experience captured within the [figure].

Text (5.41)   This stuff is so good, I look forward to waking up in the morning☕

Text (5.42)   I got my morning coffee☕

Text (5.43)   Eid Mubarak to all who are celebrating 🌙✨
               Iced coffee was the first thing I had today☕

Text (5.44)   @{User 1} @{User 2} coffee is good☕

Text (5.45)   The only way to start the day. Coffee and a good book, unless I'm
               working then it's extra strong coffee only.📚 ☕

Depending on how the scope or unit of analysis is defined, depiction involves emoji that are relatively tightly tied to the 'literal' or 'iconic' meaning made in the co-text. Emoji, however, do have the capacity to add additional ideational meaning made in the co-text by embroidering them via extension. This might occur when the emoji elaborate relatively underspecified meanings in the co-text such as the underlined entities in Text (5.46) and Text (5.47).

Text (5.46)   I've got to learn to appreciate <u>the little things</u>. 🍶 ☕ 🌸 ✳ 🌿

Text (5.47)   It's <u>the simple things in life</u> that make me the happiest!☕ 🍶👓

In these two examples the emoji sequences illustrate what the underspecified '*things*' include. For instance, in Text (5.46) the '*little things*' the author appreciates include SAKE 🍶, HOT BEVERAGE ☕, and various plants. This kind of pattern where the co-text is relatively underspecified and the emoji home in on a particular area of IDEATION is also seen in Text (5.48).

Text (5.48)   Now my room smells like **my favorite thing in the world**😊 ☕

In Text (5.48) the bolded co-text under-commits the details of the author's '*favourite thing in the world*' and the concurrent HOT BEVERAGE ☕ emoji serves to reduce the scope of the potential classification to the category of hot beverages. A similar example is Text (5.49) where the emoji unpack the '*Unexpected pleasures*', exemplifying them through a sequence of emoji.

Text (5.49)   … @{User} Unexpected pleasures are always uplifting 🕊 🌊 🍸 😎 ☕ 🍰
               🎂 🐶 🐱 https

The DOVE 🕊, WATER WAVE 🌊, HOT BEVERAGE ☕, COCKTAIL GLASS 🍸, BIRTHDAY CAKE 🎂, and DOG FACE 🐶 emoji can be interpreted as manifesting aspects of experience interpretable as pleasurable, although since there is no co-occurring linguistic specification this remains relatively under-committed.

In some examples the entire post remains relatively under-committed, even with accompanying emoji suggesting a particular field of experience, such as in Text (5.50).

Text (5.50)   @{User} Good morning 🩰💃🩰thank you kindly🩰💃🩰

Here the BALLET SHOES 🩰 emoji suggests that the post is situated within the field of discourse about ballet. In this case the repeated BALLET SHOES 🩰 emoji is not easily resolvable to a particular [entity] or [figure] within the post. It instead appears to ground the entire [sequence] within the ballet domain, possibly via concurring with an element in a previous move in the exchange.

Flag emoji were a particular type of emoji that often served to reduce the scope of the possible ideational domain in relation to the co-text. For example, in Text (5.51) the FLAG: UNITED STATES 🇺🇸 emoji identifies the particular country which is referenced via '*Patriot*' and thus we can interpret the multi-modal item as 'American Patriot'.

Text (5.51)   @{User} Good morning **Patriot**😃 ☕🇺🇸

Similarly, the flag emoji in Text (5.52) refines the ideational meaning in order to specify the reference '*4th of July*' to the American Independence Day holiday.

Text (5.52)   @{User 1} @{User 2} @{User 3} Happy 4th of July Joe and thank you. Hope you and Don are having a great 4th 🇺🇸 Stay safe and be well friend.😍 🏌 🌴☕🇺🇸

The United States flag was the most common flag emoji in the corpus, but other examples included the Italian and French flags, as seen in Text (5.53) to Text (5.55).

Text (5.53)   @{User} Good morning {name}, yes the same for me, always with adrenaline, we are fire up ! Have a wonderful day, waiting this evening to see our adversary!☕ 💙 ⚽🇮🇹

Text (5.54)   @{User} with or without sugar?☕ 😊 ☕🇮🇹

Text (5.55)   Going out for a coffee.. ☕🇮🇹🥐☕🚗 #Grasse #VilleDeGrasse 🧍🚗 #AlpesMaritimes #FrenchRiviera🧍

In these cases, the flags contextualise other emoji as well as the co-text. For instance, in Text (5.53) the SOCCER BALL ⚽ emoji suggests that the post is about an Italian soccer team. In Text (5.55) the CROISSANT 🥐 emoji in combination with the French flag and the hashtags specify where the author is going for their coffee.

5.5.2   Depict: Integrate

Returning to consider the integrate choice in more detail, as explored in Chapter 4 in terms of textual meaning, field items can be convergently realised as emoji that are inset into the discourse semantic structure. In terms of ideational meaning, as we saw in Text (5.9), this can be realised as emoji which are integrated into a [figure] or [sequence], for instance, acting in place of what would likely be a [thing entity] as in the examples, Text (5.56)–Text (5.59).

Text (5.56)   @{User} Omg, I'm a sucker for a☕

Text (5.57)   @{User} Hi @{User} I had a ☕ this morning then saw your tweet. Figured that's a sign

Text (5.58)   @{User} Not convinced it's ☕ in that jug … are you? These are Poles, after all ….

Text (5.59)   @{User 1} @{User 2} @{User 3} Double shift for @{User 4} @{User 5}. They will be drinking lots of ☕ ☕.

In these posts, without co-textual clues the emoji are underspecified in terms of the type of hot beverage they index. Text (5.59) is an example where multiple emoji are used to indicate plurality since emoji have no other means of expressing quantity, although in this case the plurality redounds with '*lots of*' ([GRADUATION: force: up-scale]) in the verbiage.

Less frequently emoji also act as classifiers of [entities]. For instance, in Text (5.60) to Text (5.62) the HOT BEVERAGE ☕ emoji classifies the type of [time entity].

Text (5.60)   @{User} ☕ Break❣ ☺

Text (5.61)   When the dev stack is broken by dependency team, time for a ☕ break☺

Text (5.62)   ☕ time

In these examples, the HOT BEVERAGE ☕ emoji may be read as a Classifier that modifies the Thing ('*break*', '*time*'), resulting in nominal groups such as 'coffee break' or 'tea time'.

[Occurrences] and [activity entities] can also be inset into the discourse semantic structure. For example, in Text (5.63) the RED HEART ♥ emoji substitutes for an [occurrence] such as '*love*' or '*adore*'.

Text (5.63)   I♥ @{User} !!!
Happy Birthday & cheers to many more ☕ !!

Other kinds of resources can also be integrated, for instance, expletives.

Text (5.64)   @{User} Oh 💩 I forgot the litter boxes yesterday.
I know what's first after ☕ of course.

In Text (5.64) the PILE OF POO 💩 emoji replaces the position where we would expect the expletive, 'shit'.

In practice users can switch between the choices to illustrate and integrate seamlessly in their tweets. For example the HOT BEVERAGE ☕ and the FACE VOMITING 🤮 emoji are integrated into Text (5.65), substituting for a linguistic [thing entity] and [occurrence], respectively, while the THOUGHT BALLOON emoji illustrates the [occurrence] '*thinking*'.

Text (5.65)   I drink so much ☕ I feel like 🤮 even thinking 💭 bout it

We will now shift to considering examples where there is a much less congruent relation between emoji and their co-text, which illustrates how emoji are capable of expressing abstract concepts and rendering metaphorical meanings that extend beyond the largely literal meanings explored in this section.

5.6   Embellish

Another way of adding meaning to a post is through relations of embellishing, for instance, through drawing on figurative meanings. The relations involve incongruency, that is indirect meanings, where emoji activate meanings from the context that are not explicitly co-realised in the written verbiage. These meanings will be more or less interpretable depending on the kind of interactive negotiation occurring between social media users or the kind of ambient communion happening in the social stream. For instance, in contexts where people have close relationships, 'there are large amounts of shared knowledge between participants, which allows them to make use of vague, underspecified language, and a shared understanding of metonymic links' (Littlemore & Tagg, 2018, p. 482). Thus, emoji that index localised shared symbols are more likely to occur.

Two types of embellishing were observed in the corpus. The first was metaphorising, an incongruent relation where an emoji represents something other than its congruent interpretation in relation to the co-tex. The second was

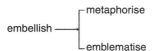

Figure 5.4 The system of embellish

emblematising, where an incongruent relation has stabilised to the extent that it comes to stand as a symbol for an idea or concept from the cultural context. For example, consider the difference in meaning between Text (5.66) and Text (5.67).

Text (5.66)   @{User} Homa, I spy bagels w/cream cheese!•• 😋 😋 😖

Text (5.67)   @{User} Omg who??😋 😋 😋

In Text (5.66) the EYES •• emoji has a metaphorising relation of metonymy (specifically synecdoche) with the process '*spy*': the representation of just the human eyes stands for the entire activity of looking (which in reality involves an entire human, a head, a brain, etc.). On the other hand, the HOT BEVERAGE ☕ in Text (5.67) activates meanings about gossip and intrigue by functioning as an emblem for the idiom 'spilling the tea' (which we will cover in more detail in terms of interpersonal meaning in the next chapter). In other words, rather than making direct meanings about a hot beverage such as coffee or tea, it encapsulates the idea of revealing salacious gossip or interesting hidden information.

5.6.1   Embellish: Metaphorise

A frequent kind of metaphorising seen in the corpus is metonymy, as introduced in the previous section. This occurs where an aspect or dimension of something comes to stand for that thing. For instance, while Text (5.68) involves simple depiction (e.g. the HOT BEVERAGE ☕ emoji depicts '*coffee*' and the SHORTCAKE 🍰 emoji depicts '*cake*'), this post also incorporates more complicated types of metaphoric ideational concurrence.

Text (5.68)   Morning bookophiles 📚. I am not at work today 😊 👍. I am having a day off, about to head out for coffee ☕ and cake 🍰 but there might be breakfast 🍳 🥓 🐷. Spending quality time with #DaddyTwoSpoons😊 😊 🥄

In this post, '*bookophiles*' concurs with the BOOKS 📚 emoji through metonymy. A bookophile is a type of person represented here simply by a book. Similarly, the relation between '*breakfast*' and the COOKING 🍳 and BACON 🥓 emoji is metonymic, with these objects appearing to stand for the broader concept of breakfast rather than necessarily specifying the particular breakfast items consumed. To a certain extent metonymic relations are always somewhat ambiguous in emoji usage, since it is difficult to disambiguate with actual identification. For example, in some instances the emoji following a general term such as '*breakfast*' might in fact identify the particular foods that were consumed, and then the relation would be one of depiction rather than metaphorising.

There was a tendency observed in the corpus toward over-elaborated metonymy. An example is the extended sequence of emoji in Text (5.69) concurring with '*a drive through*'.

Text (5.69)   Get ready Red Mill and VB peeps! Town Center Cold Pressed is opening its 4th location with a drive through 🚗 🚗 🚗 🪟 🥤 ☕ ☕ 🍴 🍩 🍩 🥛 🥣 I got a sneak peek 👀 [images]

The emoji sequence in this post comprises the AUTOMOBILE 🚗, SPORT UTILITY VEHICLE 🚗, WINDOW 🪟, CUP WITH STRAW 🥤, HOT BEVERAGE ☕, FORK AND KNIFE 🍴, DONUT 🍩, GLASS OF MILK 🥛, and BOWL WITH SPOON 🥣 emoji, all of which are potential aspects of the experience of watching a movie and eating food at a drive-through cinema. Thus, there is a metonymic metaphorising relation between these emoji and the linguistic '*drive-through*' [entity]. In addition, in a similar way to Text (5.66), the EYES 👀 emoji is in a metonymic relation of synecdoche with the process '*sneak peek*'.

Other examples of this kind of pattern include the EYES 👀 emoji representing meanings such as searching in Text (5.70) and interest or attention Text (5.71):

Text (5.70)   if anyone in IC is looking for a part-time barista gig, I may know a guy and would be happy to put in a good word for the right person☕ 👀 ✨

Text (5.71)   I AM VERY VERY INTERESTED👀 ☕ 💚 💚 💚

From an interpersonal perspective the EYES 👀 emoji is often used to suggest '"pervy eyes" to indicate approval of an attractive photo posted online; or "shifty eyes" to convey a deceitful act' (Emojipedia®, n.d.) or some form of shame, self-deprecation, or generalised embarrassment (often ironic). For instance, this often occurred in the corpus in conjunction with the emblematic usage of the HOT BEVERAGE ☕ emoji that we have noted earlier as relating to meanings about gossip.

Text (5.72)   @{User} Ooooh spill the ☕! What havoc are we wreaking today?👀

Text (5.73)   What's the tea with this drama in the Brisbane drag seven?☕ 👀

Text (5.74)   @{User 1} @{User 2} @{User 3} Nah cause they lokey spilled👀 ☕

Other body part emoji such as the EAR 👂 emoji and the NOSE 👃 emoji also involved themselves in synecdoche related to the process of listening (Text (5.75)) and smelling (Text (5.76)), though these were infrequent in the corpus.

Text (5.75)   @{User} I'm currently enjoying mine, so I'll listen in.☕ 👂

Text (5.76)   @{User} Hmmm I smelled 👃 the coffee☕

It should also be noted that to a certain extent many emoji, such as emoji depicting body parts, have a degree of synecdoche built into them via their visual affordances, and can be used where no synecdoche is inscribed.

5.6.2   Embellish: Emblematise

When a particular incongruent meaning has stabilised over time and across communities, this enables emblematising. This relation draws on recognisable emblems that activate sets of cultural implications. Idioms such as figures of speech and emoji meme sequences are examples of meanings that have stabilised to an extent that they are recognised in emoji or emoji sequences by particular communities of users. A notable example is the HOT BEVERAGE ☕ emoji to invoke meanings about disclosing gossip or revealing hidden or salacious details about something, as we have already touched on a number of times. For example, in Text (5.77)–Text (5.79) there is an incongruent relation between the emoji and the co-text, and the HOT BEVERAGE ☕ emoji does not directly illustrate any coordinating IDEATION in the written verbiage.

Text (5.77)   @{User} ☕ that sounds like a very interesting dynamic• • •• ••

Text (5.78)   It's far too entertaining knowing things i probably shouldn't and just sitting back and letting the universe do it's thing☕

Text (5.79)   @{User} I agree with you girl … but you'd be surprised at how much flexing these dudes do for a woman's attention. Not to mention how much they do for other men☕

In these instances, the HOT BEVERAGE ☕ emoji instead acts as an emblem representing the concept of 'spilling the tea' (meaning disclosing gossip). In some examples, the incongruent meaning is explicitly unpacked by the written verbiage (bold), for instance, in Text (5.80)–Text (5.82).

Text (5.80)   **What's the tea with this drama** in the Brisbane drag seven?☕ • •

Text (5.81)   @{User} Eeeeek! I can feel **the drama brewing** …..⚗ ☕

Text (5.82)   Omg **teaaa** ☕ [link to interesting proposition about Jung]

In these cases, the emoji and the written verbiage together enact the multimodal emblem rather than the emoji alone activating the incongruent meaning in relation to the meanings made in the rest of the post. Here the congruent ideational meaning (i.e. the meaning of some kind of hot beverage) is semantically bleached or backgrounded, and another less congruent meaning is foregrounded (e.g. the meaning of gossiping).

This kind of bleaching can also occur with forms of linguistic play such as the use of homonyms, as can be seen in Text (5.83), but these were very infrequent in the corpus.

Text (5.83)   @{User} I felt that {name} I felt that to a tea☕ ☕ ☕ ☺ ☺ ☺

In Text (5.83) the HOT BEVERAGE ☕ emoji concurs with '*tea*' to construe a play on the idiom 'to a tee' (meaning exactly or perfectly) in which 'tea' and 'tee' are homophones.

A final example of emoji realising metaphoric and emblematic meaning worth unpacking is Text (5.84).

Text (5.84)   Educated, vaccinated, caffeinated and dedicated! 🍎 💉 ☕ #bfrocks @ bfes_ltps @{User 1} @{User 2} @User 3

Here we can see how the sequence of emoji RED APPLE 🍎, SYRINGE 💉, and HOT BEVERAGE ☕ coordinate with the three ideational [qualities] listed in the co-text: the RED APPLE 🍎 emoji emblematically references the tradition in western societies of students gifting teachers with apples, and thus CONCURS with '*Educated*'; the SYRINGE 💉 emoji realises a metonym of the instrument employed to deliver vaccines, and thus metaphorically concurs with '*vaccinated*'; and the HOT BEVERAGE ☕ emoji, as observed numerous times in the preceding chapters, emblematically references energy and hard work, thus CONCURRING with '*dedicated*'.

5.7   Emoji Meme Sequences

Emoji which reference memes are a special case of emblematising that draws on pre-accrued cultural meanings that have arisen through the mass use of memes. This includes phrasal template memes and memes involving visual/verbal templates known as image macros (Zappavigna, 2020). The emoji in these cases function like emblems which need to be recognised for the meaning to be interpreted. Thus, their usage is difficult to identify in a corpus without existing knowledge of the memes. They otherwise might only be detected via emoji sequences that appear unusual in terms of their relationship with the co-text. While technically ideational in the sense of the way in which the emoji index the meme, the overall meaning that is made is typically interpersonal since the memes are usually making some kind of attitudinal comment. In other words, the ideational emblem activates interpersonal meanings.

The most common example of an emoji meme sequence in the corpus is the 'Kermit the Frog Drinking Tea' meme (freq. = 144). This is most likely because the meme itself involves tea in the visual component of the image macro, thus it is typically referenced via the HOT BEVERAGE ☕ emoji. The meme usually occurs as an image macro where the 'TT [Top Text] is a critical or at least puzzled remark on people's behaviour, and BT [Bottom Text] plays the role of a sort of "suit yourself" attitude', commonly associated with the phrase 'but that's none of my business' (Dancygier & Vandelanotte, 2017, p. 557). The FROG + HOT BEVERAGE 🐸 ☕ emoji meme sequence is used to reference this meme, for example in Text (5.85).

Text (5.85) Lmfao reminder you can be 150 and purely muscle bc muscle weighs more than fat since we seem to have forgotten🐸 ☕

In this example the meanings made with the 🐸 ☕ emoji sequence function as an evaluative meta-comment on the rest of the post in a similar way to the kind of evaluative aside afforded by hashtags. In this instance the emoji sequence negatively judges the putative voice that has asserted that a person who weighs 150 pounds is overweight and to which this post appears to be a reaction. Thus, while identification of the ideational pattern is required to interpret the reference to the meme, the function of the emoji sequence is itself ultimately interpersonal (via backgrounding the relevant IDEATION).

In the corpus the 🐸 ☕ emoji meme sequence most often indexed negative [judgement] on the part of the author in a similar manner to Text (5.85). For instance, Text (5.86) incorporates a quoted tweet about inaction on diversity and inclusion in organisations with the emoji sequence indicating the user's reactive stance.

Text (5.86)   🐸 ☕ [quoted tweet]

Similarly, Text (5.87) incorporates a quoted tweet about difficult customers and the emoji meme sequences negatively judges this customer behaviour.

Text (5.87) Lmao I got a complaint from a customer one time and my boss and I literally stood in the back room laughing about it, so go ahead and write your complaints we could not care less🐸 ☕

Other examples such as Text (5.88) to Text (5.90) involve more underspecified co-text, making it difficult to interpret the specific target of the criticism.

Text (5.88) If the shoe fits wear it🐸 ☕

Text (5.89) @{User} I'm just like..🐸 ☕

Text (5.90) @{User 1} @{User 2} come and hear this🐸 ☕

In others still, such as Text (5.91) to Text (5.94), there are clues in the co-text that interpersonally resonate with the negative [judgement] activated by the emblem (shown in bold).

Text (5.91) @{User 1} @{User 2} @{User 3} Didn't you **lose** this game?🐸 ☕

Figure 5.5 The images used in the 'this is fine' meme

Text (5.92)   The fact that she **don't know**.. .....😕 💀

Text (5.93)   @{User} [initials] you **survived** because you're just better!💀 😕 🔥

Text (5.94)   @{User} He **hasn't scored** and we still **never hear you stop** talking about him💀 😕

Another example of an emoji meme sequence is DOG/DOG FACE + HOT BEVERAGE + FIRE emoji 🐶 ☕ 🔥, although this was comparatively rare with only two instances occurring in the corpus. This was used to represent the 'this is fine' meme. This meme involves an image of a dog drinking a cup of coffee as its house burns down (Figure 5.5).

The meme centres on the incongruency of the depicted situation (being inside a burning house) and the dog's declaration 'This is fine' in the speech bubble. The resultant meaning that 'this is not in fact fine' is activated by using the emoji 🐶 ☕ 🔥, as can be seen in Text (5.95).

Text (5.95)   @{User} Indeed. What could possibly be a problem with requiring anyone who wants access to a web site to be registered with Google? We can trust Big Tech, so why worry? A human is what a corporation says it is. This is fine.
🐶 ☕ 🔥
#SurveillanceCapitalism

In Text (5.95) the emoji sequence emblematises the meme, concurring with the phrase in the post '*This is fine*'. This in turn enacts the evaluative meta-judgement, in tandem with the hashtag '*#SurveillanceCapitalism*' that the situation described in the post is not a positive one. The other example in the corpus (Text (5.96)) is less far-reaching, instead applying the meme to a personal misadventure in the everyday activity of washing hair.

Text (5.96)   I feel like an eighth of my hair just came out of my scalp after washing it. This is fine🐶 ☕ 🔥

Again, the emoji sequence functions as a meta-comment on the rest of the post, in particular flipping the ATTITUDE expressed in '*This is fine*' and suggesting that the situation has had an undesirable outcome.

5.8   Conclusion

This chapter has explored relations of concurrence between emoji and their co-text. We began by considering why it is important to consider emoji as more than a catalogue of types, positing instead that we need to consider how emoji coordinate with the IDEATION construed by the rest of a social media post. After considering some of the most frequent emoji that appear relevant to the main fields of experience that are traversed in the corpus, we introduced our CONCURRENCE network for describing the kinds of ideational relations at stake. We covered two main kinds of relations: depiction and embellishment. depiction is where emoji congruently illustrate their co-text or integrate themselves into the IDEATIONAL structure of the post. embellishment, on the other hand, is where emoji make less congruent meanings by either metaphorising through figurative meanings or emblematising through symbols that activate preconfigured meanings for particular communities. These less congruent relations tend to background the ideation through which they are initiated and instead foreground interpersonal implications. We now turn to considering such interpersonal meaning in the next chapter.

6   Emoji Resonating with Interpersonal Meaning

6.1   Introduction

This chapter explores how emoji and text work together to make interpersonal meanings, in particular, attitudinal meanings relating to emotion and opinion. In terms of the kinds of CONVERGENCE introduced in Chapter 3, our focus is on interpersonal RESONANCE. We will also consider interpersonal meanings related to engaging with the stances of other discursive voices. However, we will leave detailed exploration of the role of emoji in the construction of alignment to Chapters 7 and 8, where we explore DIALOGIC and COMMUNING AFFILIATION. The model of evaluation we will draw upon for exploring linguistic meaning is the Appraisal framework (Martin & White, 2005), as introduced in Chapter 3.

Most studies of emoji recognise their significant involvement in expressing attitudes and sentiment, and social media is resplendent with evaluative language with which emoji can coordinate (Zappavigna, 2017a). In particular, pragmatic studies have considered the role of emoji in modifying the tenor of a message through adjusting the meaning of linguistic co-text. Emoji have been observed to adjust the illocutionary force in texts by modifying the tone of the message (Dresner & Herring, 2010, 2014; Herring & Dainas, 2017). Emoji can also be used to 'align with the interlocutor, to express informality or to enhance phatic communion and expressive speech acts, especially greetings' (Sampietro, 2016, p. 109). Other interpersonal functions that have been noted include marking sarcasm or irony (Escouflaire, 2021; Yus, 2021)), as well as the involvement of emoji in the expression of personal identity (Ge, 2019).

Before we proceed to explore the kinds of interpersonal meaning in which emoji can involve themselves, it is important to reflect on some of the semiotic constraints built into emoji due to their affordances that are relevant to how interpersonal meanings are expressed. Many emoji have some degree of attitudinal polarity built into their representation, for instance, the FACE WITH SMILING EYES 😊 emoji versus the FROWNING FACE ☹ emoji or the THUMBS UP 👍 emoji versus the THUMBS DOWN 👎 emoji. This should, as we have noted throughout this book, not be confused with the 'meaning' of the emoji; while some emoji may be able to construe generalised positive or negative ATTITUDE in isolation, more delicate meanings (including reversals in polarity such as irony and sarcasm) can only be interpreted in coordination with the co-text. It does, however, represent some loose modal constraints on emoji meaning potential, inflected by the design choices that particular vendors implement in the visual glyphs developed (e.g. how large a smile or how furrowed a brow is represented). As has been noted in relation to the different affordances of images compared with language (Martin, 2011), emoji's semiotic valeur reflects their modal realisation as 'picture characters'. Emoji are inherently representational due to these affordances, with their palette limited to objects and symbols (at times adjusted through the use of action lines to suggest motion), as we explored in Chapter 2. Thus, they must represent emotional states and opinions via these resources that are usually associated with representing ideational meanings.

For example, in the CAT FACE 🐱 emoji, there is a fairly clear semiotic link between the pictographic depiction (albeit, simplified and stylised) of a cat's face and the potential interpretation of the emoji as construing ideational meaning about cats. However, if we look to the TWO HEARTS 💕 emoji, the potential interpretation of this emoji as being related to interpersonal meanings about [affect] is more complex. This complexity arises from the semiosis 'stepping through' an ideational/emblematic encoding before arriving at its affective meaning. Representationally, the TWO HEARTS 💕 emoji construes the emblematic ideational [entity] of a 'heart', and this meaning is backgrounded or bleached as the interpersonal connotations of this emblem are foregrounded via its conventional association with meanings about love or romance. This kind of backgrounding is seen even with an emoji such as the FACE WITH SMILING EYES 😊 where the interpersonal meaning of generalised positive [affect] eclipses the representation of the ideational [entity] of a smiling face. Other studies of emoji have noted how emoji such as the FACE BLOWING A KISS 😘 are used to signal intersubjective aspects of intimacy rather than their literal or iconic meaning of actually blowing a kiss, and as such, engender a 'semantic bleaching of the original iconic meaning, suggesting a process of pragmaticalization and discursive conventionalization' (Wiese & Labrenz, 2021, p. 281). As we will explore in this chapter, when coordinating with interpersonal meanings of the linguistic co-text in this way, emoji manifest a pattern of common usage where ideational meaning is discharged while interpersonal meaning is charged.

6.2   Frequent Interpersonal Patterns in the Corpus

Before introducing our system network for describing interpersonal RESO-NANCE we will consider some of the most frequent interpersonal meanings in the Hot Beverage Emoji corpus. The most frequent linguistic collocates of the

Table 6.1 *Most frequent collocates of the HOT BEVERAGE emoji that likely have an attitudinal function (window span = 5)*

N	Collocate	Rank	Freq (Scaled)	FreqLR	FreqL	FreqR	Example
1	good	3	30,180	2,650	1,536	1,114	@{User} Good Morning 🌸🌴🌴☕ ☕☕
2	happy	14	7,770	546	319	227	@{User} Happy Wednesday {name}. ☕ 🌸
3	great	17	5,080	338	281	57	@{User} Good morning {name}, have a great day ! 🌸 ❤ ☕ 🍃 😊
4	fantastic	30	860	100	93	7	@{User} Good morning {name}, hope you are having a fantastic day ☀ ☕
5	dear	32	1,670	134	82	52	@{User} Thank you so much my dear friend {name} 🍃 ☕ 🌷 💕

HOT BEVERAGE emoji in the corpus that likely have an interpersonal function are shown in Table 6.1. As the examples in this table suggest, a range of emoji including facial expressions, gesture, symbols, and object emoji could all involve themselves in interpersonal RESONANCE. For this reason it is ill-advised to approach emoji as a catalogue of types, and instead in this chapter we will explore how emoji can function as an interpersonal resource for making attitudinal meanings along with their co-text.

The most frequent type of interpersonal pattern, visible via inspecting the most frequent linguistic 3-grams (Table 6.2), was greetings and thanks. This pattern tended to involve formulaic phrasing that has become conventionalised and bleached of specific attitudinal meaning. For instance, in the greeting 'good morning' (Text (6.1) to Text (6.6)), the emphasis is on fostering generalised positive social alignment with the interlocutor rather than necessarily positively appreciating the day.

Text (6.1)   Good morning ☕ 💕 🌼 ☕ 🏴

Text (6.2)   @{User} Good morning sweetheart ☕ ☕ 🎵 ❄ ❄ hope you slept well and have a wonderful day 😊 🌸 🐸

Text (6.3)   @{User} Have a good one Pauline!! 🦋 ☕ 🍂 😌

Text (6.4)   @{User} bonghendy198585 Good afternoon. Have a nice afternoon. ☕ ☕ 🐌 🎵

Text (6.5)   @{User} Good morning dear friend ☕ ☕ 🐌
             Thank you ☕ 🍂 🌸 🌿

Text (6.6)   @{User} Good Morning {name}
             Have a Wonderful Tuesday My Friend
             Take Care Stay Safe Love and Hugs 😊 🌴 ❤ 🦋 🌿 🌹 🕯 💕 ☕ ☕ 🐸

Table 6.2 *Most frequent 3-grams with a likely interpersonal function*

N	Freq.	3-gram
1	284	have a great
2	236	a great day
3	174	you have a
4	165	have a wonderful
5	133	a wonderful day
6	101	hope you have
7	83	have a good
8	77	i hope you
9	72	enjoy your day
10	70	good morning my

The emoji that co-occurred with 'good morning' support this positive alignment. For instance, the representation of hearts in the TWO HEARTS 💕 (Text (6.1), Text (6.6)), SMILING FACE WITH HEARTS 🥰 and FACE BLOWING A KISS 😘 emoji (Text (6.2), Text (6.6)) coordinate with the greeting to construe positive solidarity via their emblematic meaning of love or affection. In addition, the SMILING FACE WITH OPEN HANDS 🤗 (Text (6.2), Text (6.3), and Text (6.6)) and the SMILING FACE WITH SMILING EYES 😊 emoji (Text (6.1), Text (6.4), and Text (6.5)) support meanings relating to camaraderie. Moreover, the HOT BEVERAGE ☕ emoji, in its [metaphoric] relation with 'morning' (explored in Chapter 5), invokes positive meanings from the cultural context relating to conviviality (Page et al., 2014).

Similar meanings relating to solidarity and camaraderie were apparent in the most common linguistic 3-grams in the corpus 'HAVE A GREAT', 'A GREAT DAY', and 'YOU HAVE A' as can be seen in Text (6.7) to Text (6.14).

Text (6.7)   @{User} Good morning {name}!! Have a great weekend!🥰 ☕

Text (6.8)   @{User} Hope you have a great one too {name}!😊 ⬇ ☕

Text (6.9)   @{User} Good Morning @{User}. Have a great day. 😊 ☕ 🌸

Text (6.10)   @{User} Good morning my friend. Have a great day.😊 🥰 🤗 ☕

Text (6.11)   @{User 1} @{User 2} Happy Friday {name}! Have a great day my friend!🇺🇸 ⛰ ☕ 🙏

Text (6.12)   @{User} Good Morning {name}. Have a great day 🌸 ☕ 😎

Text (6.13)   @{User} Good Morning {name} ☕ ☕, have a great Sunday🌼 ☕ 🙏

Text (6.14)   @{User} Thank you! Have a great day too, Good Morning {name} 😎 ☕

Text (6.15)   And you have a great Wednesday also {name} 😃 😄

This chapter considers the kinds of emoji–text relations that are involved in these and other frequent interpersonal meanings in the corpus.

6.3   A System Network for Emoji–Text RESONANCE

Figure 6.1 displays the system network for interpersonal emoji–text RESONANCE. The main distinction in meaning is between emoji which [enmesh] with the interpersonal meaning in the post or evaluatively [imbue] the written verbiage with interpersonal meaning. For example, emoji can [enmesh] with the linguistic interpersonal meaning by [echoing] the ATTITUDE in the co-text, as in Text (6.16).

Text (6.16)   @{User} Good morning sweetheart 😘 😊 Thank you 🙏 I'm doing positive vibes only today 👍 😄 Have a glorious day and weekend lovely and take care of yourself 💜 💜 💜

In this example, the positivity of the greeting, '*Good morning sweetheart*', [harmonises] with the FACE BLOWING A KISS 😊, and '*Thank you*' [harmonises] with FOLDED HANDS: MEDIUM SKIN TONE 🙏. Similarly, '*positive vibes*' [harmonises] with both the THUMBS UP 👍 and the BEAMING FACE WITH SMILING EYES 😄 emoji. In addition, the three RED HEART 💜 emoji at the end of the post coordinate with the general positivity globally across the tweet, as well as more locally with '*glorious*', '*lovely*', and '*take care*' in the final [sequence]. By way of contrast, an example of the alternative choice, to evaluatively [imbue] the co-text with attitudinal meaning, occurs in Text (6.17).

Text (6.17)   drinking an iced al pacino 😘 😌

In this example the RELIEVED FACE 😌 suggests a positive evaluation of the [occurrence figure] in the body of the tweet ('*drinking an iced al pacino*').

We will now consider the more delicate choices in this network in more detail.

6.4   Imbue

We will begin our discussion of emoji–text RESONANCE with the [imbue] feature, as it allows us to introduce the concept of an interpersonal–ideational coupling that will be referred to in the following sections. When emoji [imbue] linguistic co-text, the emoji are not echoing the linguistically construed interpersonal meaning but are instead infusing linguistic ideational meaning with interpersonal evaluation. For example, consider the interaction between emoji and language in Text (6.18) where the emoji target particular IDEATION in the co-text.

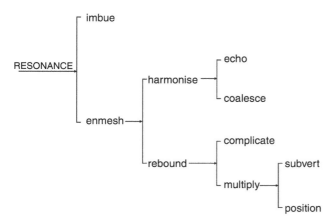

Figure 6.1 Interpersonal emoji–text RESONANCE

Text (6.18)   That first sip of coffee in the morning

Here, the linguistic co-text '*That first sip of coffee in the morning*' does not contain any inscribed ATTITUDE but rather is targeted by the positive evaluation realised by the SMILING FACE WITH SMILING EYES 😊 emoji that concludes the post.

Due to the parallel division of meaning by metafunction and by mode, instances of [imbue] constitute illustrative examples of intermodal couplings. By 'coupling' we refer to the fusion that occurs when interpersonal and ideational meaning interact in a text. This unit of analysis is valuable when describing how interpersonal meaning is realised as it allows for contrasts among interpersonal resources to be cross-referenced with their ideational targets, thus providing more complex and nuanced explanations of how meaning is made within texts. Take, for instance, the couplings of emoji and language in Text (6.19).

Text (6.19)   Hedge cut 💪 now to have a cuppa ☕ and read the newspaper 📰 for a
               few minutes😊

Here we have FLEXED BICEPS 💪 realising positive ATTITUDE interacting with '*hedge cut*', while the FACE WITH SMILING EYES 😊 emoji realises positive ATTITUDE interacting with '*have a cuppa ☕ and read the newspaper 📰 for a few minutes*'. By interpreting these interactions as ATTITUDE–IDEATION couplings, we can more delicately describe the ATTITUDE features being realised. FLEXED BICEPS 💪, as a response to the accomplishment of a task, is likely to index positive self-evaluation; this realises a coupling of positive [judgement] targeting the author and triggered[1] by the [figure] '*hedge cut*'. FACE WITH SMILING EYES ☺, as a response to activities associated with leisure and relaxation, is likely to index positive [affect] targeting the author and triggered by the [figures] '*have a cuppa* ☕ *and read the newspaper* 📰 *for a few minutes*'.

Another example of emoji targeting linguistic ideational meaning occurs in Text (6.20).

Text (6.20)   Hot tea ☕ and listening to the rain … ☺ ❣

Here we can see how the PLEADING FACE 🥺 and HEART EXCLAMATION ❣ emoji target the [sequence] in the post: '*Hot tea* ☕ *and listening to the rain* …'. The combination of the attitudinally ambiguous PLEADING FACE 🥺 with the typically more positive HEART EXCLAMATION ❣ suggests the author is indexing nuanced emotional states such as contemplation or wistfulness with which they [imbue] the co-text. However in this case, the absence of linguistic interpersonal meaning and possibility of the ideational targets to be targeted by multiple ATTITUDE resources (e.g. the rain might sound beautiful ([appreciation]), but it also might make the author feel wistful ([affect])) limits our interpretation of the emoji's meaning to generalised, slightly positive ATTITUDE.

As the examples above illustrate, in analysing [imbuing] it can often be challenging to determine whether the emoji are targeting [affect], [judgement] or [appreciation] at the co-text. However, the type of IDEATION targeted can assist with this kind of disambiguation. For instance, in Text (6.21), [judgement] is typically targeted at human participants or their behaviours (underlined).

Text (6.21)   … Did <u>she throw a rock at herself and knocked herself out</u> 🤦 …

Here we have evidence to suggest the PERSON FACEPALMING 🤦 emoji is critiquing the expressed behaviour in terms of [capacity] (a judgement of ability) since the activity sequence is about a person causing their own injury. On the other hand, [appreciation] is typically directed toward things (underlined), as can be seen in Text (6.22).

Text (6.22)   Ok, my taste buds haven't matured or <u>my coffee</u> ☕ is just bad 😵

Thus, the WOOZY FACE 😵 is likely realising [reaction] as a type of [appreciation]. Sometimes co-occurring features in the text such as hashtags can also aid in determining the kind of attitudinal meaning the emoji may be realising. For instance, consider Text (6.23), which contains a hashtag.

---

[1] In coupling theory, a distinction is made between instances where an attitude resource targets ideation and instances where an attitude resource is triggered by ideation.

Text (6.23)   First cup of coffee in the new house 😌 ☕ 💜 #feelingblessed

In the absence of the hashtag, we might decide that the FACE WITH SMILING EYES 😌 and RED HEART 💜 are positive reactions to '*First cup of coffee in the new house*'. However, at the same time, the hashtag '*#feelingblessed*' harmonises with these emoji and foregrounds the affective dimension of the evaluation. Since emoji are relatively underspecified, it appears that they can accommodate this duality and mean something somewhere in between these two choices of [appreciation] and [affect] that are much more delineated in language.

6.5   Enmesh: Harmonise

Within the [enmesh] branch of the RESONANCE system network (Figure 6.2), emoji which [harmonise] with the interpersonal meanings in the co-text coordinate closely with these meanings in terms of polarity, reinforcing their general positivity or negativity, and often also coordinating with any inscribed or invoked evaluation or expression of solidarity.

As Sections 6.5.1 and 6.5.2 will detail, the main distinction in meaning within this system is between emoji which [echo] interpersonal meaning, coordinating with it throughout a post, and emoji which [coalesce] interpersonal meaning by encapsulating it in some way, typically washing evaluation backwards across the entire post, and sometimes also enhancing it in terms of GRADUATION. For example, consider the difference between the emoji in Text (6.24) and Text (6.25).

Text (6.24)   @{User} Good morning my darling 😘 ☕ Thank you so much 🙏 Have a gorgeous day lovely and enjoy the match tonight 🎉

Text (6.25)   @{User} Morning my friend 🌹 🌹 ✨ 🍀 🌺 🌸

In Text (6.24) the emoji coordinate with the more committed expressions of positive [affect] and solidarity (underlined) in the [figures] preceding them, while in Text (6.25) the solidarity construed in the greeting is condensed in a sequence of six object emoji: HOT BEVERAGE ☕, ROSE 🌹, SPARKLES ✨, FOUR LEAF CLOVER 🍀, HIBISCUS 🌺, and BLOSSOM 🌸, all of which have positive associations. Here the emoji commit only generalised positive ATTITUDE, rather than realising more committed positive [affect] in coordination

Figure 6.2 The harmonise system

with '*friend*'. These different options are supported by textual synchronicity: [echo] is coordinated by [isolate], while [coalesce] is coordinated by [cluster].

6.5.1   Harmonise: Echo

Emoji which [echo] the interpersonal meaning in the co-text coordinate closely with this meaning, most often by interweaving with linguistic evaluation throughout a post. For example, as noted earlier, the most frequent interpersonal pattern in the corpus is greetings and expressions of thanks and well-wishes. These often involve emoji that continuously coordinate with the positivity in the posts, such as in Text (6.26).

> Text (6.26)   @{User} Good Morning my sweet {name}!! 💜 ☕ 🌺Have a lovely
> day, Darling! God Bless You!! 🙏 Btw. you are looking beautiful!!🌹

> Text (6.27)   Thank you so much 💙Happy Friday and a great weekend🎉 😋 💙

In Text (6.26) the GROWING HEART 💜 and the FOLDED HANDS 🙏 emoji both [echo] the positive [affect] realised by greeting and well-wishes in the co-text. In addition, the HIBISCUS 🌺 and the ROSE 🌹 emoji are both representations of flowers that are associated with positive meanings and with beauty. The rose in particular [echoes] the positive [appreciation] '*beautiful*' in the co-text. Thus, we can see that the emoji are coordinating not only with a generalised positive ATTITUDE but with more delicate features of ATTITUDE; in terms of commitment, both emoji and language are committing a similar degree of attitudinal meaning.

Similarly, in Text (6.28) the underlined emoji and co-text all support positive meanings regarding the tenor of the relationship, with solidarity inscribed in the vocative '*mate*'.

> Text (6.28)   @{User} <u>No problem mate</u> 👍 <u>it's the best coffee</u> ☕ <u>in the world</u>🌹 💯

The close coordination between adjacent realisations of linguistic and emoji interpersonal meaning in instances of [echo] also allows for more varied and dynamic coordination across a post. As Text (6.29) demonstrates, the unfolding coordination of the emoji and the linguistic attitudinal meaning can shift in polarity in tandem throughout a post as the emoji ESCORT the co-text. In this example, as the author consoles the message recipient '*Oh, that's a really pity ...*', the emoji shifts polarity from the previous SMILING FACE WITH SMILING EYES ☺ to the WORRIED FACE 😟.

> Text (6.29)   @{User} Good morning my dear friend ☺ 🎶 ☕ ❄ Oh, that's really
> pity ... Every day can't be the best 😟 🙏 Hope Wednesday is much
> better 😊 ❄ ☁ 🌸 Good night lovely⭐ ✦ ✦

Similarly, in Text (6.30) the emoji shift polarity back and forth in coordination with the linguistic ATTITUDE.

Text (6.30)   @{User 1} @{User 2} @{User 3} @{User 4} @{User 5} @{User 6} @{User 7} @{User 8} @{User 9} @{User 10} @{User 11} Good morning 😎 😍 #BrewCrew 😍 😍 😋I ran out of #coffee 😠 😢 😢 😭 😭 😭 having😒 Tea instead 😭 😭 😭 😭 😭 but if this is worst thing … I'm good 😊 & #grateful I have everything else I need 😊 have a blessed day!🙌 💜 😊

Here the SMILING FACE WITH SUNGLASSES 😎 coordinates with the positive interpersonal meaning in the greeting '*Good morning*'. The SMILING FACE WITH HEART-EYES 😍 and the SMILING FACE WITH HEARTS 🥰 coordinate with the hashtag '*#BrewCrew*', which invokes solidarity by naming a community. As the linguistic meaning shifts to invoking negative ATTITUDE when the user describes running out of coffee, so too does the polarity of the emoji, with an emoji sequence comprising FROWNING FACE 😠, CRYING FACE 😢, PLEADING FACE 😢, and repetition of the LOUDLY CRYING FACE 😭 emoji. The next figure '*having Tea instead*' includes the UNAMUSED FACE 😒 emoji before the [thing entity], again coordinating with invoked negative [affect]. An alternative coding would be to analyse these emoji as targeting the IDEATION in the [figures]; however, given the context provided by the hashtag it is likely that these figures invoke negative ATTITUDE rather than expressing neutral IDEATION. The [echo] analysis is also supported by the coordination back and forth in the polarity of the linguistic ATTITUDE with the emoji in the rest of the tweet, and overall, we can say that this post manifests an oscillating attitudinal prosody.

Another example of coordination of attitudinal polarity, this time featuring non-face emoji, is Text (6.31), where the THUMBS DOWN 👎/THUMBS UP 👍 emoji coordinate with the linguistic ATTITUDE '*Least interesting*' /'*Most interesting*'.

Text (6.31)   Gooood morning😎
               Tell me the LEAST interesting thing you're working on this week, then the MOST interesting. I'll start:
               👎 Least: Cleaning up an old Wordpress site.
               👍 Most: Setting up my new work laptop to start next week.

This example illustrates how [echoing] emoji can also precede linguistic interpersonal meaning with which they interact, thereby jointly realising the Theme of these intermodal clauses.

Instances where emoji [echo] language can also result in a calibration of the intensity of interpersonal meaning. An example of this occurs in Text (6.32).

Text (6.32)   When your wife leaves the house for work, and the last thing that she
says as she leaves is 'Oh by the way, there's no milk left!' 😳 😫 Surely
that's grounds for divorce?🙈 👄

Here the linguistic co-text makes a causal connection between finishing the
milk in a household and divorce, which realises a relatively strong negative
evaluation targeting the absence of milk and the author's wife. However, the
interaction between the negative ATTITUDE targeting the wife and the SEE NO
EVIL MONKEY 🙈, which carries connotations of non-serious shock or dis-
belief, suggests that this ATTITUDE is non-seriously exaggerated. Thus, while
it seems likely that the author does to some, probably minor extent negatively
evaluate their wife, the intensity of this sentiment is reined in by the linguistic
realisation's interaction with the emoji. We can speculate here that even in the
absence of emoji, the negative evaluation of the wife might be interpreted as
non-serious; however, the inclusion of the emoji explicitly calibrates the intensity of the language, thus the emoji is [echoing] the interpersonal meaning realised in the linguistic co-text while de-intensifying it.

6.5.2   Harmonise: Coalesce

When emoji [coalesce] with the interpersonal meanings in the co-text, they con-
solidate this meaning in a single 'burst', often [clustered] at the end of the post
(in terms of textual PERIODICITY). In this role they also reinforce other resonant
interpersonal meaning in emoji that may be scattered throughout the post (via
the [echo] choice, as explained in the previous section). The most common example in the corpus is multiple emoji interpersonally [coalescing] and textually
[clustering] after a greeting or well-wishes, as in Text (6.33) to Text (6.37).

Text (6.33)   Hope ur day is warm & ur coffee hot☕ 😊 🌹 🐝 ☕ ⬇ ☕

Text (6.34)   @{User} Good morning🌹 💨 ⬇ 📖 💤 ☕

Text (6.35)   @{User} {name}, have a great weekend too.🌅 😺 ☀ 💤 😄 🧺

Text (6.36)   @{User} Balloons!!🎈🎈🎈
Happy birthday,{name}. It is my delight to read your wake-up message
every morning. Thank you so much for everything. Have a wonderful
birthday and a wonderful year ahead!✨ ☕ 😫 🥀 🍸 💐 🍸 💦 🌸 ✨ ✨ ✨ ✨ ✨

Text (6.37)   @{User}
Morning {name}
You have a Fabulous Monday and a Beautiful Week My Friend
Take Care Much Love and Hugs🌹 🌿 🌴 💤 ⛲ 💐 🐦 💦 ☕ 💤 🐌

In these examples a string of emoji which invoke positive association
are appended to the end of the post. While some of these are the kinds

of face emoji that are most obviously associated with positive sentiment
and solidarity (e.g. the PARTYING FACE 🥳, FACE BLOWING A KISS
😘, SMILING FACE WITH OPEN HANDS 🤗, and the SMILING FACE
WITH HEARTS 🥰 emoji) or are emblems suggestive of positive emotion
(e.g. the TWO HEARTS 💕 emoji), other emoji are objects which invoke
positivity. For example, the BALLOON 🎈 emoji and the BIRTHDAY
CAKE 🎂 emoji, at the same time as concurring with IDEATION in the co-
text, invoke positive, celebratory connotations. Similarly, the BOOKS 📚
and PALM TREE 🌴 emoji can activate meanings relating to relaxation such
as reading and holidays. In addition, the SPARKLES ✨ emoji contributes
positive meanings relating to beauty or excitement, and the repetition [up-
scales] the general enthusiasm or emphasis with which these meanings are
construed.

In contrast to [echo], emoji coalescing in a post will not commit the same
delicacy of meaning as found in the language. Clustering emoji typically only
commit either generalised positive or negative ATTITUDE, thereby encompassing and generalising the more delicate linguistic realisations of ATTITUDE
in the post. Thus in Text (6.36) and Text (6.37), the positive [affect] realised
by '*Happy*', '*delight*', and '*Love*', and the positive [appreciation] realised
by '*wonderful*', '*fabulous*', and '*beautiful*' are collectively coalesced by the
generalised positive ATTITUDE of the emoji. Moreover, the repetition of multiple emoji realising positive ATTITUDE serves to reinforce and up-scale the
positive ATTITUDE. Indeed, such repetition of emoji in culminative position
to emphasise or condense the sentiments echoed throughout a post was a frequent choice in the corpus. For example, in Text (6.38) to Text (6.42) the repetition of the RED HEART ❤️ emoji 'washes' positive, up-scaled interpersonal
meanings backwards across the entire post.

Text (6.38)   @{User} Morning sweet pea ☕ 🌸 Finally, finally Friday 🙌 📷 😌 Have
                a perfectly smooth and sweet day lovely and take care❤️ ❤️ ❤️

Text (6.39)   @{User} Good morning sweetheart ☕ 🌸 Oh, I hope you're right 🙏 ☕
                Have a fabulous day lovely and look after yourself❤️ ❤️ ❤️

Text (6.40)   @{User} Good morning my darling ☕ 🌸 Thank you 🙏 Have a
                fabulous day and weekend lovely and look after yourself❤️ ❤️ ❤️

Text (6.41)   @{User} Good morning my darling friend 🌸 ☕ Beautiful, thank you
                so much 🙏 🥰 Another day with the potential for miracles … Have a
                beautiful and happy day my lovely, take care and look after yourself❤️
                ❤️ ❤️

Text (6.42)   @{User} Good morning my darling friend ☕ 🌸 Thank you so much for
                all the sweetness 🙏 🥰 Have a blessed and glorious day lovely, treasure
                every moment of your day and take care. Much love to you❤️ ❤️ ❤️

Across these examples, we can see how emoji echoing linguistic interpersonal meaning realise more delicate features of ATTITUDE, such as FACE BLOWING A KISS 😘 coordinating with the interpersonal closeness suggested by the vocatives, '*sweet pea*', '*sweetheart*', '*darling*', '*friend*', and '*sweetness*'. This closeness, along with other features of positive ATTITUDE such as '*fabulous*', is then bundled up and reinforced by the repeated emoji that cluster at the end of a text.

6.6   Enmesh: Rebound

Converse to the congruent polarity between emoji and linguistic interpersonal meaning found in [harmonise] features, emoji which rebound diverge from the interpersonal meaning in the co-text or layer evaluative commentary over it, potentially adding sarcastic or ironic meanings, or adjusting dialogic positioning. Within the [rebound] system (Figure 6.3) a distinction can be made between [complicate], where emoji diverge from the polarity or intensity of interpersonal meaning realised by linguistic co-text, and [multiply], where emoji coordinate with linguistic resources to introduce new perspectives into the text. Within multiply, emoji can either [subvert] the co-text by indicating that linguistic interpersonal meaning is in some way transgressive or nonserious and is intended to provoke a humour response, or they can [position] the co-text to modify its dialogic positioning.

To illustrate the difference between [complicate] and [multiply], consider how emoji are interacting with language in Text (6.43) and Text (6.44).

Text (6.43)   Enjoy your Sunday #NFT peeps! 😜 👄

Text (6.44)   It's coffee ☕ time …. shhhhh 🤫 enjoy 🍫

In Text (6.43), the linguistic co-text suggests positive ATTITUDE. However, FACE WITH UNEVEN EYES AND WAVY MOUTH 😖 realises negative ATTITUDE, which diverges from the linguistic co-text. Here this divergence is interpreted as signalling two different ideational targets of evaluation – the linguistic co-text is realising positive ATTITUDE directed at the community of '*NFT peeps*', while, given the timing of when the corpus this post occurred

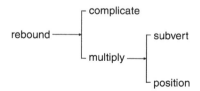

Figure 6.3 The rebound system

in was collected, the 😵 emoji probably refers to instability in the NFT (non-fungible tokens) market in April 2021. As such, in this post the emoji complicates the positive ATTITUDE realised in the language by introducing divergent interpersonal meaning. We can take this interpretation a step further to consider how the negative ATTITUDE realised by the emoji is functioning as a shared value within the community positively evaluated by the language – thus in common sense terms, the post is enacting camaraderie within a community sharing a negative experience. Note, however, that while there are divergent interpersonal resources distributed across emoji and language in this post, the text maintains a consistent voice, as the author expresses divergent ATTITUDES for different ideational targets. In essence the emoji's relation to the co-text shows how '*enjoy*' is meant both ironically, and that this understanding is limited to members of a particular community.

Conversely, Text (6.44) is an example of a post containing emoji that subvert co-textual meaning, which seems to refer to the figure of speech 'Don't talk to me before I have had my morning coffee'. In this post the FACE WITH TEARS OF JOY 😂 emoji that follows the command for silence signals that the author is aware of the potentially transgressive meaning of the linguistic co-text and is laughing this off, thus signalling that they do not in fact consider themselves in a position to tell the reader to be quiet. Unlike the consistent voice of Text (6.43), where the divergent interpersonal meaning represents the author's attitudes to different ideational targets, in Text (6.44) the linguistically realised interpersonal meaning is disaligned from by the author. In so doing, emoji that subvert linguistic co-text serve to introduce a new voice into the text that reveals the author's true sentiments.

Similarly, in Text (6.45) the THINKING FACE 🤔 emoji interacts with the linguistic modality resource '*maybe*' to position an alternate perspective in the text.

Text (6.45)   @{User} Yes lots and lots of coffee ☕ was instructed by @{User 2} to get up and give you hell today 😈 Maybe later 🤔 😈 Love 😊

However, unlike in instances of [subvert], in instances of [position] the author does not align with one particular perspective in the text over another, they simply acknowledge their plurality.

Thus, while instances of [complicate] introduce divergent interpersonal meaning in addition to linguistic co-text, instances of [multiply] introduce plural perspectives that can either subvert and reverse the interpersonal meaning in the linguistic co-text or position linguistically realised perspectives within a polyphony of other possible perspectives. Given the more nuanced interaction between linguistic and emoji resources realising [rebound] features, the descriptions of how they jointly make meaning are more detailed than in Section 6.5 and include references to the ideational targets of interpersonal resources, which previews the discussions of couplings and bonds that will be expanded on in the two chapters on affiliation which follow.

6.6.1   Rebound: Complicate

Emoji that complicate interpersonal meaning diverge from the polarity of ATTITUDE in the linguistic co-text but do not contradict it, often resulting in layered, complex interpersonal meaning being realised by the post. For example, in Text (6.46) the interaction between '*good morning*' and the SMILING FACE WITH OPEN MOUTH AND SMILING EYES ☺ emoji realises positive ATTITUDE; however, the SMILING FACE WITH OPEN MOUTH AND COLD SWEAT ☺ emoji diverges from this by introducing an element of negative ATTITUDE.

Text (6.46)   Good morning all☕ ☕ ☕ ☺ ☺

In combination with the repeated HOT BEVERAGE ☕ emoji and their connotations of hard work and maintaining alertness despite fatigue, we can interpret this negative ATTITUDE as referencing some sense of stress or urgency. We can interpret these divergent ATTITUDE resources as reflecting the differing ideational targets they interact with; '*Good morning*' and the SMILING FACE WITH OPEN MOUTH AND SMILING EYES ☺ realise positive [affect] targeting '*all*': the audience of the post, while ☕ ☕ ☕ ☺ do not have any obvious ideational target, so we can interpret them as realising generalised negative [affect] felt by the author of the post. In sum, we can describe the interpersonal meaning made in this post as reflecting on the one hand the author's solidarity with their social media community, and on the other their sense of stress. In contrast to the [harmonise] features described earlier, the SMILING FACE WITH OPEN MOUTH AND COLD SWEAT ☺ emoji is incongruent with, and thus does not echo, the linguistically realised interpersonal meaning. Moreover, compared with the strings of emoji which collectively coalesce generalised positivity at the end of posts, in this case the ☺ and ☺ emoji realise distinct, although related meanings.

Text (6.47)   Felt so good to sleep in. Now, enjoying my coffee☕. Happy Monday☺

Text (6.48)   Morning losers☺ send for my morning coffee ☕ ☺

6.6.2   Rebound: Multiply: Subvert

Emoji that subvert construe meanings that are incongruent with the polarity of the interpersonal meaning realised by linguistic co-text. In instances of [subvert], emoji serve to signal that linguistically realised meaning construes values or perspectives that the author does not align with. Consequently, this disaligned-from meaning can be laughed off, as the author of the post is implying that they (and their audience) in fact align with an alternate value or perspective.[2] This 'laughing off' is typically indexed by emoji depicting a humorous response, usually FACE WITH TEARS OF JOY 😂 or ROLLING ON THE FLOOR LAUGHING 🤣. Because emoji serve to index an alternate alignment to that realised by language, texts where emoji realise instances of [subvert] can be described as polyphonic, as the emoji are introducing a new voice into the text that reveals the author's 'true' alignment. This stands in contrast to instances of [complicate], as in these cases the emoji serve to add to or modify the interpersonal meaning of linguistic co-text and remain part of an intermodally consistent authorial voice.

An illustrative example is found in Text (6.49). Here the linguistic text includes a pun, where 'been' is written as the homophone '*bean*' so as to reference the ideational field of coffee that the text realises.

Text (6.49)   I've always bean a coffee girl 🤣 Never could Aquire a taste for tea☕

The [figure] wherein the pun occurs is followed by the ROLLING ON THE FLOOR LAUGHING 🤣 emoji, which can be interpreted as the author laughing off the notion that they are positively evaluating the pun. In common-sense terms, we can interpret the emoji as signalling that the author of the post understands the pun they made is banal and is aligning with a recipient that shares this perspective.

In Text (6.50), '*I'm unfollowing you*' realises negative evaluation targeting the User at whom the post is addressed.

Text (6.50)   @{User} I thought I knew you. I'm unfollowing you.😂 😂 😂 ☕

However, the FACE WITH TEARS OF JOY 😂 😂 emoji that conclude the post index the non-seriousness of the linguistic negative ATTITUDE, indicating instead that the author is not in fact unfollowing the addressee of the post, while the SMILING FACE WITH OPEN HANDS 🤗 emoji confirms that the author does still positively evaluate the addressee. The FACE WITH TEARS OF JOY 😂 😂 emoji in particular index a humour response provoked by the previous linguistic negative ATTITUDE, suggesting the author is aware that this negative evaluation is transgressive and thus needs to be 'laughed off' so as to resolve the tension it creates. In so doing, the emoji introduce a new voice into the text (that we broadly define as that of a meta-author) that subverts the interpersonal meaning in the linguistic co-text and invites alignment from the interactant, as it reveals the author's true sentiments.

We can speculate here that in the context of the relationship between the interactants, even the linguistic co-text by itself could be interpreted by the

---

[2] See Knight (2010a) for more detail on how laughing affiliation is modelled in SFL.

addressee as non-serious. However, we must also consider the public visibility of posts made on Twitter, and that the author of the post may be accounting for how others who might see the post will interpret it. As such, the inclusion of the emoji to more clearly index the non-seriousness of their negative evaluation and their implicit positive ATTITUDE for the addressee ensures that the post is interpreted as intended by the author, not just by the addressee but by the post's broader audience.

Another interpersonal dynamic found in instances where emoji [subvert] meaning made in the co-text concerns the use of potentially negative ATTITUDE to signal solidarity among interactants. Such a case is found in Text (6.51).

Text (6.51)   Good morning, you fucking fucks! 😘 😗

Here, the linguistic co-text realises both positive ATTITUDE ('*good morning*') and negative ATTITUDE ('*you fucking fucks*'). Thus, if viewed in isolation, the linguistic co-text collectively realises a somewhat ambiguous ATTITUDE. However, when the interaction with the FACE THROWING A KISS 😗 is considered, it becomes clear that the negative ATTITUDE of '*you fucking fucks*' is disaligned from, and that the collective ATTITUDE expressed by the text is a positive one. The emoji representation has a directional component (throwing a kiss towards someone) that converges with the addressing function of the vocative realising solidarity. The reversal of the polarity of seemingly negative attitudinal resources could be interpreted as signalling even greater solidarity among the interactants in this post, as the author is confident enough of the strength of their rapport with the recipient that they know the semiotic resources which typically signify negative ATTITUDE will be interpreted as positive.

Another example of emoji indexing a humour response occurs in Text (6.52).

Text (6.52)   You're better than him Jimmy! He wouldn't have made me a brew 😭?
              Oh you didn't either😭

Here the FACE WITH TEARS OF JOY 😭 emoji follows a [figure] that invokes negative evaluation for the addressee of the post, and thus the emoji serves to index the author's disalignment from this negative evaluation.

A final noteworthy example of emoji echoing and subverting linguistic interpersonal meaning is found in Text (6.53).

Text (6.53)   Reverse that, sorry.
              Coffee hasn't kicked in yet. 😜 😴

Here we can see how the GRINNING FACE WITH ONE LARGE AND ONE SMALL EYE 😜 emoji coalesces the negative self-evaluation of '*sorry*', while serving to make explicit the negative self-evaluation invoked by 'coffee hasn't kicked in yet', which references the widely shared association of coffee as promoting alertness and mental capability. However, the 😌 emoji also carries connotations of playful non-seriousness, thus signalling that the intensity of the negative self-evaluation is intended to be mild. Thus, in Text (6.53) the emoji at once summarises and calibrates the overall interpersonal meaning construed in the post.

6.6.3   Rebound: Multiply: Position

The final feature of emoji–text RESONANCE involves the use of emoji that converge with language to modify the dialogic positioning of linguistic co-text. By dialogic positioning we refer to resources of the ENGAGEMENT system introduced in Chapter 3 in the section on linguistic evaluation. Within this system, a primary distinction is made between resources that realise [monoglossia] (a single voice) and [heteroglossia] (multiple voices). A further distinction is then made among heteroglossic resources, distinguishing between those that expand the dialogic space by allowing for alternative perspectives, and those that contract it but dismissing them. In the dataset analysed here, emoji were found to converge with language to realise heteroglossic expansion.

An example of emoji and language interacting to realise heteroglossic expansion can be found in Text (6.54).

Text (6.54)   @{User} Happy Friday To You Miss {name} 😴😴

Today's goals:-
Coffee ☕ and being kind to YOU

Am I Always Kind To YOU?
Maybe two ☕ ☕ coffees, and then kindness 🤔
Enjoy Your Day😴😴😆

Here, we can see the linguistic resource for heteroglossic expansion '*maybe*' converging with the THINKING FACE 🤔 emoji, which in this context indexes consideration for possible alternatives. Together, they signal the possibility for the day's goals to include either one or two coffees, thus introducing plural perspectives into the post.

Another example where emoji and language converge to dialogically position a perspective found in the text occurs in Text (6.55).

Text (6.55)   if they haven't deleted all the pictures with their ex out of their phone, blocked them on social media, and deleted their phone number

Their NOT DONE with them ° ° 😌💆☕

#ImJustSaying #TheTruthShallSetYouFree
#SomebodyGoingToBeMadAtThisTweet

In this example, we see how the hashtag '*#ImJustSaying*' realises heteroglossic expansion by positioning the perspective contained in the post as one among many. This expansion then RESONATES with the MAN SHRUGGING: DARK SKIN TONE 🤷🏿 emoji, which indexes the author's hesitance at being overly assertive. We can also see how the HOT BEVERAGE ☕ emoji can be used emblematically to index the communicative context of conversation unfolding while drinking tea or coffee, which carries connotations of informal intimacy. In turn, this register is associated with dialogic heteroglossia (as opposed to formal, institutional registers), thus its evocation further contributes to the heteroglossic expansion of the perspectives contained in the post. In common-sense terms, the meaning construed by ☕ can be described as 'this is something said in an informal, intimate environment, so it is just one subjective opinion among many potential others'.

This kind of emblematic meaning of 'sophisticated nonchalance' was encountered in the corpus when emoji serve to target the text with dialogic meaning. For instance, the NAIL POLISH 💅 emoji was also used to evoke the communicative context of conversation unfolding while a person is applying nail polish or having it applied in a nail salon, which carries similar connotations of informal intimacy and heteroglossic expansion. The use of NAIL POLISH 💅 to construe heteroglossic expansion and position a perspective found in the co-text as one among many can be seen in Text (6.56) to Text (6.59). In these texts the NAIL POLISH 💅 emoji combines with the HOT BEVERAGE ☕ to reinforce the dialogic positioning indexed by the emoji. Text (6.59) also features the sequence of FROG and HOT BEVERAGE 🐸 ☕, which references the 'Kermit tea meme',[3] another resource for emblematically construing heteroglossic expansion that was described in the previous chapter.

Text (6.56)   You can't be canceled if you don't got clout☕ 💅

Text (6.57)   {name} is messy AF on the circle but I'm absolutely obsessed with him! He's the kind of person that turns up to brunch late just to spill the Tea and leave before the bill!• • ☕ 💅

Text (6.58)   @{User} Sad to see you survived sweaty💅 ☕

Text (6.59)   @{User} You definitely deserve a deal with one of these streaming services. Especially since they handing them thangs out like candy to folks that arent half as funny or intelligent as you are.💅 🐸 ☕

---

[3] This is a meme that originated from a still image from the television show *The Muppets*. The image features the Muppet character Kermit the Frog sitting at a table, drinking tea, and looking relaxed. The text associated with the meme typically includes a caption that starts with 'but that's none of my business' followed by a witty comment or observation, often as a sarcastic remark. The meme is used to convey a tone of pretended disinterest or feigned ignorance about a situation or event.

Further to these instances where emoji coordinate with linguistic resources for dialogic positioning, it is worth noting that many emoji, by depicting a sentient body part, potentially reference alternate perspectives. Indeed, if we revisit the examples discussed in the previous section describing the [subvert] feature, we can see how depictions of faces or body parts that index meaning that diverges from that found in the linguistic co-text realise this kind of heteroglossic expansion. For instance, returning to Text (6.49), we can see how the ROLLING ON THE FLOOR LAUGHING 🤣 emoji introduces a new perspective into the text, one that is aware the 'bean'/'been' pun is banal.

Text (6.49)   I've always bean a coffee girl 🤣 Never could Aquire a taste for tea☕

Similarly, the FACE BLOWING A KISS 😘 emoji in Text (6.51) indexes the author's positive ATTITUDE for the addressee of the post, thus realising a differing perspective to the negative evaluation found in the linguistic co-text via the expletives.

Text (6.51)   Good morning, you fucking fucks!💭 😘

As a final observation on the heteroglossic meaning of emoji depicting sentient body parts, it should be noted that the potential for emoji to realise alternate perspectives is only realised in instances where the emoji ATTITUDE diverges from linguistically realised ATTITUDE.

6.7   Up-Scaling Attitude through Emoji Repetition

Turning now to resources for intensifying interpersonal meaning, emoji can up-scale ATTITUDE through strings of repeated emoji functioning as a GRADUATION resource in the posts. GRADUATION was explained in Chapter 3 as part of the appraisal framework and a region of meaning concerned with modulating (upscaling and downscaling) linguistic ATTITUDE. Corpus studies of emoji n-grams have suggested that emoji sequences typically comprise repetitions of the same emoji (e.g. 💜 💜 💜) or combinations of semantically similar emoji (e.g. 💭 😘) (McCulloch & Gawne, 2018; Medlock & McCulloch, 2016). The repetition that is possible in strings of repeated emoji have been likened to beat gestures in embodied paralanguage (McCulloch & Gawne, 2018), and this kind of paralanguage can also function as a form of emphasis.

The most frequently repeated emoji in our corpus are shown in Table 6.3. A 'greedy match' method was used to construct this frequency table and ensures that every emoji is only counted once in the table. For example, a string of five RED HEART emoji would only be counted in the RED HEART row with a span of five and would not be included in the span of six. In other words, any smaller spans that are part of a larger span are not counted within that larger

Table 6.3 *The five most frequent repeated emoji in the*
Hot Beverage Emoji corpus

N	Emoji	CLDR Short Name	Span	Count
1		HOT BEVERAGE	2	631
2		HOT BEVERAGE	3	183
3		RED HEART	3	69
4		HOT BEVERAGE	4	67
5		FACE WITH TEARS OF JOY	2	38

span. The reason for our desire to only count each emoji once is to avoid the
problem of overcounting due to overlapping spans.

Repeated emoji in the corpus most frequently occurred as part of textual
clustering after greetings, examples of which we have seen earlier. Further examples include Text (6.60) to Text (6.64), which feature repeated emoji that
intensify the expression of solidarity in the greeting (underlined) and any co-
occurring positive ATTITUDE (bold):

Text (6.60)   @{User} Good morning **beautiful** <u>friends</u> … I wish you all a **pleasant**
Sunday ...

Text (6.61)   @{User} Good morning {name}

Text (6.62)   @{User} Good Morning V!K

Text (6.63)   @{User} Morning have a good day

Text (6.64)   <u>@{User} Good morning & happy Thank Crunchie day</u> **beautiful**
special {name} & **dear loverly special** mama <u>Wishing you a</u> **<u>super</u>**
<u>sparkly</u> <u>fabby</u> <u>fun-filled</u> <u>day</u> Keep cool Lots of **love** & **hugs** from me
& da pups

In these examples emoji repetition both coalesces with and up-scales the
positive interpersonal meanings in the co-text. For example, Text (6.64)
includes a clustering of a long string of repeated emoji triples: FACE
BLOWING A KISS , SMILING FACE WITH OPEN HANDS ,
SPARKLING HEART , UNICORN , ROSE , and SHAVED
ICE which up-scale the positive [appreciation] '*super sparkly fabby fun-*
filled' as well as the positive [affect] '*love & hugs*'. As these examples show,
the repeated emoji could span a range of emoji types across face, symbol and
object emoji which tended to both resonate with the interpersonal meanings
but also concur with the relevant ideational field. For instance, in terms of field,
the SHAVED ICE emoji appear to coordinate with the command to '*Keep*

cool' (possibly relating to shared context about hot weather in this exchange) and also appear to intensify its interpersonal dimension by acting like a virtual gift for keeping cool. Indeed, many of the examples, particularly those including flowers, seem to draw on gift-giving associations to intensify the expressed solidarity, as can be seen in Text (6.65) to Text (6.68).

Text (6.65)   @{User} Good morning

Text (6.66)   @{User} Morning {name}!

Text (6.67)   @{User} Good morning & Happy Wednesday. Hope your day is amazing!!

Text (6.68)   @{User} Good Morning dear friend {name} Hope you had a restful sleep, so Wednesday can Start with a smile. Happy Wednesday for you {name}.

Other examples, which were not directly associated with a greeting, often included repeated face emoji to emphasise co-occurring ATTITUDE (bold), such as Text (6.69) to Text (6.72).

Text (6.69)   @{User} Here you are, Darlin'!!!!! I **hope** it will tide you over

Text (6.70)   I **need** coffee

Text (6.71)   I be going to Target to see what new coffee mugs they be having **lol**

Text (6.72)   @{User} **Awesome** …

Coalescing could also group emoji by field, with emoji from the same semantic domain being repeated. For instance, Text (6.73) makes a joke about sport and music through a parody of the company name 'Spotify' which is a major music streaming service.

Text (6.73)   It's a vibe at Spotify

In this example the repetition of the sport-related emoji, BASKETBALL, AMERICAN FOOTBALL, and BASEBALL up-scale the humorous positivity invoked by '*vibe*' in the co-text, at the same time as reinforcing the sports as the field needed to express the joke.

6.8   Radiating Interpersonal Meaning through Iconisation

In additional to resonating with interpersonal meanings in the co-text, emoji can function as symbols or emblems which reverberate interpersonal meanings drawn from the cultural context. This is the interpersonal dimension of the emblematising function of emoji that was explored in Chapter 5 from the perspective of ideational meaning. Emblems radiate interpersonal meaning through what has been referred to in social semiotic research as a process of 'iconisation' (Martin, 2004). Iconisation occurs when the experiential dimension of everyday activities or objects recedes and the attitudinal or emotional importance they hold for a particular community as something that unifies them is foregrounded. Martin (2008b, p. 19) positions iconisation as the interpersonal equivalent of the ideational process of technicalisation where complex IDEA-TION (such as the technicality of science) is condensed in technical terms:

> The comparable condensation process as far as interpersonal meaning is concerned is iconisation – a process whereby bondicons accrue value which they in turn radiate outwards for people to align around. Among well-known bondicons are peace symbols (the dove and the peace sign) which anchor communities of protest against war. Symbols of this kind illustrate the way in which values can be materialised as images; further examples of iconisation would include ceremonies, proverbs, slogans, memorable quotations, flags, team colours, coats of arms, mascots and so on. Iconisation can also involve people, including well-known embodiments of peaceful protest and of liberation such as Gandhi and Mandela respectively (see Martin & Welsh to appear for discussion). (Martin, 2008b, p. 19)

In this way, activities, such as eating an election day 'democracy sausage' (a barbecued sausage in bread) at an Australian election day polling venue (Zappavigna, 2014c) and objects, for example a morning cup of coffee (Zappavigna, 2014a), function as 'bonding icons' that align members of a community around the particular values that that activity or object has accrued (Stenglin, 2008). This kind of accrual is perhaps most recognisable in images in the form of national emblems or corporate logos, in material objects such as statues, flags, or awards, and in certain kinds of regularised social practices such as rituals or ceremonies. For instance, memorabilia can function to 'rally visitors around communal ideals' within museum exhibitions (Martin & Stenglin, 2006, p. 216) and artefacts such as academic gowns and testamurs are important symbolic icons in graduation ceremonies which help to rally participants around academic ideals (Stenglin, 2012).

The most obvious example of a bonding icon in the corpus is the HOT BEVERAGE ☕ emoji itself, particularly where it construes meanings about coffee. Coffee has been shown to be a topic of social media discourse that aligns different kinds of communities around shared experiences and feelings (Zappavigna, 2014b, 2019b). This is because coffee has accrued a range of associations such as inducing creativity, wakefulness, and productivity through the process of iconisation (Zappavigna, 2014a). For example, the corpus contained many examples such as Text (6.74) to Text (6.78) where the HOT BEVERAGE ☕ emoji radiated positive meanings about enabling increased work and productivity.

Text (6.74)   I even borrowed my cousin's coffee machine! I am ready to both relax
               AND work my ass off!☕ 💚

Text (6.75)   This is the face of someone who worked a 15 – hour shift; (barely)
               made it though 7-rush peaks, 2 meltdowns, and 1 30-minute break …
               #whatafuckingday ☕ [selfie of a woman in a mask]

Text (6.76)   ☕Good Morning!☕ Lots of admin work to do this Saturday!   ☕   ☕
               ☕ [selfie of a woman drinking a takeaway coffee]

Text (6.77)   Up with enough time for a coffee before a disgustingly early start at
               work☕ ☕

Text (6.78)   Working, taking my braids out, micromanaging kids, and peeping this
               Khaled album all before 9am☕

The HOT BEVERAGE ☕ emoji was also invoked as a remedy for tiredness
through associations with inducing alertness, as can be seen in Text (6.79) to
Text (6.81).

Text (6.79)   Someone send coffee ☕ my back is stiff and I'm so tired. Class
               tonight☕

Text (6.80)   work starts now but im already tired and sleepy☕

Text (6.81)   It's nights, living on coffee ☕ #tired [image of steering wheel from the
               driver's seat of a car]

These posts do not explicitly state that coffee has the property of inducing
wakefulness but instead rely on the emblem to activate these iconised meanings
which coffee has accrued from the cultural context over time. In other words,
they invoke the meaning that the reason the author needs coffee is because it
wakes them up. Even posts such as Text (6.82) to Text (6.85) that draw on the
popular trope 'I need coffee' associated with enacting a 'coffee addict' persona
(Zappavigna, 2014a), do not make explicit the reason why coffee is required.

Text (6.82)   A decade ago I could pull few all-nighters before a deadline. Don't
               think this is working anymore
               ☕ ☕ Maybe more ☕ ☕ is needed?

Text (6.83)   Afternoon tweets ☕ ☕ ☕what a hectic morning -all i need now is plenty
               coffee and chocolate☕ ☕ ☕
               #AcademicChatter

Text (6.84)   #MondayCoffee ☕ It's a brand new week. I'm just going to need a lot
               of caffeine to get me started. Y'all have a great day!

Text (6.85)   Whew I'm tired this morning! I need COFFEE☕

Instead, these posts also rely on the interpersonal meanings about wakefulness
and productivity that are infused in coffee as a bonding icon and activated by

the HOT BEVERAGE ☕ emoji. Somewhat paradoxically, coffee is also associated with stimulating relaxation as in examples Text (6.86) to Text (6.88).

Text (6.86)   Summer morning coffee with a good book☕📖 on the deck, and
no rush to race off to work! This is what I've been waiting for!
#SummerVibes #CoffeeTime #TheseViolentDelights #TeacherLife
[inferred selfie of hand holding a book and a cup of coffee on a table in
front of a pool]

Text (6.87)   How peaceful it is when i am working at home all alone☕

Text (6.88)   Get to have a late start today and tomorrow as I'm working a split
1st/2nd for a few days to cover co-worker's vaca time so a nice slow
start with ☕ ☕and 📖📖Happy Monday

Again, while these examples forge meanings about a relaxing situation in the co-text, they do not explicitly inscribe the meaning that 'coffee induces feelings of relaxation'.

6.9   Conclusion

This chapter has explored the interpersonal function of emoji as they resonate with the linguistic ATTITUDE and negotiation of solidarity expressed in social media posts. We have introduced a system network for describing the ways in which this resonance can occur, making a distinction between emoji which imbue the co-text with interpersonal meaning (usually through attitudinally targeting particular IDEATION), and emoji which enmesh with the interpersonal meanings made in the co-text (usually through coordinating with linguistic ATTITUDE). We then explained the more delicate options in this RESONANCE network where emoji can harmonise with the co-text by either echoing or coalescing interpersonal meaning, or can rebound from the co-text, either complicating, subverting, or positioning interpersonal meaning. Following this traversal of the RESONANCE network, we considered two important dimensions of interpersonal meaning noted in the corpus: the role of emoji in modulating attendant interpersonal meanings in the co-text by upscaling GRADUATION and emoji's capacity to radiate interpersonal meaning through emblematic usage as bonding icons.

The next logical step after having considered emoji's role in such interpersonal meaning is to consider their potential in negotiating social relations, given that interpersonal meaning is oriented to the negotiation of relationships. Thus in the next two chapters we turn to exploring how emoji function as a resource for affiliation by exploring how they can support social bonding in social media discourse.

7   DIALOGIC AFFILIATION
The Role of Emoji in Negotiating Social Bonds

7.1   Introduction

Chapters 3 to 6 have progressively outlined our model for analysing how emoji coordinate with language to realise meaning across the textual, ideational, and interpersonal metafunctions. This analytical framework is valuable in its own right for exploring discrete regions of emoji–language semiosis, in other words, for understanding in detail how emoji make meaning with their co-text through textual SYNCHRONICITY, ideational CONCURRENCE, and interpersonal RESONANCE. The details of this coordination are also critical for generating a solid foundation on which to build claims about how emoji function as resources for social bonding. The emoji–text relations explored thus far enable a principled investigation of the role emoji play together with language in negotiating and enacting identity and community in social media discourse. Our focus in this and the following chapter is on how emoji support DIALOGIC and COMMUNING AFFILIATION, two key aspects of the 'ambient affiliation' at the heart of social media discourse (Zappavigna, 2011).

The affiliation framework was developed within social semiotics to describe how social relations are enacted in language (Knight, 2010b; Martin, 2010). Affiliation encompasses both social bonding and social alienation (disaffiliation). For instance, language can be used to forge solidarity, togetherness, and camaraderie, or alternatively, to create discord, estrangement, and enmity. It can also be used to negotiate everything in between, for example the complex relations underlying humour. For an overview of current social semiotic research into affiliation the reader is directed to Logi and Zappavigna (2022).[1] The affiliation framework was originally developed to account for written and face-to-face communication and was further developed to account for online contexts where social relations can be negotiated beyond the level of conversational exchanges through the kinds of mass communion of feeling seen in 'searchable talk' such as hashtag use and the spread of memes

---

[1] For further work on how affiliation is related to a more general SFL model of Tenor as a resource for enacting social relations, see Doran, Martin, and Zappavigna (forthcoming).

(Zappavigna, 2018). This led to the development of the concept of 'ambient affiliation' to account for both interactive bonding and such mass communing (Zappavigna, 2011). This is the model which we will apply in this chapter on interactive bonding and in the following chapter on COMMUNING AFFILIATION.

7.2   Negotiating Bonds in the Quarantine Hotel Food Review TikTok Corpus

This chapter explores the role of emoji in direct exchanges between users through what we refer to as 'dialogic'[2] affiliation. The corpus we will use to explore the role of emoji in negotiating social bonds is the Quarantine Hotel Food Review TikTok Comment corpus, hereon in this chapter, simply the corpus. This is a specialised corpus of TikTok comments made on a video series (c. 40 videos; c. 60,500 words) about the food delivered to the room of a TikTok Creator over their fourteen-day hotel quarantine stay in New Zealand in 2021. Since the topic of quarantine itself is controversial, and because food choices offer fertile ground for discussion, the comments feeds of these videos incorporated a relatively high degree of interaction between people, making it a useful dataset for considering the negotiation of values. While most of the TikTok videos in the corpus received around 100,000 views, three were more popular, with 2.4, 1.4, and 3.1 million views, respectively.

7.2.1   Social Bonds and IDEATION–ATTITUDE Couplings

The reader might be surprised that any further analysis is required to understand the role that emoji play in enacting social relations, given that Chapter 6 dealt extensively with interpersonal meaning. However, while interpersonal meaning is crucial to enacting relationships, affiliation involves more than emotion or opinion: 'We don't after all simply affiliate with feelings; we affiliate with feelings about people, places and things, and the activities they participate in, however abstract or concrete. We align through the bonds we make as we share these couplings' (Martin, 2008a, p. 58).

Thus according to the affiliation framework, a key way in which social bonds are expressed in language is through 'couplings' of ideational and attitudinal meanings (Zappavigna, Dwyer, & Martin, 2008) which were introduced in Chapter 6, hereon IDEATION–ATTITUDE couplings. The framework is also concerned with the ways in which couplings can be negotiated in discourse. Of particular interest to us are instances where IDEATION and ATTITUDE are

---

[2] While this might seem like a tautology, this term distinguishes interactive bonding from the kind of non-interactive communing that can occur in social and mass media contexts.

apportioned across modes, such as in the instances where attitudinal emoji [imbue] ideational language (see Chapter 6). For example, in Text (7.1) we can see how the linguistically realised [sequence] '*Her sister was getting married and she can't go*', which does not contain any inscribed linguistic evaluation, is imbued with negative ATTITUDE by the PLEADING FACE 🥺 emoji:

Text (7.1)   Her sister was getting married and she can't go 🥺

This constitutes an IDEATION–ATTITUDE coupling which can then be negotiated as a potential bond through interaction. Similarly, in Text (7.2) the FLUSHED FACE 😳 emoji imbues the linguistic [element] '*Meanwhile in Korea*' with negative ATTITUDE:

Text (7.2)   Meanwhile in Korea ... . 😳

While instances where emoji [imbue] language with ATTITUDE provide illustrative examples of how emoji participate in IDEATION–ATTITUDE couplings, this is the marked choice among intermodal couplings.

More common in the corpus were instances where emoji coordinate with linguistically realised ATTITUDE to interact with linguistically realised IDEATION. For instance, the FLUSHED FACE 😳 emoji was frequently used in combination with linguistic ATTITUDE to realise a number of more delicate ATTITUDE features, as can be seen in Text (7.3) to Text (7.5).

Text (7.3)   I was so lucky 😳 😳 😳

Text (7.4)   Fitting I thought 🔪 🔪 bloody evil quinoa coming for me 😳 😳

Text (7.5)   Wow that actually looks top tier 😳 🤤

In Text (7.3), 😳 complicates the positive judgement of '*so lucky*' to realise negative ATTITUDE targeting an ideational [entity] the author was relieved to have avoided. In Text (7.4), 😳 echoes the negative appreciation of '*bloody evil*' targeting '*quinoa*'. And in Text (7.5), 😳 forms part of an emoji sequence that coalesces the linguistic positive ATTITUDE of the post targeting '*that*'.

Identifying IDEATION–ATTITUDE couplings such as these provides linguistic evidence for the description of how bonds are negotiated. However, as we will see in the following sections, the interpretation of which meanings are being construed by emoji in social media texts becomes more nuanced and delicate once these texts are analysed in the context of exchanges among social media users. In particular, once the interactive dimension is factored in, it becomes clear that further to enmeshing with ATTITUDE realised linguistically, emoji also serve to index interactants' own affect, and thus constitute a simultaneous, parallel vector for interpersonal affiliation.

7.3   Quarantine Hotel Food Review TikTok Comment Corpus

Hotel quarantine is a system used in many countries during the COVID-19 pandemic to allow travel across borders, with people completing around fourteen days of isolation to ensure they did not spread the virus at their destination. During their isolation travellers usually had their meals delivered directly to their rooms, ensuring minimal contact with others during their stay. The hotel staff would deliver the meals to the door without any personal interaction with the quarantined individuals. Some travellers documented their experiences on social media, including posting videos that reviewed the food delivered to their rooms. In the videos related to the present corpus, the meals often came in brown paper bags, which the Creator unpacked in front of the camera. The corpus saw a high level of engagement, with many comments receiving replies from both other users and the Creator, who may have been more actively engaging with comments due to the monotony of quarantine.

The comment section of these hotel quarantine food review videos became a platform for negotiating bonds about food, daily life, and the impact of the pandemic. Most comments involved convivial alignments around shared values, with the occasional heated exchange regarding whether quarantine was a justifiable approach. There were also more light-hearted controversies regarding food preferences, including the negotiation of [GOOD FOOD][3] bonds, with users deliberating on light-hearted issues such as whether Snickers is a popular chocolate bar brand and whether or not it is good practice to put milk or water on Weetabix/Weet-bix (a type of cereal popular in Australia, NZ, and the UK). Alongside this food discourse was discussion of values relating to appearance and overeating in which users discussed their feelings towards how much they eat and their body weight.

Table 7.1 provides an overview of the most common emoji in the corpus.[4] The most frequent emoji, FACE WITH TEARS OF JOY 😂, matches other quantitative studies noted in Chapter 1.

Previewing the analysis to be undertaken in this chapter, this emoji, alongside other frequent emoji, such as ROLLING ON THE FLOOR LAUGHING 🤣 and GRINNING FACE WITH SWEAT 😅, functioned as laughter tokens. They were involved in negotiating humorous meanings and with 'laughing off' bonds that could not be immediately shared in the interaction due to other prominent bonds that interactants appeared to share. Other frequent emoji such as SMILING FACE WITH HEARTS 🥰, SMILING FACE WITH HEART-EYES 😍, HEART SUIT ♥, and RED HEART ❤ were used to enact solidarity

---

[3] As explained in the conventions section and later in this chapter, we will use square brackets to demarcate bonds realised as IDEATION–ATTITUDE couplings in the textual analysis.

[4] These emoji were originally encoded and rendered on the TikTok platform; however, for sake of consistency they are displayed here in the Twitter rendering.

Table 7.1 *Most frequent emoji in the Quarantine Hotel Food corpus*

#	Emoji	Frequency
1	FACE WITH TEARS OF JOY😂	700
2	SMILING FACE WITH HEARTS🥰	660
3	PLEADING FACE🥺	309
4	GRINNING FACE WITH SWEAT😅	283
5	ROLLING ON THE FLOOR LAUGHING🤣	204
6	FLUSHED FACE😳	177
7	HEART SUIT♥	166
8	SMILING FACE WITH HEART-EYES😍	133
9	LOUDLY CRYING FACE😭	128
10	RED HEART❤	107

through sharing common bonds. In addition, the corpus contained instances where users debated values about food preferences, the validity of quarantine, and other issues relevant to life during the COVID-19 pandemic. In general, this debate was relatively low stakes and non-serious, and, as we will see, the emoji played an important role in maintaining a sense of conviviality in the comments feed.

7.4   Dialogic Affiliation

IDEATION–ATTITUDE couplings provide linguistic evidence for social bonds, which are the key unit of analysis in the AMBIENT AFFILIATION framework. The concept of an IDEATION–ATTITUDE coupling was first used by Knight (2008, 2010a, 2010b, 2013) to understand affiliation in casual conversation, specifically the complex nuances of meaning involved in conversational humour shared between friends. Further work using IDEATION–ATTITUDE couplings as a unit of analysis includes research into academic discourse (Hao & Humphrey, 2009; Hood, 2010), business writing (Szenes, 2016, 2021), terrorist discourse (Etaywe & Zappavigna, 2022), misinformation and disinformation (Inwood & Zappavigna, 2021, 2022), political discourse (Makki & Zappavigna, 2022), and stand-up comedy humour (Logi, 2021; Logi & Zappavigna, 2019, 2021a). The fundamental premise of these studies is that tabling a bond (a social variable) involves rendering it in language as one or more IDEATION–ATTITUDE couplings (a linguistic variable) or through some implied meaning shared by a group (usually invoking an IDEATION–ATTITUDE coupling from the context or previous co-text).[5]

---

[5] This approach is currently being explored at the level of Tenor in Doran et al. (forthcoming).

Examples of linguistic IDEATION–ATTITUDE couplings are the coupling of the [thing entity], '*snickers*', with the positive [affect] ('*love*') in Text (7.6) and with negative [affect] ('*YUCK*', '*doesn't like*') in Text (7.7).

Text (7.6)   I love snickers 🖤 😊

        [IDEATION: [thing entity] ('*snickers*')/ATTITUDE: positive [affect]]

Text (7.7)   Looool 😊 you showed the snickers and I was like YUCK SNICKERS[1]..
        then you proceeded to say I know no one who doesn't like snickers[2] ...
        welp ...

        [1][IDEATION: [thing entity] ('*snickers*')/ATTITUDE: negative [affect]]
        [2][IDEATION: [thing entity] ('*snickers*')/ATTITUDE: positive [affect]]

The square brackets encompassing the resources interacting to form a coupling in this notation are intended to represent the fusion of IDEATION and ATTITUDE into a single bundle of meaning that is available for negotiation, for instance, in the next move in an exchange. Since many posts contain multiple couplings, a superscript notation is used to number them and is placed next to the relevant ideational meaning in the text (e.g. snickers[1], snickers[2] in Text (7.7)), as well as next to the relevant notation below the text. In some cases the ideational or attitudinal resources interacting in a coupling cannot be mapped on to specific lexical items in the text (for instance, when ATTITUDE in invoked as opposed to inscribed); in these cases the relevant lexis will be omitted from the coupling notation or glossed for clarity. Figure 7.1 describes a variety of strategies

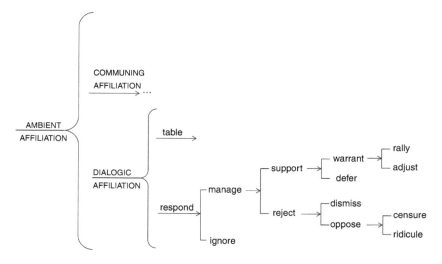

Figure 7.1 DIALOGIC AFFILIATION strategies

for negotiating social values, feelings, and opinions in interactional exchanges (Zappavigna, 2019a). The analysis and annotation of how these strategies unfold begins with the identification of the social bonds being negotiated, as these constitute opportunities for interactants to either affiliate or disaffiliate from each other.

Couplings form the linguistic evidence for bonds, thus the annotation of bonds is informed by the couplings that enact them. Since posts often contain many couplings, only those that relate to the emoji under analysis will be annotated in the examples. For instance, in Text (7.8), which responds to a TikTok food review video, linguistic (and emoji) resources realise the coupling: [IDEATION: [thing entity] (*food*)/ATTITUDE: positive [appreciation] (*yummy*, 😋)]. Given the field of discourse established by the original video, this coupling is interpreted as tabling a [GOOD FOOD] bond.

Text (7.8) Wow the food looks yummy😋

[IDEATION: [thing entity] (*'food'*)/ATTITUDE: positive [appreciation] (*'yummy'*, 😋)]
table × [GOOD FOOD]

We will adopt a similar display convention to the previous chapter for laying out our affiliation analysis. For instance, an exchange will be annotated as per Exchange 7.1.

Exchange 7.1

Text (7.9) **User 1:** That song 🎵 😍 🎶

[IDEATION: [thing entity] (*'song'*)/ATTITUDE: positive (😍 🎶)]
table × [GOOD SONG]

Text (7.10) **Creator:** Such a classic😍 😍 😍

[IDEATION: [thing entity] (*'song'*)/ATTITUDE: positive [appreciation] (*'classic'*, 😍 😍 😍)]
[rally] × [GOOD SONG]

In Exchange 7.1, the interaction is labelled as an exchange incorporating two posts, Text (7.9) and Text (7.10). The affiliation strategies (derived from Figure 7.1) are shown in square brackets, together with the relevant bond in [ALL CAPS]. For instance, in Exchange 7.1, the sequence of three SMILING FACE WITH HEART-EYES 😍 emoji in Text (7.10) acts in concert with the rallying affiliation resource, supporting the [GOOD SONG] bond. For the sake of simplicity, we will specify bonds, and unpack the specific IDEATION–ATTITUDE couplings only where they are necessary in terms of explaining the function of the emoji in the post.

Once a bond has been tabled, the fundamental distinction in the affiliation strategies described is between [manage], where a bond is actively negotiated, and [ignore], where a bond goes unaddressed. If the bond is actively negotiated, the main choice is between supporting or rejecting it, which distinguish between instances where interactants affiliate around a shared tabled bond or disaffiliate by rejecting a tabled bond they do not share.

Within the [support] subsystem, a further distinction can be made between [warrant], where interactants affiliate around the bond tabled, and [defer], where interactants affiliate around a bond implicated by the tabled bond. Finally, within [warrant], interactants can either rally with the tabled bond itself, or adjust, by tabling a bond related to the original tabled bond.

To illustrate the difference between these features, consider the following examples: in Exchange 7.2, a [GOOD PAVLOVA] bond tabled by User 1 is rallied by the Creator in Text (7.12), who repeats the coupling of positive [appreciation] (via the ATTITUDE token of positive [affect]) evaluating pavlova (a popular dessert dish in Australia and New Zealand). In Exchange 7.3, User 1 tables a [GOOD NEW ZEALAND] bond via an ellipsed reference to New Zealand and positive [affect]; in the following post, the Creator adjusts this bond by sustaining the positive evaluation for the same ideational target but selecting a different sub-type of ATTITUDE: [appreciation].

Exchange 7.2

Text (7.11)   **User 1:** God I miss a good pavlova☺ ☺

[IDEATION: [thing entity] (*'pavlova'*)/ATTITUDE: positive [appreciation] (*'good'*)]
[table] × [GOOD PAVLOVA]

Text (7.12)   **Creator:** I love pavlova☺ ☺ ☺

[IDEATION: [thing entity] (*'pavlova'*)/ATTITUDE: t^6- positive [appreciation]]
[rally] × [GOOD PAVLOVA]

Exchange 7.3

Text (7.13)   **User 1:** i wanna move so bad☺ ☺ ☺ ☺ ☺

[IDEATION: [occurrence figure] (move to New Zealand)/ATTITUDE: positive [affect] (*'want to'*)]
[table] × [GOOD NEW ZEALAND]

---

[6] Here the *t*-notation indicates that the affect (*love*) is a token of appreciation, construing the meaning that it is a good pavlova.

Text (7.14)   **Creator:** Haha yes our country is awesome

[IDEATION: [thing entity] (New Zealand)/ATTITUDE: positive
[appreciation] (*'awesome'*)]
[adjust] × [GOOD NEW ZEALAND]

The final option for supporting a tabled bond is [deferral]. [Deferral] occurs when a tabled bond is interpreted as playful or non-serious, thus pro-
voking a humour response among interactants who simultaneously defer
the tabled bond they don't share and rally around an opposing, implicated bond they do share. For example, in Exchange 7.4, User 1 tables a
[GOOD QUARANTINE] bond in Text (7.15), which is in tension with
the commonly shared [BAD QUARANTINE] bond. In response in Text
(7.16), User 2 responds with an initialism indexing the humour response
of laughter (*'lol'* = laugh out loud). This humour response signals that
User 2 has interpreted User 1's original bond as non-serious and is deferring it by 'laughing it off' while rallying around the implicated [BAD
QUARANTINE] bond.

Exchange 7.4

Text (7.15)   **User 1:** I'd like to book a vacation to the New Zealand government
quarantine facility

[IDEATION: [thing entity] (NZ quarantine)/ATTITUDE: positive
[affect] (*'like'*)]
[table] × [GOOD QUARANTINE]

...⁷

Text (7.16)   **User 2:** literally lol

[IDEATION: [thing entity] (NZ quarantine)/ATTITUDE: negative
[affect]]
[defer] × [GOOD QUARANTINE]
[rally] × [BAD QUARANTINE]

Turning now to affiliation strategies that involve rejecting tabled bonds,
the first option in the framework is to dismiss a bond by not engaging with
the coupling through which it is realised, and by expressing generalised
negative ATTITUDE. For example, in Exchange 7.5 User 1 tables a [BAD
FOREIGNERS ENTERING NEW ZEALAND] bond in response to the
Creator's quarantine food review TikTok video.⁸ User 2 then responds to

---

⁷ The ellipsis indicates that some intervening moves have been omitted for the sake of brevity since
this exchange involved many moves as multiple users added additional comments responding to
User 1.
⁸ 'tangata whenua' translates to "local people, hosts, indigenous people" in the Māori language,
and is used to refer to people of Māori ancestry.

User 1's comment with generalised negative ATTITUDE realised by '*shut up*', which does not engage with User 1's coupling of negative [judgement] targeting the Creator's entry into New Zealand and thus dismisses User 1's bond. The '*hahah*' that concludes User 2's post signals their desire to de-intensify the potential conflict arising from the dismissal by deferring any excessive aggression construed in their post.

Exchange 7.5

Text (7.17)   **User 1:** Why are you coming to NZ when there are tangata whenua trying to get home?

[IDEATION: [thing entity] (Creator)/ATTITUDE: negative [judgement]] [table] × [BAD CREATOR]

...

Text (7.18)   **User 2:** Girll shut up hahah

[IDEATION: [thing entity] (User 1)/ATTITUDE: negative [judgement]] [dismiss] × [BAD CREATOR] [defer] × [EXCESSIVE AGGRESSION]

Proceeding to the features of the [oppose] subsystem, these are distinguished between [censure], where a tabled bond is criticised, and [ridicule], where the bond is parodically imitated. For example, returning to Exchange 7.6, we can see how User 3 responds to User 1's post by reversing the polarity of the [judgement] targeting the Creator, and thus censures the [BAD CREATOR] bond tabled by User 1.

Exchange 7.6

Text (7.19)   **User 1:** Why are you coming to NZ when there are tangata whenua trying to get home?

[ideation: [thing entity] (Creator)/attitude: negative [judgement]] [table] × [BAD CREATOR]

...

Text (7.20)   **User 3:** Why can't she come to nz? She's paid she's from here. She has every right to come !

[ideation: [thing entity] (Creator)/attitude: positive [judgement]] [censure] × [BAD CREATOR]

Finally, Exchange 7.7 is an example where a [BAD QUARANTINE] bond tabled by User 1 is ridiculed by the Creator, who mocks User 1 by hyperbolically exaggerating the negative ATTITUDE of their post via ALL CAPS and the infantilising reference to a baby's cry ('*WAAAAAAAH*'). A [DELUDED CREATOR] bond is also dismissed by reversing the negation of the implied answer to the rhetorical question in User 1' post '*you're all just chill with it?!*', '*yes I'm chill*'.

Exchange 7.7

Text (7.21)   **User 1:** A facility?! WTH? This is normal there and you're all just chill with it?! That is insane.

> [IDEATION: [thing entity] ([quarantine] ('*facility*')/ATTITUDE: negative [affect] ('*WTH?*')]
> [IDEATION: [relational entity] (*you're all just chill*)/ATTITUDE: negative [judgement] (*insane*)]
> [table] × [BAD QUARANTINE]
> [table] × [DELUDED CREATOR]

Text (7.22)   **Creator:** MY RIGHTS WAAAAAAAH. I made choices. & this is the result of my choice so yes I'm chill.

> [IDEATION: [semiotic entity] (User 1's post)/ATTITUDE: negative [judgement]]
> [IDEATION: [occurrence entity] (quarantine in a facility)/ATTITUDE: positive [judgement] (*chill*)]
> [ridicule] × [BAD QUARANTINE]
> [dismiss] × [DELUDED CREATOR]

The rest of this chapter explores how emoji coordinate with these kinds of dialogic affiliation strategies.

7.5   The Role of Emoji in rallying around Shared Bonds☺

As Table 7.1 detailed, the most frequent emoji found in the TikTok comment corpus denote largely positive attitudinal meanings, which in terms of affiliation correspond to their mainly occurring in posts that enact solidarity among interactants. While these emoji enmesh with ATTITUDE found in the linguistic co-text of a post, in the context of interaction among social media users, they can also be used to index an interactant's emotional state by imbuing the authorial persona with [affect]. This, as we have already noted, allows emoji to simultaneously realise evaluations targeting the ideational content that comprises the field of discourse, as well as realising interpersonal contact and solidarity.

In many exchanges interactants rally around a [GOOD FOOD] bond, with emoji coordinating with the positive attitudes in the couplings that realise the bond. For example in Exchange 7.8, User 1 tables a [GOOD FOOD] bond via the coupling [IDEATION: [thing entity] ('*food*')/ATTITUDE: positive [appreciation] ('*GOOD*')] and the Creator responds by rallying around this bond through a response expressing their agreement ('*I know*'), together with a sequence of five SMILING FACE WITH HEART-EYES 😍 emoji. These emoji coordinate with the language of Text (7.23) and Text (7.24) to echo the positive [appreciation] of '*GOOD*'. They also imbue the [thing entity] '*I*' with positive [affect], thus indexing the Creator's pleasure in response to the quality of the food. Our coding of these emoji as realising [affect], as opposed to more generalised ATTITUDE, is justified by the target/appraiser being a sentient entity, as mentioned in Chapter 6, Section 6.3.

This added dimension of positive [affect] in response to a positively evaluated ideational [entity] (the food) comprises a further coupling that supports the [GOOD FOOD] bond, one where food is the trigger for the ATTITUDE realised, rather than the target of the evaluation.[9] Consequently, in this exchange the emoji both sustain the linguistically realised couplings and introduce a new dimension of positive ATTITUDE that further supports the bond around which the interactants are rallying. Worth noting here is that compared to the examples of emoji–language interaction within posts described in the preceding chapters, when the scope of analysis is broadened to include exchanges comprising multiple posts, we can see how emoji may interact with linguistic resources found in other posts as long as they satisfy the principles of minimum mapping and prosodic correspondence that govern their interaction. As such emoji in exchanges can index parallel or mirrored [affect] among interactants that further supports solidarity and shared alignment, the region of interpersonal meaning described in SFL as INVOLVEMENT. This region is 'especially tuned to the negotiation of group membership (thus solidarity)' (Martin & White, 2005, p. 34).

Exchange 7.8

Text (7.23)   **User 1: SALMON BROCOLINI POTATOES?! THATS GOOD FOOD[1]**

> [1][IDEATION: [thing entity] ('*food*')/ATTITUDE: positive [appreciation] ('*good*')]
> [table] × [GOOD FOOD]

Text (7.24)   **Creator: I[1] KNOW[2]😍 😍 😍 😍 😍**

> [1][IDEATION: [thing entity] (Creator)/ATTITUDE: positive [affect]]
> [2][IDEATION: [thing entity] (food)/ATTITUDE: positive [appreciation]]
> [rally] × [GOOD FOOD]

Exchange 7.9 is a similar example, with the SMILING FACE WITH HEARTS 😍 emoji again enmeshing with positive ATTITUDE to realise rallying affiliation relating to a [GOOD FOOD] bond, as well as imbuing the Creator with positive [affect] resulting from the food being positively evaluated:

---

[9] For a full discussion on the different relations between ideational meaning and attitudinal features, see Martin and White (2005)

Exchange 7.9

Text (7.25)   **User 1:** nice af[1]

[1][IDEATION: [thing entity] (*food*)/ATTITUDE: positive [appreciation]]
[adjust] × [GOOD FOOD]

Text (7.26)   **Creator:** It was so good

[1][IDEATION: [thing entity] (Creator)/ATTITUDE: positive [affect]]
[2][IDEATION: [thing entity] (food)/ATTITUDE: positive [appreciation]]
[rally] × [GOOD FOOD]

It is common on YouTube and TikTok for commenters to positively evaluate the Creator in terms of their appearance or aesthetic dimensions of their videos. These kinds of posts typically feature bonds that are realised through couplings incorporating positive [appreciation]. The PLEADING FACE emoji is a common choice among instances where emoji coordinate with these couplings. It is frequently used to simultaneously positively evaluate the interactant's compliment and index that the author is emotionally moved by it. An example of this can be seen in Exchange 7.10. Here we have both the SMILING FACE WITH SMILING EYES and SMILING FACE WITH HEARTS emoji in the User's post and the PLEADING FACE emoji in the Creator's response contributing to the affiliation among the interactants. In the User's post, the language realises positive [appreciation] for the Creator's voice, while the emoji adds an affective dimension denoting the User's positive emotions arising from the Creator's voice. In the Creator's response, the emoji coordinates with the positive [appreciation] to the compliment as well as indexing the Creator's positive emotions arising from the compliment.

Exchange 7.10

Text (7.27)   **User 1:** Your voice[1] is so pretty[2]

[1][IDEATION: [thing entity] ('*voice*')/ATTITUDE: positive [appreciation]]
[2][IDEATION: [thing entity] (User)/ATTITUDE: positive [affect]]
[table] × [GOOD VOICE]

Text (7.28)   **Creator:** Thank you[1] [2] I hate my voice[3]!!! I feel like everyone does tho unless you amazing singer or something hehe

[1][IDEATION: [thing entity] (compliment)/ATTITUDE: positive [appreciation]]
[2][IDEATION: [thing entity] (Creator)/ATTITUDE: positive [affect]]
[3][IDEATION: [thing entity] ('*voice*')/ATTITUDE: negative [affect]]
[dismiss] × [GOOD VOICE]
[rally] × [GOOD COMPLIMENT]

Thus across this exchange, the emoji serve both to coordinate with the linguistic evaluations for entities (the Creator's voice and the User's compliment) as well to add a second layer of support for the resulting bonds in the form of the interactants' positive emotions. In particular the Creator's positive [affect] following the User's compliment is noteworthy as they then proceed to reject the User's [GOOD VOICE] bond (the Creator states, '*I hate my voice*'). As such, the affiliation realised in this exchange does not relate to shared evaluation of an ideational entity so much as to reciprocal positive [affect], where the User's bond is re-interpreted by the Creator as an act of positive interpersonal evaluation and rallied around. By indexing the emotional states of the interactants, the emoji in this exchange are productive resources in foregrounding this affective dimension of the affiliation.

A similar affiliative dynamic is found in Exchange 7.11. Here User 1 positively evaluates the Creator's original video as well as the food shown within it ('*favourite*', '*yummy*'), and in response the Creator positively evaluates the User and their activity of watching the video ('*thanks*'), as well as indexing their own positive [affect] via the SMILING FACE WITH SMILING EYES and SMILING FACE WITH HEARTS 😍 emoji. In terms of affiliation, the Creator reinterprets the User's tabled [FAVOURITE VIDEO] bond as the [GOOD VIEWER] bond, which they then rally around. As with Exchange 7.10, the emoji multiply the ATTITUDE resources that the interactants align around, resulting in an affiliative dynamic where generalised, reciprocal interpersonal positivity eclipses the more specific bonds being negotiated.

Exchange 7.11

Text (7.29)   **User 1:** Out of all the quarantine videos I've watched so far yours[1] is by far my favorite! everything[2] looks yummy!

> [1][IDEATION: [thing entity] (Creator's video)/ATTITUDE: positive [appreciation]]
> [2][IDEATION: [thing entity] (food)/ATTITUDE: positive [appreciation]]
> [table] × [FAVOURITE VIDEO]
> [table] × [GOOD FOOD]

Text (7.30)   **Creator:** Thanks[1] so much for watching[2] 😊 😍[3]

> [1][IDEATION: [thing entity] (User)/ATTITUDE: positive [affect]]
> [2][IDEATION: [occurrence entity] (watching the video)/ATTITUDE: positive [affect]]
> [3][IDEATION: [thing entity] (Creator)/ATTITUDE: positive [affect]]
> [rally] × [GOOD VIEWER]

An important point to note is that people do not just align around bonds incorporating positive assessments, but can also enact solidarity regarding bonds that involve negativity, as is clear in work on conversations incorporating gossip

(Eggins & Slade, 1997/2005). An example of this kind of pattern found in the corpus was users aligning around shared complaint about workplace bosses in the United States. For instance, in Exchange 7.12 the commenters rally around a shared [BAD US BOSSES] bond and relating bonds regarding the UK and unfair bosses who demand employees physically attend work despite being sick with COVID.

Exchange 7.12

Text (7.31)   **User 1:** In the us they[1]'ll be like 'You're still coming to work, right?'

[1][IDEATION: [thing entity] (US boss)/ATTITUDE: negative [judgement]]
[table] × [BAD US BOSSES]

Text (7.32)   **User 2:** my old boss[1] literally made people who had COVID come into work … . we[2] had to work while we were being 'confirmed' with COVID☹

[1][IDEATION: [thing entity] (US boss)/ATTITUDE: negative [judgement]]
[2][IDEATION: [thing entity] (User)/ATTITUDE: negative [affect]]
[table] × [BAD US BOSSES]

Text (7.33)   **User 1:** What THE HELL[1] 😡[2] UGHHH

[1][IDEATION: [thing entity] (US bosses)/ATTITUDE: negative [affect]]
[2][IDEATION: [thing entity] (User)/ATTITUDE: negative [affect]]
[rally] × [BAD US BOSSES]
…

Text (7.34)   **User 3:** This is also the uk[1] 😂[2]

[1][IDEATION: [thing entity] (UK bosses)/ATTITUDE: negative [judgement]]
[2][IDEATION: [thing entity] (User)/ATTITUDE: negative [affect]]
[rally] × [BAD US BOSSES]
[table] × [BAD UK BOSSES]
[defer] × [INTENSIFIED COMPLAINT]

Text (7.35)   **User 4:** 😂 😂 😂[1] … .. but seriously. [2]Not false!!!

[1][IDEATION: [thing entity] (User)/ATTITUDE: negative [affect]]
[2][IDEATION: [thing entity] (UK bosses)/ATTITUDE: negative [judgement]]
[defer] × [INTENSIFIED COMPLAINT]
[rally] × [BAD UK BOSSES]

In Text (7.31) and Text (7.32) the POUTING FACE 😡 and FACE WITH ROLLING EYES ☹ emoji resonate interpersonally with negative attitudes targeting work and bosses and thus coordinate with the negotiation of the [BAD US BOSSES] bond. As we saw with the earlier exchanges, these emoji also index the interactants' negative [affect] arising from the situations they describe, which multiplies both the negative evaluation of those circumstances as well as the vectors for interpersonal alignment between the interactants.

Similarly in Text (7.33) and Text (7.34) the FACE WITH TEARS OF JOY 😂 emoji is used to both resonate with the negative evaluations the interactants are aligning with in previous posts, and to index the interactants' emotional state of laughing at an undesirable situation (what might be colloquially termed 'gallows humour'). Viewed together, we can see how in Text (7.33) the 😂 emoji follows what is otherwise a relatively reserved stretch of discourse that only realises negative ATTITUDE by ellipsing it from previous posts. As such, the 😂 introduces the interactants' negative [affect] targeting the circumstance they describe, as well as their deferral of the intensity of this negative [affect], coded here as the [INTENSIFIED COMPLAINT] bond (we can speculate that this represents the stereotypical British cultural trait of deflecting intense feelings with humour, thus deferring the [INTENSIFIED COMPLAINT] bond through humour allows the interactants to avoid a socially transgressive degree of emotional intensity). Then in Text (7.34), the interactant begins by repeating this deferral before rolling back the humorous deflection to rally around the negative evaluation of UK bosses. Across these posts, the 😂 emoji gives nuance to interactants' sentiments regarding the circumstances they describe, allowing for affiliation to occur both in terms of how these circumstances are evaluated (negative [appreciation]), how the interactants feel about them (negative [affect]), and the intensity of their feelings (de-intensified).

7.6   The Role of Emoji Invoking Laughter😂

Further to realising the kind of solidarity and mutual evaluation for ideational meaning that corresponds with rallying around a shared bond, emoji can also be used in the more complex affiliative resource of deferring a tabled bond by indexing a humour response. Emoji functioning as tokens of laughter have been noted as prevalent in digital discourse (Gibson, Huang, & Yu, 2018). In this way they have similar functions to other typed laughter-derived expressions such as '*lol*' that often occur at the end of social media posts but which, while more likely to include a direct addressee, do not necessarily follow the offer/acceptance pattern for negotiating non-seriousness often seen in face-to-face exchanges (McKay, 2020). As we saw with Exchange 7.12, emoji indexing humour such as FACE WITH TEARS OF JOY 😂 can construe an interactant's humour response targeting their own post even in the absence of interaction.

Emoji such as FACE WITH TEARS OF JOY 😂 and GRINNING FACE WITH SWEAT 😅 that functioned as tokens of laughter in the corpus were very frequent, as suggested in Table 7.1. This was likely due to the prevalence of humour in the corpus, possibly triggered by the unusual context of hotel quarantine, and the odd experience of having food delivered to a room without human contact. In addition, the field of food discourse when combined with this context is likely to be relatively low stakes, unlike, for instance, a review of an expensive restaurant by a food critic, thus allowing for playful mockery. Examples of posts containing emoji acting as laughter tokens included Text (7.36) to Text (7.39).

Text (7.36)   Do they knock then sprint away or😩

Text (7.37)   I wanna quarantine in NZ omg😩

Text (7.38)   honestly I would be dead already 😩 😩 I'm allergic to a lot of the things in there lol

Text (7.39)   Omfg this made me crack up so hard 😂 😂 😂I think I'm going to watch that Documentary today what a shit show😂 😂

Determining the function of these emoji in terms of affiliation involves examining the co-text, including the bond that is at stake in the post in relation to the text to which it is responding. For example, Text (7.40) enacts a [DESIRABLE QUARANTINE] bond realised via the coupling [IDEATION: [thing entity] (*'here'*)/ATTITUDE: positive [appreciation] (*'I would ... anytime if I could ... '*)]. However, the language in this post only captures part of what is going on in the interaction in terms of affiliation, and we need to consider the emoji to understand the full meaning. It is not that the user baldly tables this bond as something around which the Creator or other commenters can unreservedly align around. Quarantine is generally viewed as an undesirable experience since the person quarantining is not permitted to freely leave quarantine as they are under a public health order restricting them from physically interacting with the rest of the community in order to stop the spread of disease. Thus, if we take up Knight's (2010a) definition of deferral as an affiliation resource for signalling that a bond is unshareable in a particular context (but might be shareable in others) and thus that the tension that it generates among interactants can be discharged through laughter, we can interpret this post as 'laughing off' a [DESIRABLE QUARANTINE] bond, while implicitly [rallying] around an [UNDESIRABLE QUARANTINE] bond.

Text (7.40)   I would quarantine anytime if I could stay here[1]😩 😩
          [1] [IDEATION: [thing entity] (*'here'*)/ATTITUDE: positive
          [appreciation] (*'I would ... anytime if I could ... '*)]
          [defer] × [DESIRABLE QUARANTINE]
          [rally] × [UNDESIRABLE QUARANTINE]

Similar examples in the corpus which involve deferring a [DESIRABLE QUARANTINE] bond in conjunction with a laughter token emoji include Text (7.41) to Text (7.46).

Text (7.41)   I rly want u to go into quarantine again just for the vids😂

Text (7.42)   Low-key wanna be in hotel quarantine cos I'd probably eat better than I do at home😂

Text (7.43)   damn I wanna stay there😂

Text (7.44)   Dang! I want to be in quarantine from my kids😂

Text (7.45)   now just to get into one of the local quarantine facilities😂

Text (7.46)   dude I wanna go into quarantine on purpose now I have taken a look at that food.. lmao😂 😂

The use of emoji to index laughter responses as part of deferring affiliation is an especially rich resource for DIALOGIC AFFILIATION in the dataset, and often combines with other affiliation resources across longer exchanges. In order to explore the nuances of how instances of deferral interact with other affiliation resources, two case studies have been isolated from the dataset, each illustrating how emoji contribute to the negotiation of bonds among interactants.

7.6.1   Hot Water on Weet-Bix Controversy

Within the corpus, a subject that attracted intense and often humorous debate was whether hot water is an appropriate liquid to add to Weet-bix – the canonical liquid being cold milk. Across exchanges where this 'controversy' was debated, emoji were frequently used to index humorous responses and thus defer wrinkling bonds, as well as to enact shared ATTITUDE and solidarity among interactants. For example, in Text (7.47) User 1 expresses negative evaluation for adding hot water to Weet-bix and employs multiple resources for intensifying this evaluation ('*violently*', '*!!*', '*!!!*'). However, the GRINNING FACE WITH SWEAT 😅 and ROLLING ON THE FLOOR LAUGHING 🤣 emoji which conclude the post signal that a bond realised in the post is being laughed off. Given the low emotional stakes typically associated with this field of discourse (Weet-bix preparation methods) and the intensity of the interpersonal resources interacting with this field, this bond has been labelled as [WEET-BIX ORTHODOXY]. Consequently, by indexing a deferral of this bond via a humorous response, the interactant acknowledges that their language is excessively negatively intensified for the subject being discussed, and that they implicitly share a more measured, tolerant view of how Weet-bix can be prepared ([WEET-BIX ECUMENISM]).

Exchange 7.13

Text (7.47)   **User 1:** Watching you make that weetbix[1] made me violently ill 😕 yogurt!! Hot water!!! GURL😕 🥴

                [1][IDEATION: [occurrence entity] (Weet-bix method)/ATTITUDE: negative [affect]]
                TABLE × [INCORRECT WEET-BIX METHOD]
                [defer] × [WEET-BIX ORTHODOXY]
                [rally] × [WEET-BIX ECUMENISM]

Text (7.48)   **Creator:** HAHAHHA SOMEBODY STOP ME😂

                [1][IDEATION: [occurrence entity] (Weet-bix method)/ATTITUDE: negative [affect]]
                [dismiss] × [INCORRECT WEET-BIX METHOD]
                [defer] × [WEET-BIX ORTHODOXY]
                [rally] × [WEET-BIX ECUMENISM]

In their response to User 1's post, the Creator of the original TikTok video follows this pattern of bond negotiation by simultaneously dismissing User 1's [INCORRECT WEET-BIX METHOD] bond and then repeating the table/ deferral of the [WEET-BIX ORTHODOXY] bond and the rallying of the [WEET-BIX ECUMENISM] bond, with the [defer]/[rally] resources signalled by the humour response of the FACE WITH TEARS OF JOY 😂 emoji. What is worth noting across this exchange is that while a superficial bond relating to the Creator's preparation method for Weet-bix is not being shared, the interactants are jointly deferring and rallying the [WEET-BIX ORTHODOXY] and [WEET-BIX ECUMENISM] bonds. Thus, despite not sharing the same views on how to eat Weet-bix, the interactants are affiliating around their shared opinion that Weet-bix preparation does not merit strong opinions.[10]

A similar affiliative dynamic unfolds across Exchange 7.14, which occurs in the comment section for the same TikTok video as discussed in Exchange 7.13. Here we can see how in Text (7.49) User 1 positively evaluates the Creator's method for preparing Weet-bix by calling it '*the right* way' and thus tables a [CORRECT WEET-BIX METHOD] bond. However, the '*lol*' that concludes the post shows that User 1 recognises that their post tables a potentially transgressive bond, and that they are laughing off the wrinkle caused by this bond. As for the previous exchange, this deferred bond is interpreted as a [WEET-BIX ORTHODOXY] bond, which is realised by the coupling of ATTITUDE (especially [up-scaled] ATTITUDE) with specific methods of preparing or consuming Weet-bix.

---

[10] We might speculatively define this as a 'meta' bond comprising attitudes towards attitudes about ideational meaning.

Exchange 7.14

Text (7.49)   **User 1:** Thank you[1] for making your weetbix the right way[2] lol

> [1][IDEATION: [thing entity] (Creator)/ATTITUDE: positive [affect] (*'thank you'*)]
> [2][IDEATION: [occurrence entity] ([Weet-bix method])/ATTITUDE: positive [appreciation] (*'right'*)
> [table] × [CORRECT WEET-BIX METHOD]
> [defer] × [WEET-BIX ORTHODOXY]
> [rally] × [WEET-BIX ECUMENISM]

Text (7.50)   **Creator:** 😍 👏 [1]

> [1][IDEATION: [thing entity] (User 1's post)/ATTITUDE: positive [affect]]
> [rally] × [CORRECT WEET-BIX METHOD]

Text (7.51)   **User 2:** Yess

> [1][IDEATION: [thing entity] (User 1's post)/ATTITUDE: positive [affect]]
> [rally] × [CORRECT WEET-BIX METHOD]

Text (7.52)   **User 3:** NOOOOOOOOOOOO 🥺

> [1][IDEATION: [thing entity] (User 1's post)/ATTITUDE: negative [affect]]
> [dismiss] × [CORRECT WEET-BIX METHOD]
> [defer] × [WEET-BIX ORTHODOXY]
> [rally] × [WEET-BIX ECUMENISM]

The posts that follow Text (7.49) sustain the negotiation of these bonds, with the Creator of the original TikTok post rallying around the [CORRECT WEET-BIX METHOD] bond via the sequence of SMILING FACE WITH HEART-SHAPED EYES 😍 and CLAPPING HANDS 👏 emoji. These emoji are interpreted as indexing the Creator's own positive [affect] in response to User 1's previous post. As such, Text (7.50) realises a kind of inter-move coalesce feature, where the emoji reflect the positive ATTITUDE in the previous post back onto their equivalent ideational targets. As we saw in Section 7.5, these ATTITUDE resources also serve to both positively evaluate an ideational target (User 1's post) as well as index the author's positive [affect]. In combination, the ensuing couplings rally around the [CORRECT WEET-BIX METHOD] bond.

This exchange then proceeds though Text (7.51), where User 2 also rallies around the [CORRECT WEET-BIX METHOD] bond, and Text (7.52), where User 3 dismisses it. Worth noting in Text (7.52) is how the upscaling of the negation via capitalisation and repetition of the 'o' coordinates with the FACE WITH PLEADING EYES 🥺 emoji to defer the [WEET-BIX

ORTHODOXY] bond. This interpretation is guided by the earlier deferral of this bond, thus the intensification of the language and inclusion of an emoji that indexes the interactant's negative [affect] serve to reference, and then defer, the kind of inappropriately strong opinions regarding breakfast cereal playfully mocked in Text (7.49).

7.6.2   Snickers Controversy

The [GOOD FOOD] controversy generating the most comments in this dataset is reflected in the most common 3-grams in the corpus (Table 7.2), and more obvious in the most common linguistic 5-gram in the corpus: I DON'T LIKE SNICKERS. Snickers is a brand of chocolate bar, and at issue was whether or not it has broad appeal. This discussion was in response to the Creator's proposition, 'I don't know anyone who doesn't like a Snickers', made in her Day 3 video when showing the ambient audience a Snickers brand chocolate bar that had been included in that day's meal.

This debate about Snickers' popularity most often involved a [GOOD CHOCOLATE] bond, realised in posts featuring *t*-[appreciation], that is, posts where [affect] (dis/liking chocolate) functions as a token of [appreciation] (chocolate is good/bad):

Text (7.53)   **Love** Snickers

Text (7.54)   I **don't like** snickers lol

Text (7.55)   I **don't like** snickers because I'm allergic to all nuts

Text (7.56)   I'm the rare person that **hates** snickers

Text (7.57)   I **don't like** snickers. Now you know someone who **doesn't like** snickers

Table 7.2 *The most common 3-grams in the corpus*

#	3-gram	Frequency
1	I DON'T	159
2	DON'T LIKE	112
3	'T LIKE SNICKERS	69
4	I'M SO	67
5	THANK YOU FOR	64
6	YOU HAVE TO	58
7	YOU SO MUCH	58
8	THANK YOU SO	51
9	ALLERGIC TO PINEAPPLE	48
10	IT'S A	47

The emoji in Text (7.53) to Text (7.57) not only coordinate with the *t*-[appreciation] in the post but are involved in how DIALOGIC AFFILIATION is being enacted.

This role that emoji can play in DIALOGIC AFFILIATION is best explored in the context of a defined exchange such as a distinct set of comments made in response to Text (7.58).

Text (7.58)   **Creator:** I¹ WAS WRONG ABOUT EVERYONE LIKING SNICKERS² OK! I just assumed it being chocolate that everyone loved it!

> ¹[IDEATION: [thing entity] (Creator)/ATTITUDE: negative [judgement] (*'wrong'*)]
> ²[IDEATION: [relation entity] (Snickers universally liked)/ ATTITUDE: negative [appreciation] (*wrong*)]
> [table] × [INCORRECT SELF]
> [table] × [DISLIKE SNICKERS]

This post was made by the Creator as a reaction to ongoing comments where Users expressed their dislike of Snickers bars. In the post, the Creator tables an [INCORRECT SELF] bond in relation to tabling a [DISLIKE SNICKERS] bond. The comment received thirty-seven replies, twenty-six of which included an emoji. It also received 2,654 'likes', suggesting that it dealt with a noteworthy issue in the ongoing conversation. Most of the replies to Text (7.58) supported the bonds tabled in the post, most commonly via rallying around the [DISLIKE SNICKERS] bond. Interestingly, however, emoji acting as laughter tokens were used frequently in these posts, signalling the authors of the posts are also deferring a potentially transgressive bond. In the context of the exchange, this is interpreted as the [INCORRECT SELF] tabled by the Creator. As the interactants rally around the [DISLIKE SNICKERS] bond, they could be interpreted as implicitly also rallying around the [INCORRECT SELF] bond to which it is related in the original post, which carries the potentially aggressive meaning of negative [judgement] for the Creator. Thus, the interactants include emoji indexing humorous responses to 'laugh off' this bond and sustain interpersonal solidarity. In other words, the commenters are agreeing that the Creator was wrong but want to express that they still like them. This description also accounts for the GRIMACING FACE 😬 emoji in Text (7.59), which can be interpreted as both enmeshing with the linguistic negative ATTITUDE of the post (*'don't like'*) and indexing the interactant's concern that the post might be read as implicitly criticising the Creator.

Text (7.59)   **User 1:** I don't like snickers lol 😅 😬

> ²[IDEATION: [thing entity] (*'Snickers'*)/ATTITUDE: negative [affect] (*'don't like'*)]
> [defer] × [INCORRECT CREATOR]

Text (7.60)   **User 2:** lol I don't really like chocolate and I do not like nuts so.. lol😊

      [IDEATION: [thing entity] (Snickers)/ATTITUDE: negative [affect] (*'don't … like'*)]
      [rally] × [DISLIKE SNICKERS]
      [defer] × [INCORRECT CREATOR]

Text (7.61)   **User 3:** I do not like snickers lol or Reese cups😊

      [IDEATION: [thing entity] (*'snickers'*)/ATTITUDE: negative [affect] (*'do not like'*)]
      [rally] × [DISLIKE SNICKERS]
      [defer] × [INCORRECT CREATOR]

Text (7.62)   **User 4:** I hate snickers and I'm not allergic to nuts. Also not everyone likes chocolate😊

      [IDEATION: [thing entity] (*'Snickers'*)/ATTITUDE: negative [affect] (*'hate'*)]
      [rally] × [DISLIKE SNICKERS]
      [defer] × [INCORRECT CREATOR]

Text (7.63)   **User 5:** I love snickers😊 😊

      [IDEATION: [thing entity] (*'Snickers'*)/ATTITUDE: positive [affect] (*'love'*)]
      [dismiss] × [DISLIKE SNICKERS]
      [defer] × [INCORRECT USERS]

As a final observation on this exchange, it is noteworthy that in Text (7.63) the interactant includes the FACE WITH TEARS OF JOY 😊 emoji despite dismissing the [DISLIKE SNICKERS] bond rallied around by the other users. In the context of the exchange, we can interpret this as deferring a potential [INCORRECT USERS] bond that might be inferred by User 5's post, thus the laughter emoji here are also being used to stave off tension arising from disagreement.

7.7   The Role of Emoji in Negotiating Gendered Bonds about Appearance

The corpus contained examples reminiscent of bonds about diet and appearance that were identified by Knight (2010b, p. 329) in casual conversations among young female university student friends, in particular:

… a 'happy fatness' bond, instantiated as the coupling [ideation: eating/attitude: + appreciation]. This wrinkles with a shared, implicated 'beautiful thinness' bond, commensurate with other body-conscious values that they share, and the tension generated by this wrinkle is discharged through laughter.

The corpus contained exchanges between interactants where they negotiated gendered meanings about gluttony and body weight. These exchanges often included emoji functioning as laughter tokens used to 'laugh off' weight-related bonds. For example in Text (7.67) of Exchange 7.15, the FACE WITH TEARS OF JOY 😂 emoji functions to defer a [FAT SELF] bond construed by User 1, who has intervened in an exchange about portion sizes. The bond is realised in the language as the coupling, [IDEATION: [thing entity] ('*I*')/ATTITUDE: negative [appreciation] ('*fat*')]. The FACE WITH TEARS OF JOY 😂 emoji works to defer this [FAT SELF] bond, positioning it as something that cannot be directly shared within this ambient community of commenters. User 1 responds by tabling a [HAPPY SELF] bond that they instead can share in this moment and defers the [FAT SELF] bond. The SMILING FACE WITH HEARTS 🥰 in the emoji sequence at the end of the comment appears to coordinate with the tabling and the FACE WITH TEARS OF JOY 😂 emoji with the deferring affiliation strategies, respectively.

Exchange 7.15

Text (7.64)   **User 1:** Came back to see how much you had to put away for dinner. The portions 😵 😵

[IDEATION: [thing entity] ('*portions*')/ATTITUDE: negative (😵 😵)]
[table] × [BAD BIG PORTIONS]

Text (7.65)   **Creator:** It was a lot! But I was very happy to try this! I love fish 😊 😊

[IDEATION: [thing entity] ('*portions*')/ATTITUDE: negative [appreciation] ('*a lot*')]
[IDEATION: [thing entity] ('*I*')/ATTITUDE: positive [affect] ('*happy*', 😊 😊)]
[IDEATION: [thing entity] ('*fish*')/ATTITUDE: positive [affect] ('*love*', 😊)]
[rally] × [BAD BIG PORTIONS]
[table] × [HAPPY SELF]
[table] × [GOOD FISH]

Text (7.66)   **User 1:** It looks so delicious 🥰

[IDEATION: [thing entity] (food)/ATTITUDE: positive [appreciation] ('*delicious*', 🥰)]
[rally] × [GOOD FISH]

Text (7.67)   **Creator:** See, this is why I'm fat 😂

[IDEATION: [thing entity] ('*I*')/ATTITUDE: negative [judgement] ('*fat*')]
[rally] × [GOOD FISH]
[defer] × [FAT SELF]

Text (7.68)   **User 1:** Hey, as long as you're happy😄 😄

[IDEATION: [thing entity] (Creator)/ATTITUDE: positive [affect]
('*happy*')]
[table] × [HAPPY SELF]
[defer] × [FAT SELF]

A similar pattern is apparent in Exchange 7.16. Here User 1 begins in Text
(7.69) by negatively evaluating the portion size shown in the Creator's original
TikTok video and thus implicitly tabling a [DESIRE EXTRA FOOD] bond
that is supported by the creator in Text (7.70). Then, in Text (7.71), User 1 negatively evaluates asking for extra food by suggesting it would make them seem
fat, which tables a [BAD EXTRA FOOD] bond. By implicitly associating
fatness with negative opinion, this post also tables a [BAD FATNESS] bond,
which User 1 defers by adding a sequence of FACE WITH TEARS OF JOY
😂 emoji. Finally, in Text (7.72) the Creator reinterprets User 1's bonds from
the previous post to positively evaluate quarantine. The linguistic marker for
humour '*hehe*' is used here to [defer] the [BAD EXTRA FOOD] bond recovered from previous posts, while the RED HEART ♥ emoji coalesces positive
ATTITUDE across the post, thus enacting the same kind of interpersonal positive
evaluation directed at the interactant as we saw in Section 5.

Exchange 7.16

Text (7.69)   **User 1:** That wouldn't fill me up tho are you not allowed to ask them to
                    try and get you some snacks

[IDEATION: [thing entity] (portion)/ATTITUDE: negative
[appreciation] ('*wouldn't fill me up*')]
[table] × [DESIRE EXTRA FOOD]

Text (7.70)   **Creator:** You could ask for extras!!

[IDEATION: [occurrence entity] (asking for extras)/ATTITUDE:
positive [affect] ('*!*')]
[rally] × [DESIRE EXTRA FOOD]

Text (7.71)   **User 1:** Then they would think I was just fat 😂 😂 😂 no good quarantine
                    hey

[IDEATION: [occurrence entity] (asking for extra food)/ATTITUDE:
negative [judgement] ('*they would think I was ... fat*')]
[IDEATION: [thing entity] ('*I*')/ATTITUDE: negative [judgement]
('*fat*')]
[IDEATION: [thing entity] (*quarantine*)/ATTITUDE: negative
[appreciation] ('*no good*')]
[table] × [BAD EXTRA FOOD]
[defer] × [BAD FATNESS]
[table] × [BAD QUARANTINE]

Text (7.72)   **Creator:** I doubt they would be judgmental like that – we got to eat and
for some people I'm sure food was how they got through it hehe♥

> [IDEATION: [thing entity] (quarantine workers)/ATTITUDE: positive
> [judgement] (*'doubt they would be judgmental like that'*)]
> [IDEATION: [thing entity] (food)/ATTITUDE: positive [appreciation]
> (*'how they got through it'*)]
> [dismiss] × [BAD QUARANTINE]
> [defer] × [BAD EXTRA FOOD]

Perhaps most noteworthy in the affiliation occurring in this exchange is how
deferral of the [BAD FATNESS] bond, signalled by the FACE WITH TEARS
OF JOY 😂 emoji, indexes the contradictory social values associated with
beauty standards. It is worth pointing out that the deferral here does not seem
to be a response to a self-deprecating bond, where the interactant might evaluate themselves as fat, so much as a response to how a request for more food
might be viewed poorly, with the implied gluttony or over-indulgence coded
colloquially as 'fat'. Thus, what is being deferred is the implicit association of
fatness with greed or lack of self-control. In turn, the deferral alerts us that this
is neither a bond User 1 thinks will be supported by the audience of the post,
nor a bond User 1 is actively rejecting.

7.8   The Role of Emoji in rejecting Bonds

To complete our exploration of how emoji contribute to affiliation strategies,
we will examine examples where emoji are used to reject a bond via the affiliation strategies of [dismiss], [ridicule], and [censure]. These affiliation strategies were frequently found in the more serious debate centring on personal
freedom and civic responsibility. One instance of such a debate is shown in
Exchange 7.17 (which expands on Exchange 7.7), where a (presumably)
American user (User 1) negatively evaluates New Zealand's policy during
earlier stages of the COVID-19 pandemic that international arrivals spend
fourteen days in mandatory quarantine. This user's comment then sparks a
heated exchange among multiple users, which quickly devolves into bor-
derline racist stereotypes about people from the United Stated. As noted in
Section 7.4, the exchange begins in Text (7.73) with User 1 tabling a [BAD
QUARANTINE] and a [DELUDED CREATOR] bond, which are then negotiated across the remainder of the exchange.

Exchange 7.17

Text (7.73)   **User 1:** A facility?! WTH? This is normal there and you're all just chill
with it?! That is insane.

> [IDEATION: [thing entity] (quarantine facility) /ATTITUDE: negative
> [affect] (*'WTH?'*)]

[IDEATION: [relational entity] ('*you're all just chill*')/ATTITUDE:
negative [judgement] ('*insane*')]
[table] × [BAD QUARANTINE]
[table] × [DELUDED CREATOR]

Text (7.74) **Creator:** MY RIGHTS WAAAAAAH. I made choices. & this is the
result of my choice so yes I'm chill.

[IDEATION: [thing entity] (User 1's post)/ATTITUDE: negative
[judgement]]
[IDEATION: [occurrence entity] (quarantine in a facility)/ATTITUDE:
positive [judgement] ('*chill*')]
[ridicule] × [BAD QUARANTINE]
[dismiss] × [DELUDED CREATOR]

...

Text (7.75) **Creator:** Let me guess AMERICAN😂😂😂

[IDEATION: [thing entity] (Americans)/ATTITUDE: negative
[judgement]]
[table] × [BAD AMERICANS]

Text (7.76) **User 2:** not you mocking American freedom and the right to not
be imprisoned against your will. you're right the AUDACITY of
Americans these days. Smh

[IDEATION: [thing entity] (Creator)/ATTITUDE: negative [judgement]]
[IDEATION: [thing entity] (American freedom)/ATTITUDE: positive
[appreciation]]
[IDEATION: [thing entity] (criticism of Americans)/ATTITUDE:
negative [affect]]
[table] × [BAD CREATOR]
[table] × [GOOD AMERICAN FREEDOM]
[ridicule] × [CRITICISM OF AMERICANS]

Text (7.77) **{User 3}:** It wasn't against their will, good lord. I'm so tired of being be
American. Y'all are so embarrassing.

[IDEATION: [thing entity] (Creator)/ATTITUDE: negative
[judgement]]
[IDEATION: [thing entity] (criticism of Americans)/ATTITUDE:
negative [affect]]
[rally] × [BAD AMERICANS]

Text (7.78) **User 4:** Lol she isn't wrong. Americans are whiners. They think
everyone is out to get them. A cloth over their face is the end of the
world😭

[IDEATION: [thing entity] (User 3)/ATTITUDE: positive [judgement]]
[IDEATION: [thing entity] (Americans)/ATTITUDE: negative
[judgement]]
[IDEATION: [relational entity] (opposing mask wearing)/ATTITUDE:

negative [judgement]]
[rally] × [BAD AMERICANS]
[ridicule] × [GOOD AMERICAN FREEDOM]

...

Text (7.79)   **User 5:** The last thing we are are whiners. Our government are the whiners☻

[IDEATION: [thing entity] (Americans)/ATTITUDE: positive [judgement]]
[IDEATION: [thing entity] (American government)/ATTITUDE: negative [judgement]]
[censure] × [BAD AMERICANS]
[table] × [BAD AMERICAN GOVERNMENT]

Text (7.80)   **User 4:** Very much disagree. I live in the US. Adults act like children most of the time. Anything to be kind and considerate is too much and they flip out.

[IDEATION: [thing entity] (Americans)/ATTITUDE: negative [judgement] ('*act like children*')]
[rally] × [BAD AMERICANS]
[table] × [GOOD NICENESS]

Text (7.81)   **User 5:** Cause we aren't kind ☻ that doesn't mean we whine lol ☻ nothing says I have to be nice to you.

[IDEATION: [entity] (Americans)/ATTITUDE: positive [judgement]]
[IDEATION: [quality] (niceness)/ATTITUDE: negative [appreciation]]
[ridicule] × [BAD AMERICANS]
[censure] × [GOOD NICENESS]

...

Text (7.82)   **User 6:** 'American freedom' THE MAJORITY OF COUNTRIES CITIZENS HAVE THE SAME RIGHTS AS AMERICAN get over yourself☹

[IDEATION: [thing entity] (American freedom)/ATTITUDE: negative [appreciation]]
[IDEATION: [thing entity] (User 5)/ATTITUDE: negative [judgement]]
[censure] × [GOOD AMERICAN FREEDOM]
[table] × [BAD USER 5]

...

Text (7.83)   **User 7:** Tf are you talking about? Stop, the US is embarrassing. ☹

[IDEATION: [thing entity] (User 1's post) /ATTITUDE: negative [affect] ('*tf ... ?*')]
[IDEATION: [thing entity] (USA) /ATTITUDE: negative [affect] ('*embarrassing*', ☹)
[dismiss] × [BAD QUARANTINE]
[rally] × [BAD AMERICANS]

Across this exchange, emoji converge with realisations of [reject] affiliation strategies. Most salient are the instances where the FACE WITH TEARS OF JOY 😂 emoji serves to signal an instance of [ridicule]. For example, in Text (7.78) the linguistic text establishes negative evaluation for Americans, and ends with the clause '*A cloth over their face is the end of the world*'. While the sardonic tone of this clause might be inferred from the preceding text, the 😂 emoji that follows acts as an explicit marker that this clause is intended as a parodic impersonation of opposition to wearing a face mask, and thus constitutes an instance of ridiculing the [GOOD AMERICAN FREEDOM] bond. Similarly, but more obliquely, the 😂 emoji in Text (7.81) serve to ridicule the [BAD AMERICANS] bond referenced in the language that precedes them. Text (7.82) illustrates how emoji can also enmesh with linguistic negative ATTITUDE to realise instances of [censure]; here the negative [affect] construed by the ALL CAPS of '*THE MAJORITY OF COUNTRIES CITIZENS HAVE THE SAME RIGHTS AS AMERICAN*' is coalesced in the UNAMUSED FACE 😒 emoji that concludes the post, which functions to censure the [GOOD AMERICAN FREEDOM] bond tabled by User 2 in Text (7.76). Similarly, in Text (7.83), the FACE WITH RAISED EYEBROW 🤨 emoji coalesces the negative [affect] realised linguistically by '*tf are you talking about?*', thus dismissing the original [BAD QUARANTINE] bond tabled by User 1.

A final, especially illustrative example of emoji contributing to an instance of ridicule is found in Exchange 7.18. This exchange also centres on disagreement over whether mandatory quarantine unacceptably violates personal freedom. Accordingly, in this exchange User 1 tables a [BAD QUARANTINE] bond realised by the coupling: [IDEATION: [thing entity] (quarantine)/ATTITUDE: negative [appreciation] ('*jail*')]. This is then tempered by another [GOOD FOOD] bond, realised as [IDEATION: [thing entity] (food)/ATTITUDE: positive [appreciation] (*nice*)], where despite the grammatical parallelism suggesting that the 'it' refers to jail, the presumed reference is the preceding discourse about good food.

Exchange 7.18

Text (7.84) **User 1:** its jail but its nice

    [IDEATION: [thing entity] ('*it*')/ATTITUDE: negative [appreciation] (*jail*)]
    [table] × [BAD QUARANTINE]
    [table] × [GOOD FOOD]

Text (7.85) **Creator:** Nothing like jail. But your ignorance is nice

    [IDEATION: [thing entity] (quarantine)/ATTITUDE: positive [appreciation]]

[IDEATION: [thing entity] (User 1)/ATTITUDE: negative [judgement]
(*'ignorance'*)]
[IDEATION: [thing entity] (User 1's post)/ATTITUDE: negative
[appreciation] (*'nice'*, ✦)]
[dismiss] × [BAD QUARANTINE]
[ridicule] × [BAD QUARANTINE]

The Creator responds by rejecting User 1's [BAD QUARANTINE] bond using [ridicule], imitating User 1's shift from judgement (*'jail'*) to appreciation (*'nice'*). The post begins by dismissing the [BAD QUARANTINE] bond realised as the coupling, [IDEATION: [thing entity] (*'it'*)/ATTITUDE: negative [appreciation] (*'jail'*)], which is not an unusual rejecting move. They then ridicule the [BAD QUARANTINE] bond through the coupling, [IDEATION: [semiotic entity] (*'your ignorance'*)/ATTITUDE: positive [appreciation] (*nice*)] which echoes the structure User 1 employed to construe the [NICE QUARANTINE] bond.

Across this exchange, the SPARKLES ✦ emoji interacts with linguistic ATTITUDE to intensify negative evaluations, and thus contributes to disaffiliative strategies. In Text (7.84), User 1 establishes a contrast between the negative evaluation of *'jail'* and the positive evaluation of *'nice* ✦'. Perhaps unintentional, but the use of the ✦ emoji here, with its allusion to visual lustre or reflection, evokes the idiomatic expression 'gilded cage' to refer to a circumstance that while perhaps comfortable or beautiful, nonetheless amounts to imprisonment. Collectively, these resources highlight User 1's overall negative evaluation for quarantine. This position stands in contrast to the dominant perspective shared by commenters in this dataset, which is of positive evaluation for the Creator's quarantine experience (as can be seen from the attitudinal value of the top ten most frequent emoji in the corpus, shown in Table 7.1). Indeed, the inclusion of the ✦ emoji would seem to reference the frequent use of emoji among these positively evaluating posts and could itself be interpreted as parodying this position. In common-sense language, we might describe User 1's perspective as derisive of superficial praise for food in the context of imprisonment, which they consider a much more important issue.

In response, the Creator's repetition of the SPARKLES ✦ emoji references and reflects this parodying ridicule back onto User 1. Just as User 1 references positive evaluation of the Creator's quarantine experience with the ✦ emoji, the Creator references User 1's insincere parody with their use of the emoji. Thus, when the Creator describes User 1's ignorance as *'nice* ✦', they are recovering the same ironic reversal of ATTITUDE established by User 1 in their post. Moreover, by 'flipping' the direction of the emoji's negative evaluation back onto User 1, the Creator is also implicitly mocking User 1's stylised use of the emoji itself. In common-sense language, we can describe the Creator's response as ridiculing not only the notion that quarantine is like gaol, but also User 1's attempt at cleverness by subverting the attitudinal polarity of a typically positive emoji. What is intriguing in this exchange is just how much meaning hinges from both the first, and then the second instance of the SPARKLES ✨ emoji's use.

7.9   Conclusion

This chapter has explored the role of emoji in interactive negotiation of bonds during exchanges in TikTok comment feeds. As we have seen, emoji play an extensive role in DIALOGIC AFFILIATION, interacting with linguistic resources to realise a variety of affiliation strategies. In particular, we have noted the rich meaning-making afforded by emoji to index the affective states of authors of posts, and how this interacts with the intratextual meaning made by emoji and language. To return to the comparison made by some scholars between emoji and paralanguage, while we still maintain that a direct equivalence is inappropriate, we do note here that they play a role in modulating written linguistic meaning similar to the nuance given to spoken language by gesture, facial expression, and phonology. We can speculate that it is precisely this dimension of emoji's semiotic potential that makes them such a popular resource in online discourse, as they allow for the kind of subtle, non-serious or playful meanings to be construed that are essential for negotiating social values and aligning with particular value communities.

While the contribution made by emoji to affiliation strategies is clear, just as we cannot 'read' a single semantic meaning from a given emoji presented out of context, we cannot taxonomise emoji by affiliation type. A given emoji might be used for both rejecting a bond and supporting a bond, depending on the co-text that occurs in preceding moves. Often, repetition or agreement among emoji signals the enaction of similar affiliation strategies; however, as illustrated by the use of the SPARKLES ✨ emoji in Exchange 7.18, the same emoji can reverse meaning even in the space of a single post. To reiterate a recurring motif of this book, this semiotic flexibility is itself a defining feature of emoji, that at once urges and frustrates investigation.

8 COMMUNING AFFILIATION: The Role of Emoji in Communing around Bonds

8.1   Introduction

The previous chapter dealt with the role of emoji in DIALOGIC AFFILIATION of the kind that occurs in direct exchanges between social media users. This chapter considers a different kind of affiliative scenario and examines how emoji coordinate with language in more ambient communication. This kind of communicative context occurs when bonds are tabled to an audience who may not necessarily directly reply. For instance, in mass broadcast contexts or in online environments involving large numbers of participants, people may direct their communication to large audiences which, due to the asymmetric nature of the communicative medium, typically have less opportunity to directly respond. In terms of social media discourse, the notion of 'communing affiliation' has been used to understand how social relations may be enacted even when individuals do not interact with each other on a one-to-one basis and instead engage in one-to-many or many-to-many communication (Zappavigna, 2011). For instance, users may be involved in mass communing using semiotic resources such as hashtags to forge alignments around shared or contested values (Zappavigna, 2015, 2018, 2021; Zappavigna & Martin, 2018).

This chapter explores the role that emoji play in this kind of communing by considering the ways in which they interact with how social bonds are construed in language. As with our discussion of the role of emoji in DIALOGIC AFFILIATION in the previous chapter, analysing posts for COMMUNING AFFILIATION reveals how emoji both interact with their co-text and support the tabling of bonds to potential audiences or interactants. In particular, emoji representing embodied behaviour such as facial expressions or gestures can simultaneously coordinate with meaning made in the linguistic co-text and index the affective state of the post's author. However, while exchanges of posts among interactants provide us with the details of how particular bonds are taken up by responders, in cases where the affiliation is ambient, we need to look to how the initiating posts themselves position particular values as bondable. In order to do this, in this chapter we consider how these posts CONVOKE (muster community around), PROMOTE (interpersonally high-light), and FINESSE (heteroglossically adjust) particular IDEATION–ATTITUDE couplings and the role emoji play in supporting these AMBIENT AFFILIATION strategies.

8.2   The #Domicron Corpus

The corpus considered in this chapter was collected in 2021 during the phase of the COVID-19 pandemic when the first Omicron variant was beginning to spread in Sydney, Australia. Up until this point, Australia had adopted a 'Covid zero' policy, aimed at eliminating the virus. The arrival of Omicron was a turn-ing point in government policy, away from elimination and towards a mitiga-tion strategy. The New South Wales (NSW) state government at the time had also changed leaders, with Dominic Perrottet replacing Gladys Berejiklian as premier after she resigned amid a corruption investigation. Perrottet quickly removed many of the mitigation measures that had been in place, with the aim of 'living with the virus'. This led many on social media to characterise his approach as letting the virus 'rip' through the NSW population, precipi-tating hashtags such as #Domicron (a pun merging the premier's first name, Dominic, with Omicron) and #LetItRipDon. The corpus uses these two hashtags as selection criteria, collecting all posts containing these tags from 9 December 2021 until 22 March 2022, generating a corpus of c. 130,000 posts. This corpus contained a large number of retweets which, after removal along with duplicate tweets, resulted in a corpus of 35,385 posts. Of these, 4,275 tweets contained one or more emoji and are studied in this chapter.

This smaller emoji corpus, amenable to close discourse analysis, is used in this chapter to explore the social bonds enacted by the outpouring of nega-tive ATTITUDE targeted at Perrottet and his policies. Unsurprisingly, the most frequent emoji in the corpus such as the FACE WITH SYMBOLS ON THE MOUTH 😡 are emoji that are likely to be involved with negative ATTITUDE, in particular negative [judgement] of the capacity of the premier and his govern-ment (Table 8.1). The most frequent 3-grams are suggestive of such negativity (Table 8.1). These 3-grams will be used as a starting point for exploring some of the common bonds that are communed around in the corpus. This COMMUN-ING AFFILIATION is an example where the bonds that are rallied around are negative rather than positive. This is important to note since the term 'affili-ation' can be somewhat misleading, suggesting only collective outpouring of positivity, when in fact we know from work on gossip that sharing bonds that are critical of people or events is actually a highly aligning activity (Eggins & Slade, 1997/2005). Thus, the frequency of complaining, teasing, and ridiculing in social media discourse is perhaps unsurprising.

Table 8.1 *Most frequent emoji and 3-grams in the #Domicron corpus*

	Emoji	Frequency	3-gram	Frequency
1	FACE WITH SYMBOLS ON MOUTH	1196	let it rip	80
2	POUTING FACE	477	I don't	35
3	BACKHAND INDEX POINTING DOWN	431	it's not	34
4	FACE WITH ROLLING EYES	350	the rest of	28
5	FACE WITH MEDICAL MASK	247	I can't	27
6	ROLLING ON THE FLOOR LAUGHING	234	you don't	27
7	THINKING FACE	233	won't be	24
8	FACE WITH TEARS OF JOY	218	letting it rip	23
9	CLAPPING HANDS	205	can't get	22
10	PILE OF POO	184	in the world	22

8.3   COMMUNING AFFILIATION: CONVOKE, FINESSE, and PROMOTE

DIALOGIC AFFILIATION was introduced in the previous chapter as one of the ways in which social bonds are construed in language. However, while couplings can be dialogically negotiated in interactions, they can also be communed around, particularly in contexts involving mass audiences, including broadcast media (Liu, 2018; White, 2020) and social media (Zappavigna, 2012) where the relationship to the audience is much less direct. The system of COMMUNING AFFILIATION describes the affiliation strategies by which ambient alignments are CONVOKED, FINESSED, and PROMOTED in relation to the particular bonds that are tabled in the text via IDEATION–ATTITUDE couplings. For the sake of simplicity, we include only the main bond(s) and affiliation strategies in our annotation in this chapter, without noting attendant couplings in the texts.

COMMUNING AFFILIATION applies a similar social semiotic lens to texts shared via social media to that applied by Knight's (2010a) DIALOGIC AFFILI-ATION model for interactive conversation. Social media discourse has the added complication of being inflected by the meaning potential afforded by platforms as semiotic technologies. This means that, in addition to direct negotiation of couplings via replies by other users, more indirect, ambient forms of affiliation are possible. On Twitter, this can involve resources such as shared hashtags used to forge mass alignments or generate discord. For instance, the #Auspol hashtag is commonly used in the corpus to highlight posts expressing both unity and disagreement within the domain of Australian Politics. Users frequently engage in meta-discursive commentary about the types of identities or communities that are facilitated by these hashtags, often expressing their evaluations of various groups (underlined) in Text (8.1) to Text (8.4).

Text (8.1)   The #Domicron and #LetItRipDom hashtags are demonstrating that
               people are so addicted to fear and division that they're practically
               hoping lots of people get sick just to prove a point. They're absolutely
               deranged. #auspol #COVID19

Text (8.2)   #Domicron hashtag, full of **fake** Twitter accounts and **bedwetters**😩

Text (8.3)   These **weird** #domicron hashtagers. What do they think vaccines do?
               They **think masks stop covid**? They **think QR codes are protective**?
               Please note: you may test positive despite vaccination, which is ok. It's
               very unlikely you'll get sick. That's the point!

Text (8.4)   #Domicron #ReinstateQR No QR Twitter needs a warning for anyone
               who registers in Australia, 'this site contains a large base of far left
               users & content'. Thank god only 20% of Australians user twitter. So
               Socialist Lefties Hashtag away you peanuts.

Other posts simply appraise the hashtags themselves, such as in Text (8.5) to
Text (8.7).

Text (8.5)   #Scovid and #**domicron** The hashtags that will **keep on giving &
               giving** over this Christmas time!

Text (8.6)   Gotta say, #Domicron has got to be the best rona-related hashtag-pun
               I've seen in a while. Political hashtags usually make me cringe, but
               #domicron is pretty funny.

Text (8.7)   Now there's a hashtag I'd **like to see trending**, #**Perrottwat** 😊 😊
               #nswcovid #nswpol #Domicron #auspol #Omicron

Not only do these posts table particular bonds, but they also incorporate
other resources that orient the ambient reader towards those bonds or, in other
words, work to position the bonds in certain ways. For instance, a [GOOD
HASHTAG] bond realised by the coupling [IDEATION: [semiotic entity]
(#*Domicron*)/ATTITUDE: positive [reaction]] in Text (8.6) also involves GRAD-
UATION resources, such as [force] (*the best ... I've seen in a while, pretty*) and
ENGAGEMENT resources, such as [probability] and [usuality] (*got to be, usually*), [concession] (*but*) and [attribution] (*gotta say*), which have an impact on
how the coupling is likely to be received by the ambient audience.

We conceive of all these different possible resources that might work in
tandem with a particular coupling as COMMUNING AFFILIATION strategies,
across three main regions of meaning: CONVOCATION (calling together a community to align around a bond), FINESSING (positioning a bond in relation to
other bonds held by other potential voices or groups of voices), and PROMOT-
ING (raising or lowering the stakes or scope of a bond). These simultaneous
COMMUNING AFFILIATION strategies are systematised in Figure 8.1.

Resources that CONVOKE include those which muster a community to align
around a shared bond or set of bonds realised as couplings. This includes

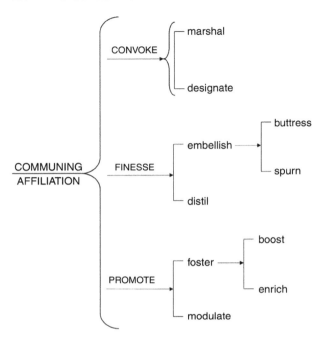

Figure 8.1 The system of COMMUNING AFFILIATION

resources such as vocatives which marshal a particular group, e.g. *New Zealanders* in Text (8.8), or tokens of membership categorisation which designate a particular group, e.g. *Lefties, sane double double vaxxed ppl* in Text (8.9).

Text (8.8)   Hi **New Zealanders**, tell us how the Covid situation is now and what we could have had in Australia if it weren't for #ScottytheFailure #LetItRip #Domicron

Text (8.9)   @{User} **Lefties** are in love with pandemic fear porn, clutching their masks, occasionally venturing out from beneath their doonas. The majority of **sane double doubled vaxxed ppl** just want to 'live with the virus' as **the lying premiers** kept promising us #Domicron #Omnicronvariant

FINESSE resources are those that establish the position of a bond in relation to other bonds that are either shared or rejected by a community. This includes heteroglossic ENGAGEMENT resources which embellish a coupling, positioning it by either buttressing and supporting a bond, or spurning and rejecting it. Other resources beyond ENGAGEMENT can be involved, for example hashtags (as discussed in Zappavigna and Martin (2018)). For instance, in Text (8.10), #ScottyThePathologicalLiar and #ScottyDoesntGiveARats buttress anti-politician bonds that occur together with the #Domicron hashtag.

> Text (8.10) Can we all agree that front line health staff & essential workers deserve a parade – like an ACTUAL parade – when this shit show is over? #COVID19 #coronavirus #auspol #AusPol2022 **#Domicron #ScottyThePathologicalLiar #ScottyDoesntGiveARats**

These hashtags target negative [propriety] (a sub-classification of [judgement] concerned with morality) at the then Australian Prime Minister, Scott Morrison, tabling [EVIL POLITICIAN] and [UNCARING POLITICIAN] bonds. On the other hand, resources that distil a coupling contract the discursive space, often through negation. An example is Text (8.11), which asserts that a vaccine hub at Homebush in Sydney is not necessarily widely accessible to the general population.

> Text (8.11) Not everyone lives near Homebush 😕 #Domicron

Here '*Not everyone*' reduces the scope of a putative [ACCESSIBLE VACCINE HUB] bond that was widely repeated in the messaging of politicians during the vaccine rollout.

The final affiliation strategy, PROMOTING, involves resources which foster or modulate the interpersonal stakes or scope of a bond by lowering or heightening the interpersonal risk. For instance, this might occur via GRADUATION where a relevant factor or attribute is boosted, such as in Text (8.12).

> Text (8.12) What the **absolute FV*CK!!!!!!!!!** 😡 😡 😡 😡 #Domicron what are you doing? This is **WRONG!!**

In Text (8.12) [GRADUATION: force: up-scale] (*absolute*, repetition of exclamation marks, and ALL CAPS font) boosts an [UNETHICAL PREMIER] bond. Another option is to enrich the bond, for instance, by further attitudinal resources contributing to an evaluative prosody, or by the addition of further voices supporting the bond. For example, in Text (8.13) the [INCOMPETENT GOVERNMENT] bond tabled via the negative [judgement] in the death toll numbers, is [enriched] by the set of hashtags which occur at the end of the post, negatively assessing the Premier and Prime Minister.

> Text (8.13) 21 people have died😢 😥 😡 #nswcovid #LetItRip #ScottytheFailure #Scottythefukwit #Domicron

Examples of tempering a bond through modulating by minimising or downscaling are infrequent in this corpus since the hashtags #Domicron and #LetItRipDon are skewed towards capturing posts by people frustrated with the Premier. Some examples did occur in posts that are ironic, mimicking negatively judged political voices such as the Premier or Prime Minister:

Text (8.14) @{User 1} @{User 2} @Dom_Perrottet @ScottMorrisonMP 'the unvaccinated present **no risk to anyone but themselves**' Errr, except for the fact that they are many times more likely to carry the virus, and so, many more times likely to spread the virus to everyone … **Just that little bit** of fact. ☺ #freedumb #Domicron #Covidiots

CONVOKING, FINESSING, and PROMOTING are simultaneous systems, and they all can occur together in a single post. The annotation convention shown below Text (8.15) is used to indicate how these systems interact with the main bonds tabled in the posts.

Text (8.15) I have been pretty angry politically since 2013 and the procession of LNP gov'ts <u>but</u> **never as pissed off as I am now**. #Domicron and #ScottyThe**Pathological**Liar are treating this pandemic and it's effects on the elderly with flippant disregard. **Not a Christian bone between them**☺
[UNETHICAL GOVERNMENT]
× CONVOKE: [marshal] → #ScottyThePathologicalLiar
× FINESSE: [embellish: buttress] → [counter]; [disclaim]
× PROMOTE: [foster: boost] → **[force: up-scale]**

This convention presents the main bond(s) underneath the post. The next line displays the COMMUNING AFFILIATION systems and features. An arrow → is used to indicate the relevant linguistic choices in the text, displayed in a coordinating style in both the extract and the annotations. For example, in Text (8.15) [GRADUATION: force: up-scale] is shown as **bold font** in both the Tweet text and the annotation below it.

8.4   Emoji Supporting Boosting and Buttressing Affiliation

The phrase 'let it rip', as used in Australian English, means to allow something to proceed at full speed without any intervention. In the context of COVID-19 management by the NSW government, this means letting the virus spread without any mitigation efforts, such as mask mandates or travel restrictions. The phrase was the most frequent 3-gram in the corpus, in part because of its coordination with the hashtag, #LetItRip. The most common emoji that occurred in posts containing the 3-gram was the POUTING FACE ☺ (often in combination with the FACE WITH ROLLING EYES ☺) and FACE WITH SYMBOLS ON MOUTH ☺ (see Table 1.2 in Chapter 1). These emoji tended to work in coordination with linguistic affiliation resources to buttress and boost particular bonds, such as [INCOMPETENT POLITICIANS] and [BAD POLICY], realised as negative ATTITUDE targeted at particular political figures and government policies.

An example is Text (8.16) in which an [INCOMPETENT POLITICIAN] bond is realised through negative [judgement] targeted at the Premier. In this post, the politician's voice is imitated through a form of mockery that acts in the service of buttressing the bond. In addition, the [force: up-scale] serves to boost the bond.

Text (8.16)   *Forget lock downs hey* #Domicron Perrottet *just let it **rip*** you **irresponsible deranged whacko! What fucking hope have we got** with this **nutter**! #nswcovid😬 🤷
              [INCOMPETENT POLITICIAN]
              × CONVOKE: [marshal] → #Domicron
              × CONVOKE: [designate] → community
              × FINESSE: [buttress] → *deny* ×😬 🤷
              × PROMOTE: [boost] → **[force: up-scale]** ×😬 🤷
              × PROMOTE: [enrich] → #Domicron

The emoji sequence GRIMACING FACE 😬 and MAN SHRUGGING 🤷 coordinate with these affiliation strategies to support the [INCOMPETENT POLITICIAN] bond that is tabled. This is achieved not just by resonating with the interpersonal meaning, although there is a clear coordination with the negative linguistic [judgement], but by coordinating with the main coupling in the text realising the [INCOMPETENT POLITICIAN] bond, and with the various resources which act upon it. For example, the emoji aid the mockery of Perrottet's voice '*Forget lock downs hey*' and '*just let it rip*' that buttress the bond, by suggesting a negative [appreciation] (😬) and dismissal (🤷) of the voice. The MAN SHRUGGING 🤷 emoji also coordinates with the [force: up-scale] of the exclamation, '*What fucking hope have we got*' by indexing the perspective of the implied answer to the rhetorical question: 'none'. As such this emoji might be interpreted as expressing a kind of exasperation through this coordination with an exclamation. In addition, the emoji sequence itself supports the boosting of the bond by coordinating with the up-scaled graduation, since the GRIMACING FACE 😬 would seem to express more negativity than other frowning face options in the emoji palette. Moreover, the choice to include a sequence of two emoji is also a choice to increase the potential strength or precision in meaning.

A similar kind of buttressing and boosting is seen in Text (8.17) where the FACE WITH SYMBOLS ON MOUTH 🤬 emoji coordinates with these affiliation strategies in a post tabling a [BAD POLICY] bond.

Text (8.17)   It hasn't kept **everyone** safe *has it* @Dom_Perrottet 🤬 you **let it rip** and people died. You *should* be held accountable. #**LetItRip** #Domicron
              [BAD POLICY]
              × CONVOKE: [designate] → #Domicron
              × CONVOKE: [marshal] → #**LetItRip**

× FINESSE: [buttress] → [Disclaim]; *[Proclaim]* ×😡
× PROMOTE: [boost] → [force: up-scale] ×😡
× PROMOTE: [enrich] → #Domicron

The symbols on the FACE WITH SYMBOLS ON MOUTH 😡 emoji may be interpreted as representing censored expletives, contributing to heightening the boosting affiliation. In terms of buttressing, the emoji supports the disclaiming of an external voice; in terms of boosting, it heightens GRADUATION, in the sense that expletives are 'explosions' of [affect]. The emoji also imbues the surrounding co-text with negative ATTITUDE, again supporting both the boosting and buttressing of the [BAD POLICY] bond.

While some emoji include visual dimensions that suggest up-scaled meanings, repetition of emoji through emoji strings is another choice that can coordinate with boosting affiliation. For example, repetition of the POUTING FACE emoji 😠 in Text (8.18) heightens the [force: up-scale] realised in the co-text.

Text (8.18)   Yup *so* ***WHO LET IT RIP??!!*** 😠 😠 **#domicron #scomicron** #nswpol #auspol #covid19AUS [image of news article]
[INCOMPETENT POLITICIAN]
× CONVOKE: [marshal] → **#domicron #scomicron**
× CONVOKE: [designate] → #nswpol #auspol #covid19AUS
× FINESSE: [buttress] → *[affirm]* ×😠 😠
× PROMOTE: [boost] → **[force: up-scale]** ×😠 😠

In this example [force: up-scale] in the co-text is realised via ALL CAPS font, repeated exclamation marks and the phrase '*let it rip*' itself. The repetition in the hashtags *#domicron* and *#scomicron* also contributes to this prosody of up-scaled GRADUATION. The emoji sequence coordinates with this prosody to boost the [INCOMPETENT POLITICIAN] bond. The emoji also contribute to the buttressing realised via the ENGAGEMENT choice [affirm] construed through the rhetorical question '*so WHO LET IT RIP??*'.[1] These resources all function to integrate into the text the voice of a critical perspective tabling an [INCOMPETENT POLITICIAN] bond.

Another example is Text (8.19); however, in this case two bonds, a [COMPETENT LEADERSHIP] bond and an [INCOMPETENT POLITICIAN] bond, are placed in opposition to one another.

Text (8.19)   @{User 1} @Dom_Perrottet @ScottMorrisonMP Pandemic leadership **certainly** does matter. We *need* governments that follow health advice, not ***purely*** the '**almighty** dollar'. It was **far worse** in America – but now that '**let it rip**' was allowed in NSW (& **spread** across Aus). Result is **catastrophic** 😠 😠 *#Domicron* ***#LetItRipScotty***

---

[1] All hashtags may also be interpreted as signalling the presence of other perspectives in the social stream. However, for simplicity we will not code every single instance in this way.

[COMPETENT LEADERSHIP]; [INCOMPETENT POLITICIANS]
× CONVOKE: [marshal] → *#Domicron #**LetItRip**Scotty*
× CONVOKE: [designate] → collective references
× FINESSE: [buttress] → [Disclaim]; [*Entertain*]; [**Concur**] ×😡 😡
× PROMOTE: [boost] → [force: up-scale]; ×😡 😡
× PROMOTE: [enrich] → *#Domicron #**LetItRip**Scotty*

Again, the repeated POUTING FACE emoji coordinates with the prosody of [force: up-scale] that functions to boost the two bonds. It also coordinates with the critical external voices entering the post via the various ENGAGEMENT choices, such as [disclaim] (*not*) and [concur] (*certainly*). Another example of this kind of pattern occurs in Text (8.20).

Text (8.20) ‛It's good that we're opening up as safely **as possible**‛ *?? If you call* #LetItRip[3] safe 😡 😡 😡 delusional **#Domicron** #COVID19nsw #nswpol
[BAD POLICY]
× CONVOKE: [marshal] → **#Domicron**
× CONVOKE: [designate] → hashtags; collective references/naming
× FINESSE: [buttress] → [*Entertain*]; **[Attribute]** ×😡 😡 😡
× PROMOTE: [boost] → **[force: up-scale]** ×😡 😡 😡
× PROMOTE: [enrich] → **#Domicron**

In this example, the repetition in the sequence of three POUTING FACE 😡 emoji coordinates with the [force: up-scale] in the boosting strategy. The choice to position these emoji in the phase of the post commenting on the quoted material (where the hashtag #Domicron, in addition to invoking negative [judgement: capacity], is used to indicate the voice attributed to the quotation), contributes to the heteroglossic buttressing of the [BAD POLICY] bond.

These kinds of sequences of emoji also often incorporate more than one emoji, enabling more nuanced heteroglossic buttressing while intensifying accompanying boosting. Such is the case in Text (8.21), which includes another example of a [BAD POLICY] bond.

Text (8.21) Morrison and #Domicron's let it rip strategy has seen Australia pass the UK to be the 4th highest case numbers country in the world. That's despite inadequate testing and asymptotic cases being asked not to get tested 🙄 😡 #auspoll
[BAD POLICY]
× convoke: [marshal] → #Domicron
× convoke: [designate] → collective references/naming
× finesse: [buttress] → [Disclaim] ×🙄 😡
× promote: [boost] → [force: up-scale] ×🙄 😡
× promote: [enrich] → #Domicron

In Text (8.21) the emoji sequence FACE WITH ROLLING EYES 🙄 and POUTING FACE 😡 work with the buttressing realised by disclaiming (*despite, not*). In this case the emoji appear to forge an 'of course they didn't enact [GOOD POLICY]' reaction, supporting the critical voice which the ENGAGEMENT resources invoke. In addition, the string of multiple emoji supports the [force: up-scale] which boosts the [BAD POLICY] bond. This post is also a good example of how much affiliation work emoji are capable of in instances of imbue where they evaluatively target their co-text. A similar pattern is seen in Text (8.22), which contrasts two bonds in order to heighten the criticism of [BAD POLICY].

Text (8.22)   @{User 1} @drkerrynphelps @Dom_Perrottet And **they knew** #COVIDisAirborne & asymptomatic spread and worked around that- Aussie **beat** Japan **big time** before #**Domicron** – as we switched to **let it rip** strategies by removing mitigation like masks QR thanks to **dumbf** @Dom_Perrottet 😡 😡 😡 😡 😩 😩 😩 😩 ✳ ✳ ✳ ✳and we are in **code**😩 😩 😩
[SUCCESSFUL AUSTRALIANS]; [BAD POLICY]
× CONVOKE: [marshal] → #COVIDisAirborne
× CONVOKE: [designate] → collective references/naming
× FINESSE: [buttress] → *entertain*; **attribute** × 😡 😡 😡 😡 😩 😩 😩 😩 ✳ ✳ ✳ ✳

× PROMOTE: [boost] → **[force: up-scale]** x 😡 😡 😡 😡 😩 😩 😩 😩 ✳ ✳ ✳ ✳

× PROMOTE: [enrich] → #**Domicron**

Text (8.22) is also an example where the emoji take on a more substantial role in the post in terms of coordinating with [force: up-scale] that supports boosting. The emoji are visually salient, taking up a large proportion of the final line of the tweet. This also supports buttressing by increasing the visual salience of the critical voice developed through the co-occurring ENGAGEMENT resources.

Other bonds in the corpus boosted and buttressed by emoji included [CRUEL POLITICIANS], realised as invoked negative [judgement: propriety] targeted at political figures, as can be seen in Text (8.23).

Text (8.23)   An 8 week old baby dead from covid. 💔 **Let it rip** is *really* the **worst** thing Perrottet could have **ever** done! We *have to* **push through**! **push through WHAT**? @Dom_Perrottet?? 😡 #Domicron #nswcovid #**LNPDeathCult**
[CRUEL POLITICIANS]
× CONVOKE: [marshal] → #Domicron, #**LNPDeathCult**
× CONVOKE: [designate] → collective references/naming ×💔
× FINESSE: [buttress] → *[Proclaim]* × 💔, 😡
× PROMOTE: [boost] → **[force: up-scale]** ×😡
× PROMOTE: [enrich] → #Domicron, #**LNPDeathCult**

In Text (8.23), the BROKEN HEART 💔 imbues the co-text about the death of a baby with negative [affect] and, in turn, supports the buttressing by introducing the trigger of this [affect] as a critical voice reacting to this death. Similarly, the

POUTING FACE 😡 buttresses, the [CRUEL POLITICIANS] bond as a negative reaction to the issues raised across the post, seeming to work alongside the hashtag as an evaluative meta-comment in a similar manner to other posts surveyed in this section. At the same time both emoji contribute to boosting the [CRUEL POLITICIANS] bond by both intensifying the negative [judgement] (e.g. *worst*) and coordinating with the exclamation marks which also strengthens the prosody of negative assessment across the post.

Emoji also boosted and buttressed critical bonds realised as negative assessment of politicians' talk. One of the key phrases that Premier Perrottet used in reference to mitigation measures such as mask wearing was 'personal responsibility'. This phrase references the neoliberal ethos that citizens should rely on their own resources, rather than coordinated assistance from the state, to ensure their ongoing health and prosperity. Many social media users reacted negatively to this phrase, mocking it in comments featuring emoji such as the FACE WITH SYMBOLS ON MOUTH 🤬, THINKING FACE 🤔, FACE WITH ROLLING EYES 🙄 and PERSON FACEPALMING 🤦 emoji together with the phrase '*personal responsibility*':

Text (8.24) So when personal responsibility results in **mass** covid testing **the government** says no we don't like that. 🤔 🤔 #Domicron #scotty*must*go #COVID19au
[BAD GOVERNMENT]
× CONVOKE: [marshal] → #scottymustgo
× CONVOKE: [designate] → collective references/naming ×🤔 🤔
× FINESSE: [buttress] → [Disclaim]; [*Entertain*]; [**Attribute**] ×🤔 🤔
× PROMOTE: [boost] → **[force: up-scale]** ×🤔 🤔

Text (8.25) So what does that **great** intellectual thinker **#GeorgieCrozier** think **now** about #Domicron and his personal responsibility? Does she **still** want @DanielAndrewsMP to make this Vic policy? Idiot 😡 😡
[BAD POLICY], [INCOMPETENT POLITICIANS]
× CONVOKE: [marshal] → #Domicron
× CONVOKE: [designate] → collective references/naming ×😡 😡
× FINESSE: [buttress] → [*Entertain*]; [**Attribute**] ×😡 😡
× PROMOTE: [boost] → **[force: up-scale]** ×😡 😡

Text (8.26) #Domicron playing right into their hands. They love this personal responsibility **shit** 🙄 #COVIDIOT #COVID19Aus [BAD POLITICIANS]
× CONVOKE: [marshal] → #COVIDIOT
× CONVOKE: [designate] → collective references/naming ×🙄
× PROMOTE: [boost] → **[force: up-scale]** ×🙄
× PROMOTE: [enrich] → #COVIDIOT

Text (8.27) Taking personal responsibility is counter to **most** public health measures because **many** people aren't responsible or community minded – hence drink driving laws, seatbelts, child seat restraints, pool

fences, smoking legislation, illicit drug controls 😏 #domicron 😕 👿
[BAD POLICY]
× convoke: [marshal] → #domicron
× convoke: [designate] → collective references/naming ×😕 👿
× finesse: [buttress] → *[affirm]* ×😏 😕 👿
× promote: [boost] → **[force: up-scale]** ×😕 👿

As examples Text (8.24) to Text (8.27) suggest emoji supported the [boosting] and [buttressing] of the [BAD GOVERNMENT], [BAD POLICIY], and [INCOMPETENT POLITICIAN] bonds that are tabled in these posts in a similar manner to the previous examples considered in this section.

8.5   Emoji Supporting with Convoking Affiliation

The examples covered so far have largely dealt with the role of emoji in supporting buttressing and boosting affiliation; however, emoji can also coordinate with convocation, whereby a particular group or community are directly or indirectly invited to align with a particular bond. This was often achieved through emoji such as flag emoji which serve as 'bonding icons' (Stenglin, 2008).[2] These are icons that serve to rally particular communities who identify with them around shared feeling. The process of iconisation whereby interpersonal meaning is foregrounded (e.g. feelings of nationalism) was discussed in Chapter 5 in terms of emblems and in Chapter 6 in terms of attitude. For example in Text (8.28), the FLAG: AUSTRALIA 🇦🇺 emoji acts as a bonding icon and coordinates with the reference to 'we' as the relevant ingroup.

Text (8.28)   Just a reminder 🇦🇺 we had the 🦠 under control before #Domicron and #MorrisonFail decided to let it rip.

[COMPETENT AUSTRALIANS]; [INCOMPETENT POLITICIANS]
× convoke: [designate] → collective references ×🇦🇺
× convoke: [marshal] → #MorrisonFail

This has a clear function in terms of ideational concurrence with the [entity] 'we', serving to delineate the community to whom the bonds are relevant. However, the function is not purely ideational, and the concurrence also acts to muster the Australian community as the ambient audience whose collective opinion the post attempts to influence. This community, cast as [COMPETENT AUSTRALIANS] (via the positive [judgement: capacity] 'under control' targeted at 'we'), is set in opposition with [INCOMPETENT POLITICIANS] (via both inscribed 'Fail' and invoked 'let it rip' [capacity]). Other examples of this kind of pattern occur in Text (8.29) to Text (8.31):

---

[2] For relevant work on bonding icons in social media discourse, see Zappavigna (2014c).

Text (8.29)   #Domicron gives me the ick! Creepy eye blinking, nodding, lip
                pursing, deflecting, fake praising, zero responsibility for his fuck ups 😡
                😷 😠 #auspol #letsvote🎬
                [UNPLEASANT POLITICIAN], [INCOMPETENT POLITICIAN]
                × CONVOKE: [marshal] → #Domicron
                × CONVOKE: [designate] → hashtags, collective references ×🎬
                × PROMOTE: [enrich] → hashtags

Text (8.30)   #auspol #ScottytheFailure is trying to blame the current supply chain
                problems on Omicron. What a #CROCKOFSHIT. He and #Domicron
                have given us Omicron and the '🇦🇺way'☺
                [IMPROPRIETIOUS POLICITIAN], [INCOMPETENT
                POLITICIAN]
                × CONVOKE: [marshal] → #ScottytheFailure #Domicron
                × CONVOKE: [designate] → hashtag, collective references ×🇦🇺
                × PROMOTE: [enrich] → #ScottytheFailure #Domicron

Text (8.31)   #covidnsw: Australia Day to Valentine's Day likely worst Hope not,
                but so many ppl may be sick/iso/caring – much may close Have your
                meds, emergency stuff on hand Get folks in elder care boosted NOW
                esp if they had AZ #Domicron + #ScottyDoesNothing = you're on your
                own 🏳 🇦🇺 💔
                [IMPROPRIETIOUS POLICITIAN], [INCOMPETENT
                POLITICIAN]
                × CONVOKE: [marshal] → #Domicron #ScottyDoesNothing
                × CONVOKE: [designate] → hashtags, collective references ×🇦🇺
                × PROMOTE: [enrich] → #Domicron #ScottyDoesNothing

In these examples the AUSTRALIAN FLAG 🇦🇺 emoji again muster together an ambient community to align around bonds that are highly critical of
Australian politicians.

Some emoji in the corpus functioned as broader emblems of CONVOCATION
that could be applied within multiple communities, for example the RAISED
FIST ✊ emoji evokes the raised fist gesture that has been used historically as
a symbol of resistance to oppression. However, again it should be noted that
emoji do not embody this meaning in the absence of co-text and context and,
depending on the co-text, can be associated with meanings such as celebration.
In Text (8.32), the ideational concurrence of the RAISED FIST: MEDIUM
SKIN TONE ✊ emoji with the [occurrence figure] about nurses striking activates the association with resistance.

Text (8.32)   NSW Nurses are on going on Strike ✊ ✊ ✊ #domicron [news article
                titled 'NSW nurses vote in favour of statewide strike, citing premier's
                'tin-eared' response to Omicron']
                [GOOD NURSES]
                × CONVOKE: [designate] –> collective references ×✊ ✊ ✊
                × CONVOKE: [marshal] –> #domicron

In this post, positive [judgement] of 'NSW Nurses' as a designated community is invoked since there is no explicit ATTITUDE inscribed in the post. Instead, the solidarity suggested by the RAISED FIST ✊ emoji supports an implicit [GOOD NURSES] bond. Another example of this kind of pattern is found in Text (8.33).

> Text (8.33)   @{User 1} @{User 2} @AnnastaciaMP Cheers from me and everyone else up here in Brisbane {name}. You've got Dan The Man. You're sorted <u>mate</u>. Same up here with Annastacia. She keeps us safe. Unfortunately we've got #Domicron in between us both. We should just cut NSW away and let it drift. Stay safe <u>mate</u>
> [COMPETENT LEADERS]; [INCOMPETENT LEADERS]; [BAD STATE]
> × CONVOKE: [designate] → collective references ×
> × CONVOKE: [marshal] → #Domicron, **vocative** ×

This post contrasts the Queensland and Victorian leadership with the NSW Premier through opposing bonds, in order to CONVOKE solidarity between members of these states and outgroup NSW. The RAISED FIST ✊ emoji coordinates with this oppositioning, supporting both the designating and marshalling affiliation.

Emoji acting in the service of CONVOCATION frequently coordinated with vocatives in the co-text addressing particular groups. For example, in Text (8.34) a string of emoji (👍 💯 😎) RESONATES with the command to '*take care*' addressed to '*folks*' (and by implication with '*Please take precautions ... *'):

> Text (8.34)   Today's figures in nsw suggest that if you become infected, you have a approx 1% chance of ending up in ICU. 😬 NOT good odds! Please take precautions against becoming the 1/100. Take care <u>folks</u> 👍 💯 😎 #COVID19nsw #Domicron #scomicron #auspol
> [BAD ODDS]
> × CONVOKE: [designate] → collective references × 😬 × 👍 💯 😎
> × CONVOKE: [marshal] → #Domicron #scomicron, <u>vocative</u> × 👍 💯 😎

Here the emoji appear to endorse the commands but also to coordinate with the vocative to muster shared positive ATTITUDE to the command. The THUMBS UP 👍 and HUNDRED POINTS 💯 in particular appear to support the direction of the command to the '*folks*'. The SMILING FACE WITH SUNGLASSES 😎 emoji appears to not only endorse this positioning of the [BAD ODDS] bond through its representation of positive [affect] (since the face is smiling) but also to suggest positive [judgement] of the folks who take the advice, with the sunglasses suggesting positive group assessment (e.g. being 'cool'). Text (8.35) to Text (8.37) are further examples where emoji follow a similar pattern of directing bonds to particular groups through coordinating with forms of address or mentions of particular communities.

Text (8.35)   Anyone who says Twitter is a nest of vipers is doing it wrong.
               ⬤ to all the HCWs who are doing it right in spite of, not
               because of, #Domicron #ScottytheFailure #BradBioHazzard or Greg
               Huuuuuuuuuuuuuuunt ™ @hg_nelson [embedded tweet about a pain
               nurse]
               [TENACIOUS HEALTH CARE WORKERS]; [INCOMPETENT
               POLITICIANS]
               × CONVOKE: [designate] → address
               × CONVOKE: [marshal] → #Domicron #ScottytheFailure
               #BradBioHazzard, address × ⬤

Text (8.36)   Thankyou frontline workers & to this fine nurse.   Free now to speak
               her story of service. #LetItRip #Domicron #covidnsw [embedded news
               article titled 'Sydney nurse quits in protest of 'chaotic and dangerous'
               hospital conditions']
               [GOOD FRONTLINE WORKERS]; [EXCELLENT NURSE]
               × CONVOKE: [designate] → address ×
               × CONVOKE: [marshal] → #LetItRip #Domicron #covidnsw

Text (8.37)   Love My tribe I found💜 #Domicron now trending 💯😎 #auspol
               #Domicron #Covid_19 [screenshot of Australian Twitter trends]
               [GOOD TRIBE]
               × CONVOKE: [designate] → collective references ×💜
               × CONVOKE: [marshal] → #Domicron #auspol #Domicron #Covid_19
               × 💯😎

In these examples, the emoji have the dual function of directing positive
ATTITUDE to these communities at the same time as endorsing cooccurring
stances. For instance, the emoji in ' 💜 ⬤ 💜 ⬤ ⭐ 💜 *to all the HCWs who
are doing it right'* CONVOKE shared feelings such as positive [affect] (through
the BEATING HEART 💜) and positive [judgement] (through the RAISING
HANDS , CLAPPING HANDS , THUMBS UP , and STAR ⭐) directed
towards the community of health care workers ('*HCWs'*). These emoji also
resonate with the positive linguistic [judgement] '*doing it right'* in the co-text.

    Similarly, the BROKEN HEART 💔 emoji often has the dual function of
resonating with negative ATTITUDE in the co-text and coordinating with CON-
VOKING affiliation integrating certain communities. These communities include the elderly, families impacted by COVID-19, and those vulnerable to
infection, as suggested in Text (8.38) to Text (8.40).

Text (8.38)   My parents announced that they arranged their funeral/cemetery cost..
               incase something happens to them … e.g. Covid. They have a good 20
               years to go. Pensioners shouldn't have to think 'letting it rip' as a death
               sentence. 💔We need to protect them #Domicron @Dom_Perrottet
               [WORTHY PENSIONERS]; [CARING COMMUNITY]
               × CONVOKE: [designate] → collective references
               × CONVOKE: [marshal] → #Domicron

Text (8.39)   Instead of health conditions, that they had for years & did not die from – Chant or Perrotett should read EACH name & their age. They deserve recognition that they lived & were loved. And their Gov failed them. 💔 🐍 #auspol #Domicron #ScottyDoesNothing #CallTheElectionNow
[WORTHY DEAD]; [INCOMPETENT GOVERNMENT]
× convoke: [designate] → collective references
× convoke: [marshal] → #Domicron #ScottyDoesNothing #CallTheElectionNow
× promote: [enrich] → #Domicron #ScottyDoesNothing #CallTheElectionNow

Text (8.40)   #covidnsw: Australia Day to Valentine's Day likely worst Hope not, but so many ppl may be sick/iso/caring – much may close Have your meds, emergency stuff on hand Get folks in elder care boosted NOW esp if they had AZ #Domicron + #ScottyDoesNothing = you're on your own 🎞 💔
[BAD SITUATION]; [UNCARING GOVERNMENT]
× convoke: [designate] →collective references
× convoke: [marshal] → #Domicron + #ScottyDoesNothing
× promote: [enrich] → #Domicron + #ScottyDoesNothing

These are examples of the groups that the authors position as relevant to the bonds shared, most often as the victims of [INCOMPETENT/UNCARING GOVERNMENT]. In these examples, Text (8.38) to Text (8.40), the BROKEN HEART 💔 emoji resonate with the negative attitude in the co-text but also inscribe what would otherwise be invoked [affect]. This then has a boosting function in terms of affiliation strategies beyond convoking.

8.6   Death-Related Emoji Promoting Bonds Critical of the COVID Response

The corpus contained a number of emoji whose visual representation was related to the field of death and mortality in terms of register. For instance, this included the COFFIN ⚰, SKULL ☠, and HEADSTONE 🪦 emoji (see Table 8.2). These emoji coordinated closely with the affiliation strategies, particular promoting affiliation. An example is Text (8.41), which features visually salient repetition of emoji in long emoji strings.

Text (8.41)   FARK!!!! ⚰ ⚰ ⚰ ⚰ ⚰ ⚰ ⚰ And this is **BEFORE COVID cases hit 25 k+ Per Day!** 🪦 🪦 🪦 ☠ ☠ ☠ ☠ 💀 💀 💀 💀 💀 💀 ⚰ ⚰ 🪦 🪦 🪦 #Domicron **WILL KILL**. [embedded tweet by NSW Health about managing COVID-19 at home]
[BAD SITUATION]; [INCOMPETENT PREMIER]
× promote: [boost] → **[force: up-scale]** × ⚰ ⚰ ⚰ ⚰ ⚰ ⚰ ⚰ ⚰ ; 🪦 🪦 🪦 ☠ ☠ ☠ ☠ 💀 💀 💀 💀 💀 💀 ⚰ ⚰ 🪦 🪦 🪦

These repeated emoji reinforce the upscaling of the negative [judgement: capacity] targeted at Perrottet that is realised via the expletive, as well as the ALL-CAPS font, explanation marks, and references to the high COVID case numbers. All of these resources work together to PROMOTE the [BAD SITUATION] and [INCOMPETENT PREMIER] bonds, along with the colourful nature of the repetition that visually dominates the post.

This pattern of visually salient emoji strings used for PROMOTING affiliation was common in the corpus. Another example is Text (8.42) in which the SKULL ☠ emoji is repeated 42 times in order to reference the 42 deaths referred to in the post:

Text (8.42)   @SkyNewsAust *What do 42 deaths in a single day matter?* As long as Alan Joyce & Graham Turner are able to buy **bigger** yachts next year. #Scomicron #Domicron ☠ = 🛥 🛥
[CORRUPT POLITICIANS]
× FINESSE: [buttress] → [Disclaim]; *[Entertain]*; **[Attribute]** × ☠ ☠ ☠
…
× PROMOTE: [boost] → **[force: up-scale]** × ☠ ☠ ☠ …

A similar example is Text (8.43) incorporating 24 HEADSTONE 🪦 emoji, which accuses Dominic Perrottet of prioritising the Australian economy over the lives of children:

Text (8.43)   @Dom_Perrottet 🪦 new headstones on the day **Barnaby** says people dying. **It should be** *obvious* **to parents by now** that #**Domicron** has decided that their childrens lives are **valueless** if protecting them affects the economy. #auspol
[IMMORAL POLITICIANS]
× CONVOKE: [designate] → collective references/naming × 🪦 🪦 🪦 …
× CONVOKE: [marshal] → #**Domicron** × 🪦 🪦 🪦 …
× FINESSE: [buttress] → *[Entertain]*; **[Attribute]** × 🪦 🪦 🪦 …
× PROMOTE: [boost] → **[force: up-scale]** × 🪦 🪦 🪦 …

Table 8.2 *Most frequent death-related emoji in the corpus*

Emoji	Frequency
HEADSTONE🪦	99
SKULL☠	83
COFFIN⚰	64
SKULL AND CROSSBONES ☠	39
FACE WITH CROSSED-OUT EYES 😵	23
FUNERAL URN⚱	1

In this example, the repeated HEADSTONE 🪦 emoji coordinate with the boosting affiliation realised by [force: up-scale] which raise the stakes of the [IMMORAL POLITICIANS] bond. In addition, the designating affiliation, realised by references to people who are dying, parents, and children, coordinates with the emoji as a visual representations of the death toll.

This kind of pattern is also visible in Text (8.44) to Text (8.46), which incorporate long emoji strings to represent the death toll [designating] people who have died, at the same time as buttressing and boosting [IMMORAL/ INCOMPETENT PREMIER] bonds, realised through negative [judgement: propriety] targeted at Dominic Perrottet.

Text (8.44)   **@Dom_Perrottet** 🪦🪦🪦🪦🪦🪦🪦🪦🪦🪦🪦🪦🪦🪦🪦🪦🪦
🪦🪦🪦🪦🪦🪦🪦🪦🪦🪦 announced today. But why is #**Domicron** concerned today – that he has overseen the deaths of **1029** people in the last 43 days? Nope, politics and his own **miserable** arse. #auspol [embedded news article titled 'NSW Premier Dominic Perrottet is putting on a brave face – he might need it later today']
[IMMORAL PREMIER]
× CONVOKE: [designate] → collective references/naming × 🪦 🪦 🪦 …
× CONVOKE: [marshal] → #**Domicron**
× FINESSE: [buttress] → [Disclaim]; *[Entertain]*; **[Attribute]**
× PROMOTE: [boost] →**[force: up-scale]** × 🪦 🪦 🪦 …
× PROMOTE: [enrich] → #**Domicron**

Text (8.45)   #Domicron **still** on track to hand down **yet another devastating blow** to our economy, businesses and, to our vulnerable, **he** thinks the pandemic just simply gone away, despite **expert** warnings. **Domicron** does not get it, pl will avoid going to places where masks are removed.🥚🥚🥚🥚🙁
[INCOMPETENT PREMIER]
× CONVOKE: [designate] → collective references/naming ×🥚🥚🥚🥚🙁
× CONVOKE: [marshal] → #Domicron ×🥚🥚🥚🥚🙁
× FINESSE: [buttress] → [Disclaim]; *[Entertain]*; **[Attribute]** ×🥚🙁
× PROMOTE: [boost] → **[force: up-scale]** ×🥚🥚🥚🥚🙁
× PROMOTE: [enrich] → #Domicron

Text (8.46)   That's **11 more** 🥚🥚🥚🥚🥚🥚🥚🥚🥚🥚🥚 #Domicron #dickhead #auspol
[INCOMPETENT PREMIER]
× CONVOKE: [designate] → hashtag, collective references/naming × 🥚 🥚🥚 …
× CONVOKE: [marshal] → #Domicron #dickhead × 🥚🥚🥚 …
× PROMOTE: [boost] → **[force: up-scale]** ×🥚🥚🥚 …
× PROMOTE: [enrich] → #Domicron #dickhead

Again, as colourful visual icons the long emoji strings visually dominate the posts: for instance, thirty-two HEADSTONE 🪦 emoji inset into a [figure] about the number of deaths in Text (8.44), four COFFIN 🖊 emoji in Text (8.45) and eleven in Text (8.46). The semiotic flexibility of emoji is once again visible in these examples by the way that they support designating through being able to symbolically represent the deceased, at the same time as supporting boosting through their visual salience and buttressing the [IMMORAL/ INCOMPETENT PREMIER] by imbuing the visual representation of the death toll with negative [judgement] as well as enmeshing with co-occurring negative ATTITUDE in the posts.

8.7   Conclusion

This chapter has explored how emoji can function as a resource operating in the service of COMMUNING AFFILIATION. We have shown the role that emoji can play in how bonds are FINESSED and PROMOTED to ambient audiences, and how they assist in CONVOCATION of potential communities to which these bonds are directed. Within the negatively charged political discourse about the NSW state government COVID response in Australia that we have explored in the specialised #Domicron corpus, emoji appeared focused around three functions in terms of how they supported the affiliation strategies. In terms of FINESSING and PROMOTING bonds that were critical of the premier and his government, the emoji tended to both buttress and boost the negative [judgement] by adding additional layers of negative assessment. This was construed through both enmeshing with existing negative linguistic evaluation in the co-text, as well as imbuing negative assessment into the text by directing it at particular political voices and stances. Finally emoji, through their ability to act as both emblems and tokens of evaluation, were used to marshal communities around the critical bonds which they had helped to enact.

Having explored the affiliative function that emoji can enact in this and the previous chapter, we now turn in Chapter 9 to considering how emoji function with semiotic resources beyond language, since these also play an important role in the how social media texts tender bonds and render reactions.

9   Beyond Emoji–Text Relations
Factoring in Images and Other Semiotic Resources

9.1   Introduction

As social media become ever more visual (Adami & Jewitt, 2016), images and other visual multimedia are playing an increasingly central role in social media posts. Indeed, many social media platforms foreground visual images or short-form video as the key semiotic resource in a post. We might interpret this as part of broader shifts toward image-centricity in contemporary digital multimodal practices (Stöckl, Caple, & Pflaeging, 2020). For example, when we consider the important role that emoji play on Instagram, they can be seen to be 'doubly image-centric: they put an image center stage and accompany it by writing that contains pictorial characters', thereby increasing the 'potential for diverse inter- and intramodal relations' (Siever, Siever, & Stöckl, 2020, p. 181). Thus, in order to adequately account for the meanings emoji make in social media posts, we need to consider their relations not only with the written text, but also with other visual paralanguage including images and various kinds of graphic devices such as GIFs and stickers; it is to these resources that we turn our attention in this chapter.

Social media is resplendent with a creative blend of non-standardised graphical resources such as images, memes, digital stickers, avatars, and GIFs that extend beyond the rigid parameters of Unicode emoji character encoding. For example, digital stickers are generally bigger and more elaborate than emoji, can include written text such as caption overlays, and may occur in different layout positions relative to written verbiage and images within a post. Memes are often configurations of both images and text, and can be embedded in social media posts as a singular media object. For instance, image macros include upper and lower captions related to the main image (Figure 9.1).

Many of these graphical resources also incorporate simple animations, which often loop indefinitely. For example, a GIF (Graphic Interchange Format) is a raster file format that is designed to support simple low-resolution images in a limited number of colours. These can be sequenced as frames to create moving images. They are a common format for memes and humorous 'reactions' across social media platforms (Sasamoto, 2022). Early examples

Figure 9.1 Example of an image–macro meme

were clip art style animations, and as bandwidth limits became less of an issue, GIFs sampled sections of video from popular culture such as iconic scenes in movies. Stickers can also be animated, such as a coffee cup with infinitely moving steam.

Herring and Dainas (2017, p. 2185) term these visual resources graphicons, 'a blend of "graphical" and "icons" (cf. Greek grafikon "graphics")' and define a number of pragmatic functions which they can enact, as summarised in Table 9.1. Just how wide we cast the net for visual resources that may be considered graphicons depends on the definition of 'icon' that is assumed. For instance, it would seem that still images and video, while articulated via the visual mode, are a move beyond icons since they adhere to established modal codes in their own rights. This distinction is porous, however, as images and video can be 'iconised', usually through simplification of images and extraction and looping of a brief segment of a video. This taxonomical porosity also applies among graphicon categories; for instance, a sticker featuring a looping animation is difficult to distinguish technically from a GIF. For the purposes of our analysis, we loosely differentiate these based on whether they are still images with animated elements, or whether they are excerpts of longer video texts; however, we are conscious many examples straddle this boundary. A further taxonomical challenge that should be noted is that while it is conceptually neat to categorise graphicons as graphic resources, they are in fact often graphic–text combinations. For instance, stickers will often incorporate words or phrases, for example an image of a popping champagne bottle with

Table 9.1 *Herring and Dainas' (2017) coding of the pragmatic functions of graphicons*

Function	Explanation
Mention (vs Use)	Metadiscursive reference to the graphicon itself, rather than use of the graphicon for a particular discursive function
Reaction	Evaluative reaction (e.g. affect) to previous discourse (e.g. a previous linguistic or multimodal move in a thread)
Riffing	Humorous reaction to previous discourse (e.g. via puns, parody or non- serious moves in a thread)
Tone Modification	Augmenting or adjusting the meaning of the co-text (e.g. functioning as a paralinguistic clue as to how the text should be read)
Action	Representing physical action, often by substituting for a verb in a textual sequence
Narrative Sequence	Sequencing used to express a simple story (e.g. graphicons expressing an activity sequence)

the words 'congratulations!' incorporated into the visual design or an image of a cute animal and the phrase 'Have a great day!'. Thus, when considering how these kinds of graphicons interact with the rest of the multimodal text in which they are embedded, we may have at least two orders of image-text relations that need to be accounted for.

Herring and Dainas' description of graphicons accurately identifies many of their most salient communicative functions. It is, however, more rhetorically oriented than the social semiotic approach we take in this book. For this reason, while we note points of intersection between our analysis and the work of other researchers, such as Herring and Dainas, who have made inroads on this topic, we will attempt here to extend the framework elaborated across the previous chapters to describe graphicon semiosis.

Accordingly, in this chapter we again adopt a trinocular approach to inter-modal CONVERGENCE. We will consider how graphicons ideationally concur, interpersonally resonate, and textually synchronise with the other semiotic resources deployed in social media posts. We will also adopt the three over-arching principles that have guided our analysis thus far: proximity, minimum mapping, and prosodic correspondence in undertaking this analysis. However, graphicons have an expansive range of affordances beyond those of Unicode emoji. They represent a wider set of graphical and animated resources spanning multiple modes (e.g. images, video snippets, animated graphics, and mul-timedia–text combinations). This means that there are many more variables that need to be considered. Thus, we will restrict our analysis to just the three types of CONVERGENCE at the most general level, without attempting to generate a more delicate network that can accommodate all of the available meaning potential. In addition, we will restrict our analysis to the most salient meanings made in the posts, since there are a very large set of relations that could otherwise be considered. For instance, if we factor in all relations within and between the various semiotic modes coming together in a social media post across written text, emoji, graphicons, metadata, layout, and other platform-specific features and parameters, we would generate a very large number of permutations and combinations. Naturally, this constrains the scope of our analysis considerably. We acknowledge this and respond that we hope the analytical framework proposed here may be of use to future scholars in undertaking more thorough investigation of how graphicons make meaning alongside other modes. Before proceeding to the analysis of graphicon examples, however, we will begin with a review of research on graphicons to date and a summary of its main conclusions.

9.2   Customisation, Personalisation, and Platform Control

In parallel with the move to image-centricity, there appear to be two competing contemporary digital imperatives that have had a significant impact on graphicon usage. These are standardisation, the impetus to create interoperable graphical communication that is machine readable by multiple platforms (e.g. emoji work wherever Unicode is recognised) and customisation, the ability to alter or personalise graphical representations to facilitate individual or community self-representation. In addition, visual repertoires involving graphicons are in a constant state of reuse and recirculation to suit changing communicative needs:

The ways in which pre-configured artefacts are appropriated and relocalised are thus shaped not only by software design but by social processes of (dis)identification, indexicality and sociolinguistic authentication. (Tagg & Lyons, 2021, p. 247)

This is often achieved by reappropriating the graphic resources offered by platforms for 'off label' uses: 'Unicode emoji are repurposed to create culturally appropriate holiday greetings on WeChat; custom images are designed by users to fulfill their own expressive needs over the design choices of platforms' (De Seta, 2018).

As we noted when exploring the technical dimensions of emoji in Chapter 2, the key principle of Unicode is standardisation. Such standardisation operates in the service of interoperability, so that Unicode characters will work across software and systems for all languages. While standardisation has many benefits, our semiotic impetus as social beings is to constantly adapt available resources to make more meanings in more functional contexts. Thus we are currently witnessing an increased 'demand for customizable glyphs' such as digital stickers (Loomis et al., 2016, p. 2). Graphicons tend to be non-standardised since they are usually either platform specific (Zhang, Wang, & Li, 2021) or semi-adjustable visual resources (e.g. Bitmoji), proprietary designed images (e.g. digital sticker sets), or entirely user-generated images.

Social media users themselves will design and sell graphicons such as sets of digital stickers, a practice that largely arose with the Japanese LINE app. LINE was originally a messaging app but has since evolved into a fully fledged social media platform and digital service provider that dominates the digital sticker economy in East Asia. Digital stickers, such as those sold via LINE, can be conceptualised within a suite of 'character merchandising strategies' that have a long predigital semiotic and commercial history (e.g. within advertising campaigns associated with television animations). They can also be seen to 'draw on emoji and deco-mail proto-stickers pioneered by i-mode, and on the wider character-centric visual culture of manga, anime, and games' (Steinberg, 2020, p. 5). Research exploring how graphicon use evolves as new resources become available, 'found considerable functional overlap between emoji and stickers, with differences being mainly ones of degree: Stickers are more pragmatically marked for expressivity, intensity, and intimacy' (Konrad et al., 2020, p. 232), with their specificity making them amenable to 'self-contained uses and self-representation' (Konrad et al., 2020, p. 232). Since digital stickers are not standardised there is less potential to build up conventions of use beyond restricted communities and they are 'more likely to be sent as single, self-contained snatches of communication rather than being integrated into a verbal sentence or strung together to form a more complex thought' (Seargeant, 2019, p. 19).

Parallel to creative development of amateur and commercial graphicon sets, there are also ongoing computational efforts to produce systems capable of generating unique and customisable emoji. Some of these efforts seek to adjust Unicode so arbitrary images could be included as some kind of embedded graphic, for instance:

… a client might behave similarly to current practice in retrieving external images in email. If the receiver already knows of the identified emoji, it can display it, but otherwise the receiver would display the fallback (base) character and ask the user to push a button before retrieving the emoji description. (Loomis et al., 2016, p. 4)

Other approaches accommodate custom images 'on the fly, especially since some messengers (such as Telegram) allow users to create their own sets of icons' (Shonenkov et al., 2021). Unicode itself has indicated that a longer-term goal of the standard is to support embedded graphics, drawing on the potential affordances of enhanced mobile keyboards:

However, to be as effective and simple to use as emoji characters, a full solution requires significant infrastructure changes to allow simple, reliable input and transport of images (stickers) in texting, chat, mobile phones, email programs, virtual and mobile keyboards, and so on. (Even so, such images will never interchange in environments that only support plain text, such as email addresses.) Until that time, many implementations will need to use Unicode emoji instead. (Unicode Consortium, 2022c)

Some services, particularly within the domain of digital messaging, allow for platform-specific graphicons that can be purchased. In this way the relevant platforms maintain some degree of control on their allowable proliferation. However other platforms, such as the instant messaging service Slack that is popular within corporate environments, allow completely custom emoji. These are created by the user and sit alongside Unicode emoji inline in the text communication. For instance, Figure 9.2 is an example of a custom emoji that has been posted in a Slack message, appearing next to a Unicode emoji (GRINNING FACE WITH SMILING EYES). Such custom emoji are not standardised characters like Unicode but are instead embedded images. Slack presents these small images as if they are characters in terms of size and location in relation to the Unicode characters that make up the rest of the post.

While memes, GIFs and most forms of digital stickers are relatively free form resources in the sense that they are manually created, other graphicons rely on machine learning. For instance, animated avatars, like the masks, lenses, and filters available in many smartphone applications, draw on facial recognition technology to create a representation of the human face as a machine-readable biometric grid. The use of this kind of machine vision has been seen as a movement towards people 'becoming biometric citizens, identified and shaped by the digital images of our faces' (Rettberg, 2017, p. 95). For example, Apple's 'Animoji' (a portmanteau of 'animation' and 'emoji') and 'Memoji' are examples of animated avatars. Animoji avatars that are visually based on emoji design (e.g. the dog, pile of poo, and unicorn) are 'worn' by users. Unlike emoji and simple stickers, they involve vocalisation by the user, moving in sync with their spoken communication and perhaps resembling the 'asynchronous audio and video messages shared in multimodal smartphone-based social media apps such as WhatsApp and WeChat' (Herring, Dainas, & Tang, 2021, p. 2). While these kinds of resources seek to visually manipulate human self-representations, their potential to 'reify and maintain extant discriminatory racial categorisations through their formal and aesthetic features' and 'to translate moments of affective and emotional expression into socially legible forms through particular, historically contingent models of

Figure 9.2 An example of an emoji graphic created with Slack (Anonymous, 2022)

classification, legibility, and discrimination' has also been noted (Stark, 2018). This is reminiscent of the issues that we explored in Chapter 2 regarding the kinds of racial biases embedded in the decisions made by Unicode regarding how to represent and categorise human diversity.

Figure 9.3 is an example of an animated digital sticker used within an Instagram story from the account of a Canadian real estate agent. The sticker is positioned in the lower right hand of the visual frame and is a pink animated coffee cup with a cartoon face, characteristic of the 'kawaii' (cute) aesthetic that tends to underpin digital sticker production (Gn, 2018). In this example, the caption below the image appears progressively on the screen, as if being typed in the moment, and is on a repeating loop. The sticker is also moving, with the animation showing coffee swilling around as the cup moves back and forth. The video that constitutes the main content of the story is a listing for a dwelling that is for sale in Canada, and the footage is largely panning shots of the various rooms in the home. Within the frame shown in Figure 9.3, which is taken from a sequence showing the kitchen, there is an ideational CONCURRENCE across the image of the coffee machine in the video, the 'Morning Coffee' in the animated caption, and the depiction of the cute coffee in the animated sticker.

Even a post with a relatively simple message such as this one is rich in inter-modal relations: we can see how an ideational field of a house and its related components and activities is realised across image, text and sticker, as well as how the text and sticker realise positive ATTITUDE that washes over the video text. In turn, these resources are collectively tabling a [NICE HOUSE] bond,

Figure 9.3 Detail from an Instagram story containing a digital sticker (Knight, 2022)

which is apposite to the social purpose of this text: to promote the sale or rent of the property.

Evoking the emoji suggestion feature available on some device operating systems, an individual's choice of graphicon is influenced by the affordances of the graphicon palette available on a particular social media platform, as discussed in Chapter 2. As Jovanovic and van Leeuwen (2018, p. 690) observe, 'Users draw on their knowledge of everyday face-to-face conversational genres, but also have to cast these in the pre-designed visually realized generic templates made available by specific social media platforms.' Figure 9.4 is an example of an Instagram story featuring an inferred selfie which includes the photographer's hands holding the items that they have purchased from the café depicted in the background of the image. This kind of visual structure foregrounds the photographer's perspective on the brand and the experience of drinking coffee. The digital sticker included in the foreground of the image is an animated 'GIPHY' of a cup of black coffee (or similar hot beverage) in which light reflections moving across the surface of the liquid are animated (and may be confused with steam, a commonly animated phenomena in stickers of hot beverages, as can be observed in the sticker palette on the left hand side of Figure 9.4). Figure 9.5 shows further examples of how GIFs and emoji can be searched for using keyword searches, linguistically defined categories or visually defined categories.

Figure 9.4 An example of an Instagram story including a 'GIPHY' selected from a palette using the search term 'coffee' (Knight, 2022)

Keyword search

Suggestions
by labelled
category

Suggestions
by visually
labelled
category

Figure 9.5   Examples of GIF and emoji palettes on Instagram

Moreover, video communication via services such as Zoom and Microsoft Teams allows users to respond to what is happening in the interactive context with a kind of reaction graphicon (which are visually similar to emoji, but which are images rather than Unicode characters). The use of emoji and other graphicons in interactions raises 'the question of which functions emojis serve in online oral communication and whether, possibly, the distinction between oral conversation (by default without emojis) and written conversation (often with emojis) must be reconsidered' (Dürscheid & Haralambous, 2021, p. 511).

Each type of graphicon is rich enough in itself for an extended corpus-based analysis. However, to manage space and complexity, in this chapter we will focus on GIFs, as these were the most frequent graphicons in the Twitter corpora, likely because of the ways in which Twitter encourages its users to load content. We will undertake a detailed analysis of how the graphicons in this corpus are involved in some of the more common discursive patterns identified in Chapters 4 to 8 and consider their roles as resources supporting the affiliation practices that are enacted by the posts.

9.3   Graphicons and Visual Grammar

Graphicons, depending on how they are deployed in a social media post, can themselves function as paralanguage, in a similar manner to Unicode emoji. However, depending on the semiotic resources employed in the graphicon, they may draw on different combinations of modalities (e.g. by including a written caption). In addition, unlike Unicode emoji that behave like

other characters in terms of text presentation and layout, graphicons have
the potential to vary substantially in terms of multimodal parameters. While
some studies have suggested that emoji 'compete' with other graphicons such
as emoticons for the communicative role of paralanguage (Pavalanathan &
Eisenstein, 2016), the nature of this interaction is inflected by whether, how,
and where different resources can co-exist in a social media post. If we consider how a graphicon relates to the rest of a post, a significant multimodal
dimension is layout, as this determines the relative visual prominence of the
graphicon in terms of size and position.

Different social media platforms, as semiotic technologies, enforce different
kinds of layout options (Djonov & van Leeuwen, 2018). Platforms also control
the various kinds of properties assigned to the different objects (e.g. interactive
buttons, display of metadata, etc.) that make up the social media post. For example, Twitter positions visual media below the body of a tweet. Figure 9.6 is a
simplified example of the kind of visual layout that Twitter imposes on tweets.
This layout includes elements incorporating graphicons such as the avatar that
appears next to the Username and the Twitter handle (e.g. @M_Zappavigna).
This static avatar is a detail of an image uploaded by the user, appearing by
default in a round format. There is a projection relation between this block
of items and the material in the body of the post (relation (1) in Figure 9.6).
This is a convention seen throughout social media and read as the origin of the
voice projecting the verbiage in the post (Zappavigna, 2017b). Posts can also
retweet or quote other posts, although in these cases the profile of the relevant

Figure 9.6 A simplified version of the relation of the body and visual media
in a tweet

users will appear in the post positioned under the original tweet, and the post is 'embedded' rather than projected.

The body of a post is constituted by the written text and emoji relations that we have explored in earlier sections of this book, which we will put aside for now. Of particular, interest in this chapter are two other kinds of relations involving graphicons: (2) the relation of the body to graphicons such as the GIF shown in Figure 9.6, and (3) the relation between any emoji/emoji sequences in the body and the graphicon. For example, the GIF in Figure 9.6 is an instance commonly referred to as a 'reaction GIF' because it shows the unfolding of a facial expression by the main visual participant.

Returning to the question of how layout interacts with graphicons' semiosis, we adapt Kress and van Leeuwen's (2006) model for analysing the semiosis of visual texts. Employing this framework, we can describe how graphicons such as GIFs contribute to the meaning of social media posts through the principles of Information value and salience. Information value is concerned with how the relative position of elements in a visual text realises textual meaning. Kress and van Leeuwen (2006) describe the semiosis of left/right placement of visual elements as realising the Given and New, while top/bottom placement realises the Ideal and Real elements of the text. However, the restricted layout imposed on social media texts, as well as their more conglomerate assembly than unitarily constructed visual texts (such as photographs and paintings), prompts us to interpret graphicons occurring at the bottom of social media posts as the New of these texts, what Kress and van Leeuwen describe as the text's central 'message, the "issue"'.

In light of this, the predominantly interpersonal meaning realised by GIFs, as well as their frequent depiction of a sentient body part, serves to foreground a particular viewpoint.[1] Due to the relation of projection between the avatar/username/handle and the body of the post (1), this viewpoint will usually be that of the author of the post. Thus, in parallel to the [coalesce] feature described for emoji–language resonance, GIFs typically contribute textual meaning to a social media post by summarising and clarifying the main interpersonal dimension of the post's message and construing it as originating from the perspective of the post's author. In this respect, the GIF can be described as functioning as a kind of multimodal comment Adjunct, 'encoding a speaker's disposition towards the message' (Martin, 2002, p. 322). In this way the GIF in Figure 9.6 radiates negative meaning across the entire post, via a kind of 'dominating prosody', to borrow the term used by Martin and White (2005, pp. 21, 24) for characterising linguistic evaluation in which an interpersonal meaning, while still enacting its own localised meaning, scopes over 'a longer stretch

---

[1] cf. how emoji index the affect of the author of the post within which they occur, as discussed in Chapter 6: Section 6.6.3.

of discourse by dominating meanings in their domain' (in this case the multi-modal social media post). This is also related to the notion of image-centricity covered earlier in the chapter. The GIF evokes these negative meanings via a range of visual resources with particular associations imported from particular cultural contexts, as per the concept of provenance introduced in Chapter 2.

The second principle we adapt from Kress and van Leeuwen (2006) is sali-ence. Salience, realised by visual features such as relative size, contrast and colour saturation, 'can create a hierarchy of importance among the elements, selecting some as more important, more worthy of attention than others' (p. 201). GIFs, by virtue of their relative size, colour saturation, and animation, are typically the most salient element in a social media post. Thus, the combina-tion of the Information value and salience of GIFs in social media posts serves to foreground the meanings of these texts that converge with those of the GIF.

To give an introductory illustration of how these features of visual grammar guide interpretation of the meaning made in posts containing graphicons such as GIFs and stickers, we can see in Figure 9.6 how the location of the reaction GIF at the bottom of the text renders it the New, and its relative size and anima-tion make it the most salient element of the text. Accordingly, we interpret the role of the GIF as foregrounding both the overall negative attitude realised by language and emoji in the post, and the heteroglossic expansion construed by the represented participant in the GIF in combination with faces in the emoji and the Username/avatar/handle. While the ideational content of this post is still relevant, we can describe this post as primarily oriented towards interper-sonal meaning. Thus, Information value and salience act in concert with the systems of intermodal CONVERGENCE described in earlier chapters, yielding an even wider spectrum of potential meanings when language, emoji and other graphicons are used together.

It is worth noting that Kress and van Leeuwen's (2006) framework for ana-lysing the semiosis of visual texts could be applied to describing how individual graphicon resources make meaning; thus we could look at the relative position and salience of elements within the reaction GIF shown in Figure 9.6 to give a more detailed explanation of its semiosis. However, given the abundance of work of this kind already published, and the focus of this book, we will con-strain our application of Kress and van Leeuwen's model to the relation among linguistic and graphiconic resources, and trust the reader is satisfied with our interpretations of the graphicons' meaning without more thorough analysis.

9.4   Greetings and GIFs in the Hot Beverage Emoji Corpus

The first set of graphicons we will analyse are GIFs found in the Hot Beverage Emoji corpus. The Hot Beverage Emoji corpus was processed to extract posts which contained some form of multimedia, resulting in a specialised corpus of 3,769 posts. These included visual resources such as GIFs, video snippets, images, and memes which fall into the graphicon category as defined earlier in the chapter. Quote tweets were another visual dimension, in the sense that they are visually embedded in the original tweet, often because they feature an image or GIF to which the user is reacting. The exact nature of this visual embedding varies depending on how the platform is accessed by the reader/viewer (e.g. via mobile app or web browser). The most frequent n-grams, aside from CUP OF COFFEE (n = 2; freq. = 55) and A CUP OF (n = 3; freq. 48), were greetings, echoing the general patterns covered earlier in the book for the entire corpus. Qualitative inspection of concordance lines suggested that most of the graphicons in these types of greetings were GIFs. CUP OF COFFEE and A CUP OF were mostly accompanied by images, including inferred selfies, for instance, images displaying the user's cup of coffee and a pleasant view. Examples of the kinds of GIFs associated with greetings in the corpus are shown in Table 9.2. The GIFs tended to feature cute, anthropomorphised animals, colourful flowers, butterflies with fluttering wings, sparkling ornamentation and lettering, and steaming cups of coffee.

As Table 9.2 shows, the most common linguistic 3-gram was 'HAVE A GREAT'. Many examples containing this 3-gram included a GIF, usually with the function of re-iterating the positivity of the greeting in the body of the post. An example is Text (9.1) which includes a GIF featuring a dark brown liquid in a red, heart-shaped cup (Figure 9.7). The steam emanating from the liquid and the sparkling star embellishment in the bottom left corner of the visual frame are both animated. The body of the post is a morning greeting with a sequence of emoji.

Text (9.1)   @{User} Good morning {name}. Have a great day my beautiful friend.☕ ☕ ☀ ♥ ♥ 🍵 ❣ [GIF]

As the numbered lines in Figure 9.7 show, there are several observable inter-modal relations in this text. Relation (1) illustrates the ideational concurrence between the HOT BEVERAGE ☕ emoji, the liquid (presumably coffee) depicted in the GIF, and the linguistic co-text '*morning*'. Relation (2) illustrates the specific interpersonal resonance between the positive [affect] of the HEART SUIT ♥ emoji, the HEART EXCLAMATION ❣ emoji and the numerous heart shapes depicted in the GIF. Relation (3) illustrates how the ensembles of the emoji sequence and the elements of the GIF realise convergent, generalised positive attitude that coalesces the positive attitude in the linguistic co-text. Further to these interactions, the GIF's contribution to the meaning of this post resides in its function as the New of the text, and its salience, which foregrounds particular aspects of the interpersonal and ideational meaning realised in the post. In combination with emoji and language, we can interpret the meaning summarised and emphasised by the GIF as a

Table 9.2 *The most frequent 3-grams in the Hot Beverage graphicon specialised corpus*

N	3-gram	Freq.	Example		
			Body	Graphicon	
				Screen Capture	Description of Animated Element
1	HAVE A GREAT	64	@{User} Good morning {name} and {name}! Have a great day! ♥ 😊 😚 😗 [GIF]		Visual participant blowing bubbles
4	A GREAT DAY	45	Good morning my friend. Have a great day. 😊 😊 😊 😊 [GIF]		Visual participant winking
5	HAVE A WONDERFUL	44	@{User} Happy Monday {name}. I hope you have a wonderful day my friend. Take care. ☕ ☕ ☀ 😊 ♥ ♥ ♥ ♥ ♥ [GIF]		Visual participant winking
6	YOU HAVE A	36	@{User} Good morning and thank you have a terrific Tuesday stay safe ☕ 😊 ☆ [GIF]		Object (leaves) blowing away
7	GOOD MORNING AND	32	Every morning when you get up from your bed, be grateful to the Almighty for the things and the precious life he has given to you. Good Morning and have a happy Saturday my friends ☕ ☀ [GIF]		Visual participant 1 (Garfield cat) walking over visual participant 2 (man sleeping) and opening his eyes
8	GOOD MORNING EVERYONE	30	Good morning everyone, let's get this day started. ☕ 🍃 ☕ [GIF]		Object (coffee cup) steaming
9	I HOPE YOU	28	Good morning David thank you ☕ I hope you also have a wonderful day and week ahead my friend 😊 ♥ 🍂 ☕ [GIF]		Visual participants' (butterflies) wings fluttering; Ornamental stars sparkling
10	A WONDERFUL DAY	26	Good morning everyone, Americans have a new national holiday , enjoy your day off to reflect on why this holiday has been created ! Have a wonderful day ! ☕ ♥ ☕ 😊 ☕ [GIF]		Object (coffee cup) steaming

Figure 9.7 An example of intermodal CONVERGENCE

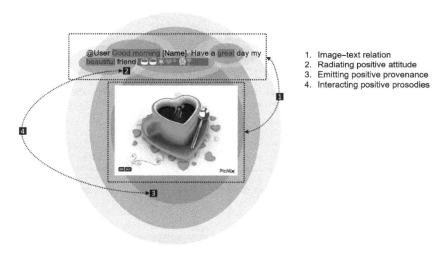

1. Image–text relation
2. Radiating positive attitude
3. Emitting positive provenance
4. Interacting positive prosodies

Figure 9.8 An example of intermodal RESONANCE

generalised [AFFECTION FOR INTERACTANT] bond, realised in turn by a number of discrete couplings including [IDEATION: interactant/ATTITUDE: positive [affect]] and [IDEATION: day/ATTITUDE: positive [appreciation]]. While we imagine this relatively general interpretation of the GIF's semiosis is uncontroversial, a closer analysis of these relations gives us a more detailed account of the semiosis occurring in this post.

Let us begin by considering the ideational relation between emoji and the GIF in more detail. The ongoing looping inherent to GIFs and animated stickers appears to enhance their abstraction, foregrounding their interpersonal meaning and rendering their ideational meaning emblematic of a general state rather than a specific occurrence. We can speculate that this dimension of GIFs' meaning is related to their indeterminate verisimilitude; they are a static image, a frozen snapshot of a specific moment, nor are they a sequence of events unfolding (once) in a conventional order (such as a narrative video text). Thus, they blend depictive reference to the subjects shown in the GIF with the meta-textual awareness provoked by departure from any particular generic schema and the timelessness of infinite repetition. Fan (2022) likens this to visual nominalisation:

What an atelic visual container enables is the cyclic processing of GIF content as visual nominalization: first, a recognition of the process, the participant(s), and the circumstance; next, an attuning to the process in an abstract manner; then, a consideration of the process in relation to the discourse setting the GIF may appear in. (Fan, 2022, p. 49)

Accordingly, in Figure 9.7 we read the hot beverage shown in the GIF not as the literal cup of coffee that the author might be consuming but as an emblem encapsulating positive solidarity with the addressee, as illustrated by the lines relating the GIF's elements to other resources for positive attitude. As such, the represented participants in GIFs would seem to background their ideational meaning while foregrounding interpersonal meaning, either implicit or explicit. This links to work on the most common linguistic and graphiconic resources found in greeting texts on social media, which Jovanovic and Jovanovic and van Leeuwen (2018, p. 683) observe can be 'formulaic and ritualistic', as well as directed to a specific addressee, yet playing out in front of an indefinite ambient audience (Reifman et al., 2020). The relationship between how GIFs depict ideational meaning and how they realise interpersonal meaning parallels the similar phenomenon we described as the [emblematise] feature in concurrent ideational emoji–language semiosis (see Chapter 5). Thus, while ideational meaning iconically associated to coffee or mornings is also construed in the GIF shown in Figure 9.7, this is eclipsed by the emblematic use of the figures to signify interpersonal meaning.

Turning now to explicit interpersonal meaning, most obvious is the specific interaction between the heart shaped emoji and the various red hearts in the GIF, as these are both symbols that evoke positive emotion. The sequence of emoji (HOT BEVERAGE, SUN, RED HEART, ROSE, SMILING FACE WITH OPEN HANDS, and HEART EXCLAMATION) at the end of the body of the post also invokes positive meanings that resonate with the positive solidarity enacted by the greeting and linguistic evaluation. In terms of the emoji–text relations that we have covered in this book, the emoji in culminative position interpersonally coalesce with the general positivity of the greeting ('*Good morning*'), as well as the positive [appreciation] ('*great*', '*beautiful*') (highlighted in dark grey). As noted above, the superficially ideational [figures] within the GIF are also emblematically realising interpersonal meaning. The sparkling of the silver embellishment evokes opulence and decoration associated with celebration, as well as carrying undertones of the kitschy, baroque ornamentation representative of unrestrained emotion. These features gather and amplify both the specific heart shaped emoji and the other emoji and linguistic resources construing positive attitude in the body of the post. This, combined with the GIF's Information value as the New of the text and its salience, serves to foreground interpersonal meaning across the entire post. The radiation of interpersonal meanings evoked by the GIF is illustrated metaphorically via the ripples of grey shading in Figure 9.8, which are intended to represent the way that the interpersonal meaning localised in each resource in the post radiates across either the body or entire post.

This post is part of a longer interaction that is saturated with positive ATTITUDE (Figure 9.9).

Text (9.2)   @{User 2} Good morning {name}. ☺ ☀ ☕ 🍸 [GIF]

Text (9.3)   @{User 1} Good morning {name}. Have a great day my beautiful friend.☺ ☺ ☀ ♥ ♦ ☺ 🍸 [GIF]

Text (9.4)   @{User 2} Thank you ☺ you do the same 🍸

The parallels in how interpersonal meaning saturates the verbiage and the GIFs in individual posts across this exchange indicates COMMUNING

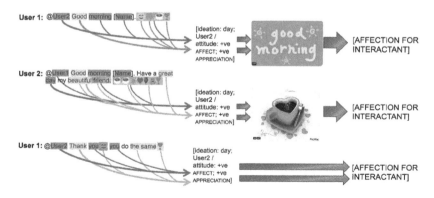

Figure 9.9 A Twitter interaction saturated with positive ATTITUDE (light grey) targeting IDEATION (dark grey)

AFFILIATION among the interactants. Figure 9.9 illustrates how couplings are realised across modes with ideational meaning shown as dark grey and attitudinal meaning as light grey (with resources realising both shaded as medium grey). The thickness of the arrows connecting resources realising related meanings shows how more specific but less salient meaning made by individual linguistic and emoji resources accumulates and percolates as the post unfolds, climaxing in the GIFs. These ideational and interpersonal meanings repeatedly realise [IDEATION: interactant/ATTITUDE: positive [affect]] and [IDEATION: day/ATTITUDE: positive [appreciation]] couplings, which in turn table and rally around a shared [AFFECTION FOR INTERACTANT] bond.

The analysis of this example shows how GIFs distil the dominant couplings of linguistic and emoji co-text, presenting a visual tableau that iconically or emblematically represents the main bond being negotiated in a social media post. In doing so, they inevitably simplify any more detailed meaning made in the co-text, privileging amplified interpersonal meaning and currency within the economy of intertextual references over the complexity of more richly grammaticalised resources. As Beckett (2016) states:

With limited power to persuade or demonstrate, the animated GIF's rhetoric is primarily epideictic. GIFs form the primary figures for the encomia of signal boosting and the vituperations of call-out culture. Reaction GIFs and their relatives overwhelmingly function as glib dismissals, enthusiastic assents, or loud expressions of incomprehension, designed to appeal to audience presumed to already agree with the GIF user's premises and prejudices.

A further dimension of how GIFs and stickers contribute to the meanings of the posts wherein they occur is that they can represent a kind of 'semiotic gift'. This conceptualisation is primarily informed by the effort required to insert graphicons into a post; this is a process that usually requires a dedicated software application to be downloaded onto a device, and then a menu of potential graphicons must be navigated until a selection is made. Of course, once an individual is familiar with the process it can be conducted quickly and easily, but it nonetheless involves a greater number of steps than the use of linguistic or emoji resources alone. As such, part of the interpersonal meaning realised by graphicons resides in their recipient's knowing that their sender undertook these extra steps in order to embellish their message. In turn, this converges with their visual salience and their richly embroidered aesthetics to further amplify the overall interpersonal meanings realised in a post.

A second example showing a similar pattern of GIFs flattening and amplifying the dominant couplings and bonds realised in the co-text can be seen in Text (9.5) to Text (9.7) and Text (9.8) to Text (9.9).

Text (9.5)   @{User} **Good Morning** {name} ☕ ☀ Hope you have a fun filled Saturday [*image of a planter box with flowers*]

Text (9.6)   @{User} Good morning {name} and Happy Thursday!!! Hope you have a great day!! ☕ ☺ ☕ [GIF of a sparkling sunrise with the words 'Good Morning' on the sun rising from the ocean]

Text (9.7)   @{User} Good morning {name}. Have a beautiful day my lovely friend. ☕ ☺ ✳ 🌹 😊 ♥ 🌸 ✳ [*GIF of the words 'June' decorated with a loop of flower designs*]

As these examples suggest, the images and GIFs tend to embroider the positive meanings aired in the greeting that tend to be directed to particular users via vocatives that either name the addressee or employ a term of endearment (e.g. '*sweetheart*' in Text (9.8)).

Text (9.8)   **User 1:** Good morning sweetheart 🐦 ☕ ☺ [GIF featuring a small, animated bird, cup of coffee with animated steam, moving gold hearts, and sparkles in front of a bouquet of red roses (as shown in Figure 9.10)].

Text (9.9)   **User 2:** Beautiful thank you my sister. 🌹 🙏

A final dimension of GIFs that should be addressed is how they can be used to realise self-referential, meta-textual meaning that riffs on their amplified, embroidered aesthetics. This use stands in contrast to the instances described above, where the typically positive interpersonal meaning is earnest. Thus, while a GIF may be used to express a relatively obvious attitudinal meaning, it can also express layered meanings: 'similar to double entendre, parody, camp, and other types of layered texts, GIFs can be (and often are) used to communicate hidden meanings in plain sight' (Miltner & Highfield, 2017, p. 2).

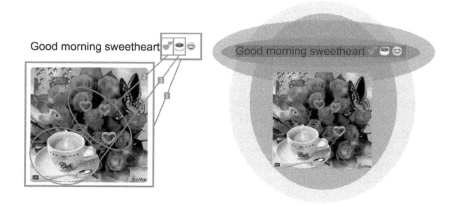

Figure 9.10 An example of a GIF saturated with emblems of positive attitude

We will conclude our analysis with GIFs related to the 3-gram 'in the morning', another common pattern in the corpus. Let us examine a final GIF where the iconisation of coffee is visually unpacked. In Text (9.10), the HOT BEVERAGE emoji and the GIF of a man sipping a drink from a mug are both involved in making meanings about coffee inducing alertness in the morning.

> Text (9.10)   There is no cup of coffee ☕ as satisfying as the first cup in the morning. I think cuz I'm always hungry and slightly thirsty. [GIF with the Alt Text: A person with wide eyes]

The GIF is a snippet from a film sequence featuring the US comedian Rodney Dangerfield, who is the main visual participant. Dangerfield is sipping what appears to be a cup of coffee, and when he finishes his mouthful, he reels around with a dizzy, wide-eyed facial expression, as shown in Figure 9.11. The full filmic sequence in fact portrays Dangerfield snorting sugar, taking a mouthful of instant coffee and then a sip of what is probably hot water from the cup, humorously making a coffee by combining these ingredients in his mouth. In addition to the humorous absurdity of the action, the sequence equates coffee drinking to illicit drug use through the inhaling of the sugar as if it is a line of cocaine. The GIF itself does not include the deconstructed coffee sequence, instead only representing the process of receiving a jolt of alertness after the first sip of a coffee.

The main emoji–text relation in Text (9.10), from an ideational perspective, is the [illustration] relation between the HOT BEVERAGE emoji and the complex nominal group, '*no cup of coffee as satisfying as the first cup in*

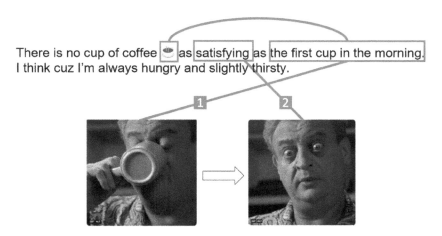

Figure 9.11 Intermodal emoji–co-text-GIF relations incorporating a bonding icon

the morning'. This emoji–text relation is itself illustrated through the text-GIF relation (relation 1 in Figure 9.11) and occurs through the visual representation of the activity sequence (drinking and reacting to a beverage). In terms of interpersonal meaning, the HOT BEVERAGE emoji and the linguistic [thing entity] (*'first cup in the morning'*) are both the target of the positive [appreciation] (*'satisfying'*). Accordingly, the GIF functions to both illustrate this state and to echo its positive evaluation. The latter function relies on recognising the humorous facial expression as an emblem of the state of increased alertness resulting from coffee consumption. It also relies on recognising the positive resonance of coffee as a bonding icon, whereby coffee is associated with alertness, and by extension with hard work and/or resisting fatigue. These broadly positive associations of productivity and endurance coordinate with the inscribed positive affect of '*satisfying*', thus the GIF in this post serves to foreground the bond tabled across modes of [GOOD COFFEE]. In turn, this bond is rallied around across the responses in Text (9.11) and Text (9.12).

Text (9.11)   Love me a #HOKKaccino in the morning!☕ [link to telegram] [image of latte art of a dog or cat]

Text (9.12)   Note to self #243: Don't start reading @ChristinaLauren's The Soulmate Equation at 10pm when you have editing to do in the morning. 4 hours sleep.☕

9.5   Conclusion

In this chapter, we have attempted to draw on the analytic principles elaborated across this book to describe, in somewhat less technical terms, how a variety of graphiconic resources are coordinating with language to realise meaning in social media posts. We have looked beyond the primary focus of previous chapters – intermodal semiosis between emoji and language – to explore some of the multitude of multimedia modes that increasingly occur alongside language in social media, including GIFs, stickers, and images. We have also attempted to give the reader a sense of how a social semiotic intermodal approach furnishes a flexible toolkit with which an analyst can approach a text, drawing on frameworks as needed to explain what meaning is being made and how.

Accordingly, a primary observation made in our analysis of the role of graphicons and images in social media posts is the relevance of layout, described through the multimodal systems of Information value and salience adapted from Kress and van Leeuwen (2006). These systems account for how graphicons such as GIFs and Stickers often realise a salient New of the posts wherein they occur, thereby foregrounding the meanings they realise. Furthermore, accounting for this textual dimension of intermodality allows for particular affiliation dynamics, such as the formation of networks of shared support for social bonds through the personalisation of generic templates.

While these observations may well be valid, we acknowledge that the analysis of graphiconic modes presented here is preliminary at best, and that, while we hope the models we propose might be of use, substantial further research of how graphicons interact with other modes to realise meaning is warranted. Indeed, given the efflorescence in multimodality across platforms and devices, we anticipate that this project will be an enduring one, fascinating and frustrating researchers for years to come. One such emergent intermodal relation that we noted but did not address, and perhaps the most novel frontier (at the time of writing) in multimodal social media posts, is the use of paralanguage in combination with animated and video texts on platforms such as Instagram and TikTok. This includes animated stickers and GIFs which can be layered over a video text for a particular duration and can move around the frame as the text unfolds. In combination with the video text (and the filters, effects, spoken language and music that might accompany it), these animated graphicons afford a truly kaleidoscopic landscape of meaning potential. In this same category of interactions we can place the relations between a video text and various face filters or Animoji on platforms such as Snapchat or iOS devices. While noting their semiotic complexity, we have not attempted to explore these kinds of texts in any depth, as they merit more focused attention than we might afford them here. We will, however, observe that in video-based platforms where we see visual modification either through digital stickers or within the video via particular kinds of gestures, these are, to a certain extent, agnate 'to the way emoji developed as an augmentation of text-based online communication' (Rettberg, 2017, p. 1). Thus, while the interaction among particular modes will yield new meaning potentials, the underlying principles that govern what meaning can be made remain constant, whether it be a HOT BEVERAGE emoji in a tweet or an animated sticker in a TikTok video.

10 Conclusion

10.1 Introduction

This book has explored how emoji coordinate with linguistic meanings in social media posts, as well as their important role in how social bonds are negotiated. The semiotic flexibility of emoji makes them powerful meaning-making resources capable of enacting this dual function – they are underspecified enough to make concrete and figurative meanings with their co-text and to support a range of types of affiliation strategies. In the early chapters we have focused on systematically defining and analysing the kinds of textual (organising text), ideational (construing experience) and interpersonal (enacting relationships) functions that emoji traverse as they interact with linguistic meanings in social media posts. Ever-present in our minds was the potential pitfall of over-privileging language and relegating emoji to some ornamental or auxiliary function at the margins of semiosis (Dreyfus, Hood, & Stenglin, 2011). With meaning as our fundamental concern, the co-construal and co-patterning of language and emoji becomes accessible even where the complexity can seem intractable.

Our key concern in this book has been the thorny issue of how to account for the ways that written language and emoji combine to make meaning. In order to address this issue, we not only needed to employ a principled approach to theorising meaning but also an understanding of how semiotic resources coordinate with each other to forge meaning. Drawing on systems for discourse analysis developed within Systemic Functional Linguistics for understanding the language with which emoji coordinate, we explored three forms of emoji–text CONVERGENCE: textual SYNCHRONICITY, ideational CONCURRENCE, and interpersonal RESONANCE. By way of reminding the reader of the details of these relations, the full system network is presented in Figure 10.1. In Chapters 4 to 6 we used this network to undertake detailed textual analysis of the ways in which emoji and their co-text converge to make meanings. This analysis revealed how such CONVERGENCE makes possible meanings that would not be possible with language alone. In social semiotic terms, CONVERGENCE allows users to 'mean more, mean new kinds of meanings never before meant and not otherwise mean-able' (Lemke, 1998, p. 92).

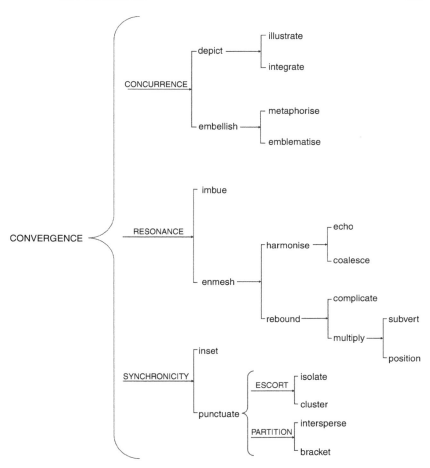

Figure 10.1 The system of emoji–text CONVERGENCE

Following on from this exploration of emoji–text CONVERGENCE, we showed how emoji are adaptable enough to not only coordinate with their co-text but to support the play of bonds in both interactive and broadcast contexts. To explore emoji's role in social bonding, we drew on technicality developed in social semiotic work on ambient affiliation, that is, research into how social bonds are negotiated or communed around in digital discourse. We traced the ways in which emoji can augment the interactive tabling and response to IDEATION–ATTITUDE couplings discursively realising social bonds through DIALOGIC AFFILIATION. We also examined their role in supporting

COMMUNING AFFILIATION even where a tabled bond receives no reply. In this case we observed the significant work that emoji do in boosting, buttressing and marshalling audiences around tabled bonds. Given how important visual meanings are to social media discourse in terms of their move towards 'image centricity' (Stöckl et al., 2020), in Chapter 9 we considered the role of graphicons such as GIFs in terms of their coordination with emoji, concluding that when we extend our framework to these resources we need to account for their relative visual salience and position in a text's layout compared to text and emoji. Accordingly, we noted how meanings across a post are both summarised and simplified by these graphiconic resources.

Further to our theoretical framework and the results of our analysis, this book also provides an appliable analytical approach that may be of use to other researchers. To carry out our analysis, we have employed a mixed methodology of corpus and discourse analysis, aiming to marry description of broad trends in emoji use with more detailed exploration of individual texts. Our application of corpus tools prompted us to grapple with a variety of challenges posed by emoji to existing corpus tools, especially with regards to handling emoji sequences. In response to these challenges, we proposed a number of solutions that other researchers might adopt or further develop to advance corpus work on emoji and other special characters. For our discourse analysis of emoji texts we employed the software WebAnno, which allowed for efficient and consistent annotation coding for both individual features and relations among these. Combined, these two approaches have allowed us to navigate our dataset, identifying both patterns and individual instances that illustrate the various features and relations we describe throughout this book.

The intricate semiotic nature of emoji as they interact with language in social media texts highlights their significance in the creation of meaning. However, their exponential rise in popularity across diverse linguistic and cultural domains and the rapid proliferation in their number and variety, coupled with their technical interdependence on the particular affordances of mobile digital devices, operating systems, and social media platforms, makes their semiosis something of a Gordian knot to unravel. In spite of this, they have elicited substantial scholarly interest that has made productive inroads in explaining how they make meaning alongside language. This book has aimed to advance this project by proposing a social semiotic theoretical framework that comprehensively accounts for emoji semiosis and systematically describes the relationship between emoji and language meanings. Where appropriate, we have attempted to incorporate relevant work in this field with the aim of both benefitting from its insights and foregrounding points of intersection between systemic functional linguistics and other linguistic approaches. Of course, we cannot presume that ours will be the definitive work on emoji–language semiosis, and we hope that the framework elaborated here might be of use to future scholars further advancing the study of this subject. In particular, as noted in Chapter 9 with regards to graphiconic resources beyond emoji, we will be intrigued to see how models developed to describe the interaction between language and emoji might be adapted and extended to account for the multimodal meanings made by the many new and mushrooming permutations of memes, GIFs, stickers, Animoji, and formats that have yet to be named. Both the fertility of the social media landscape as a crucible of new ways to make meaning and the energy of the scholarly community engaged in its study suggest this will be an exciting and challenging field for years to come.

10.2   Bringing It All Together

We are cognisant that in this book we brought to bear a significant amount of linguistic technicality from the field of Systemic Functional Linguistics in our analysis of emoji–text relations. This has included drawing on existing systems for analysing discourse semantics developed by Martin within this discipline (e.g. Martin, 1992; Martin & Rose, 2003; Martin & White, 2005). In addition, as well as developing our own system network for analysing CONVERGENCE relations, we have drawn on networks for analysing AMBIENT AFFILIATION, based on Zappavigna's research into bonding on social media (e.g. Zappavigna, 2012, 2018). Accordingly, in order to bring all of this together in a way that may be helpful to readers who are from adjacent fields and may not be avid users of this kind of linguistic analysis, we thought it would be helpful to work through a more complete analysis of a Twitter thread example to show how it might be deployed. We will also take this as an opportunity to underscore or comment on particular regions of our framework as we apply them, and to make more general observations about patterns we have observed in our data. We will begin in Section 10.2.1 by applying the three systems for describing emoji–text CONVERGENCE: SYNCHRONICITY, CONCURRENCE, and RESONANCE. Then in Section 10.2.2 we will extrapolate from these descriptions how emoji are coordinating with language to affiliate around particular value bonds, and thus how differing value communities are represented in the excerpt. We also remind the reader that we have included a glossary that explains the technical terms that have been used throughout the book.

At the time of writing this conclusion in 2022, Twitter has recently been acquired by controversial billionaire, Elon Musk. This has generated widespread concern about the future of the platform, given Musk's comments regarding 'free speech' and the significant amount of labour that social media services needed to undertake to prevent the proliferation of misinformation and hate speech on their sites. Musk fired a large proportion of Twitter employees and, concerningly, abandoned its previous policies aimed at regulating COVID-19 misinformation. In response to this upheaval many Twitter employees have been resigning and posting about their thoughts and feelings in goodbye tweets featuring the emoji SALUTING FACE 🫡 and BLUE HEART 💙. We take a thread of these tweets as an example with which to exemplify the analytical framework we have developed in this book. The original post in this thread is Text (10.1), which clearly aims to mock Elon Musk in terms of the opinion it presents as indicative of the view of the Twitter engineers (@twittereng).

Text (10.1)   From:@twittereng
               To:@elonmusk
               Subject: [Figure 10.2]

This post included the GIF in Figure 10.2, which is a sequence from the US television sitcom series *The Big Bang Theory* about a group of science geeks. The GIF displays the character Sheldon Cooper waving with the caption 'GOODBYE' at the bottom of the frame. The original author's post is followed by a thread of employees' farewell messages to which the original author replies with the SALUTING FACE 🫡 emoji (see Exchange 10.1). The emoji sequence SALUTING FACE and BLUE HEART 🫡 💙 accrued particular meaning in the many farewell posts and their respective threads.

Exchange 10.1

Text (10.2)   **Original poster:** guess I just said goodbye to the ghost of
               my dream job forever? 🫡 🫡 💙 Tweeps, you are world-class
               #LoveWhereYouWorked #OneTeam 🐦 #NoTeam

       Text (10.3)   **Original poster:** Deciding to quit was a tough choice but it
                      was the right one for me. Very proud of the work we did on
                      Embeds and will always love seeing Tweets in the news

Figure 10.2 A 'goodbye' GIF included in a popular tweet about leaving Twitter

Text (10.4)   **User 1:** 🤍 🤍 🤍 You deserve so much more than to have been treated like this. Sorry that things have imploded. ☹️ I hope wherever you are next brings joy and a supportive atmosphere.

Text (10.5)   **User 2:** Sending you so much love name, let me know if I can help with anything🤍 🤍

Text (10.6)   **User 3:** 🥺 Good luck with what's next.

Text (10.7)   **User 4:** 🤍 proud of *you*!

Text (10.8)   **User 5:** 🥺

Text (10.9)   **User 6:** 🤍

Text (10.10)   **User 7:** 🥺

Text (10.11)   **User 8:** 🤍 🥺

Text (10.12)   **User 9:** Your ass got fired.😂

Text (10.13) **User 10:** Solidarity.🤍

Text (10.14) **User 11:** 'Solidarity' [GIF of clowns dancing in a circle]

Text (10.15) **User 12:** Huge loss for Twitter😌

Text (10.16) **User 13:** It'll muddle through somehow, I'm sure.😌

Text (10.17) **User 14:** 🙄

Text (10.18) **User 15:** 😂😂😂

Text (10.19) **User 16:** This sucks, this isn't how dream jobs should end🤍

Text (10.20) **User 17:** Isn't it creepy how they talk about themselves as a world class team etc? They have done a terrible job. 7000 people, and THIS is what they done? #OneTeam 🤡 #noteam

Text (10.21) **User 18:** You'll be missed, thanks for being a positive spirit in the london office, making us laugh and pull together when needed🤍

Text (10.22) **User 19:** It was tooooo short🥺

Text (10.23) **User 20:** 🥺

Text (10.24) **User 21:** Am sorry, name! 🤍 If there is anything I can do, am here for you.

Text (10.25) **User 22:** I think she's looking for a job😂

Text (10.26) **User 23:** She can speak for herself, doesn't need you for directions so🤡

Text (10.27)   **User 24:** Why do you all look exactly the same? ☺
[image of Elon Musk holding a baby with the face of
a crying democratic supporter used in many memes
mocking left wing voters]

Text (10.28)   **User 25:** New world class eng just dropped ✦

Text (10.29)   **Original poster:** ☁

Text (10.30)   **User 26:** So sorry. Cheering you onward to happier times. ♥

Text (10.31)   **User 27:** I'm sure there's plenty of openings elsewhere for
election manipulators. Good luck ☺

Text (10.32)   **User 28:** ☺

Text (10.33)   **User 29:** I am beyond grateful for the time I've had on this
bird app. I never realized how many people were behind
making sure this thing ran efficiently. Already, just in the
past two weeks we've seen the cracks beginning to form in
the foundation. You will be missed. ☺

Text (10.34)   **User 30:** You can always learn to code as your next job ☺

Text (10.35)   **User 31:** ♥ so sorry the dream had to end like this

Text (10.36)   **User 32:** 🥀

Text (10.37)   **User 33:** ♡

Text (10.38)   **User 34:** ☺

Text (10.39)   **User 35:** I'm so deeply sad for you ☺

Text (10.40)   **User 36:** ♡ ♡ ♡ ♡ ♡ I'm really sorry

Text (10.41)   **User 37:** Bye bye 🦋 🦋 🦋 🦋 🦋

Text (10.42)   **User 38:** I'm so sorry ♥

10.2.1   Emoji–Text Coordination: SYNCHRONICITY, CONCURRENCE, and RESONANCE

The posts shown in Exchange 10.1 are only an excerpt of the replies (and
replies to replies, etc.) to the original post that contained emoji, but they are
illustrative of the major ideational and interpersonal meanings made in the
thread. Moreover, it is a stretch of social media discourse long enough to conduct a review of the system networks elaborated across Chapters 4 to 6 and
illustrate their features with examples. To this end, let us begin by examining
how emoji and language synchronise to make textual meaning, drawing on the
descriptions laid out in Chapter 4.

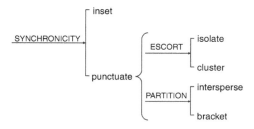

Figure 10.3 The system of emoji–text SYNCHRONICITY

At the first level of delicacy within the system of emoji–text SYNCHRONICITY (Figure 10.3) we have the distinction between [inset] and [punctuate]. Across the excerpt, [inset] appears to be the marked choice, with the only example occurring in Text (10.26), where the SHUSHING FACE emoji 🤫 substitutes a process word such as 'shush' or 'shut up' to complete the grammar of the linguistic co-text. In terms of [punctuate] features, the most common combination in the excerpt is [cluster]/[intersperse]. This reflects the repeated use of emoji to both mark the end of a clause and to summarise the main interpersonal meaning made in the post, corresponding with Danesi's (2016) adjunctive function or Ai et al.'s (2017) supplementary relation between language and emoji. Examples of this can be seen in Text (10.5), Text (10.15), Text (10.21), Text (10.34), and Text (10.39). Across these examples, emoji fall at the end of the post where they replace a full stop, and summarise linguistic attitude in the co-text, often a blend of negative [affect] for the original poster's resignation and positive [affect] for the original poster themselves. Text (10.21) exemplifies this: '*You'll be missed, thanks for being a positive spirit in the london office, making us laugh and pull together when needed* 💜.'

Text (10.4) is noteworthy here as it constitutes an example of [cluster] where the emoji sequence 💜 💜 💜 occurs at the beginning of the text, and because it is the only example containing an instance of [isolate]/[intersperse]. Here the DISAPPOINTED FACE emoji 😞 refers backwards to the negative [affect] in the linguistic co-text '*Sorry that things have imploded.*' Across the excerpt, there were no instances of [bracket].

While a dedicated corpus study would be required to confirm this observation, it bears mentioning that across our dataset, where emoji were inset the emoji tended to realise primarily ideational meaning, whereas instances of [punctuate] were more oriented to interpersonal meaning. We might interpret this as reflecting the different relations ideational and interpersonal meaning realised by emoji have to their surrounding co-text. Ideational emoji tend to respond to co-text to specify their grammatical function, thus in Text (10.26), the 🤫 emoji is constrained to an imperative form of the process 'be quiet' or 'shush' by the lexicogrammar of the clause within which it occurs. Conversely, interpersonal emoji tend to colour longer stretches of discourse with attitudinal meaning, thus in Text (10.21), the 💙 emoji interacts with various linguistic resources for interpersonal meaning targeting the original poster and the Twitter community. Of course, emoji realising primarily interpersonal meaning can also be inset so as to stand-in for a specific lexical item, and emoji realising primarily ideational meaning can summarise the broader filed of a text; moreover, as we have repeatedly argued over the course of this book, emoji frequently construe both ideational and interpersonal meaning. However, as we bring this book to a close, it seems appropriate to offer some commentary on the broader patterns we have observed over the course of our analysis, if for no other reason than to give readers suggestions for future avenues of enquiry.

In terms of the significance of this pattern, we might speculate that these two functions could correspond with the different intermodal timeframes that govern the relation of embodied paralanguage with spoken language (Ngo et al., 2021). Thus, part of the affordance of ideational paralanguage, construed primarily through gestures of the hands and arms simultaneously with spoken lexis spanning ideational [elements], is realised by inset ideational emoji that literally take the place of written lexis. Conversely, part of the affordance of interpersonal paralanguage, construed primarily by voice quality and facial expressions that accompany stretches of language spanning whole clauses, is realised by emoji that punctuate written language. As such, emoji might be seen as compensating for the absence of embodied paralanguage in written registers. Historically, this relative poverty of affordance may not have been as perceptible as these registers tended to comprise formal tenors and technical fields (consider especially the domains of written text before universal literacy) where the expressivity of embodied paralanguage would not have been as appropriate, but as digital technology and mobile devices have become ubiquitous, writing has become the default or even the preferred mode in many informal, everyday registers too.

Turning now to ideational meaning, the most evident pattern across the excerpt is the concurrence between the SALUTING FACE 🫡 emoji and the processes associated with leaving a workplace. Ideational meaning associated with Twitter was also co-realised by use of the #ONETEAM 🐦 hashflag, which references the community of Twitter employees and to a lesser extent the BLUE HEART 💙 emoji, which references the blue colour of the Twitter logo.

In terms of the specific features of emoji–language concurrence described in Chapter 5 (Figure 10.4), the majority of emoji realising ideational meaning in the excerpt fall into the [embellish] branch of the system network, as they realise ideational meaning that is incongruent with that realised by the linguistic co-text. One exception occurs in Text (10.26), where the

SHUSHING FACE emoji 🤫 realises the [occurrence element] in the [occurrence figure] co-realised with the linguistic text; as such this constitutes an instance of [depict: integrate]. A further exception comprises instances where the #ONETEAM 🌸 hashflag converges with references to the Twitter community, such as in Text (10.2), where it serves to illustrate the linguistic reference to '*Tweeps*'; this is typically a vernacular term for a Twitter user's followers, but in this case, given the solipsistic nature of using a social media platform to announce resignation from that platform to the community of followers on that platform which includes other employees at that platform, '*Tweeps*' is interpreted as a reference to the community of Twitter employees.

Returning to the SALUTING FACE 🫡 emoji, this occurs both in instances of [metaphorise] and [emblematise]. In the original poster's first post (Text (10.2)), we can see how 🫡 metaphorically concurs with the [occurrence figure] 'saying goodbye' by referencing the provenance of military salutes. Salutes carry connotations of respect and admiration, and are also customarily given at military funerals, where service women and men 'bid farewell' to their deceased comrades in arms while paying tribute to their service in the armed forces. As such, an emoji depicting one gestural element of a specific type of ceremony is used metaphorically to refer to a meaning associated with that ceremony in other contexts: in this instance, the original poster is saying goodbye to their colleagues at Twitter. Of course, the possible reference to military funerals is also heavily loaded with interpersonal meaning; this will be discussed below.

Due to the repeated use of the SALUTING FACE 🫡 emoji to index the activity of saying goodbye across the excerpt and indeed across many threads of announcements of resignation from Twitter, we would argue that this emoji has become emblematic of a specific set of cultural meanings associated with Twitter's change in management and employee resignations. Ideationally, the 🫡 emoji emblematises not only the process of a Twitter employee resigning

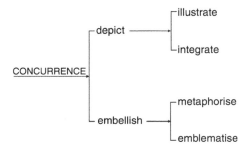

Figure 10.4 The system of emoji–text CONCURRENCE

but also the wider field of conflict between broadly left-wing media practices aimed at curtailing misinformation and hate speech and broadly right-wing media practices who privilege freedom of speech. As such, in this exchange the typically more general reference to respect and saying goodbye that is metaphorically evoked by the SALUTING FACE 🫡 emoji has become emblematic of Twitter resignation announcements, to the point where individual posts comprising solely this emoji can be interpreted as realising a specific set of meanings related to this context. As with the interpersonal dimension of the metaphorise description above, a large portion of the 🫡 emoji's emblematic meanings are also interpersonal and will be discussed presently as we describe how features of emoji–text resonance are realised in the excerpt.

Turning now to interpersonal meaning described by the RESONANCE system network (Figure 10.5), at the first layer of delicacy we can observe that the majority of instances of emoji realising interpersonal meaning in the excerpt fall into the [enmesh] branch of options, as they interact with linguistic interpersonal resources. The clearest exception occurs in Text (10.34), where the SMILING FACE WITH SMILING EYES 😊 emoji realises generalised positive attitude that imbues the ideational [relational figure] in the linguistic co-text: '*You can always learn to code as your next job.*'

Within the [enmesh] branch, the excerpt illustrates a combination of [harmonise] and [complicate] features, reflecting how emoji are used both to reinforce the polarity and coordinate closely with more specific attitude features of the linguistic co-text, and to introduce alternate or discordant interpersonal meanings. Examples of [harmonise: echo] can be seen in Text (10.4), Text (10.5), Text (10.15), Text (10.39), and Text (10.42). Looking more closely at

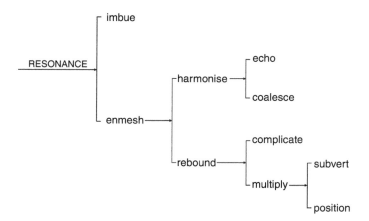

Figure 10.5 The system of emoji–text RESONANCE

Text (10.4), we can see how the opening sequence of three BLUE HEART
💙 💙 💙 emoji echoes the implicit positive [judgement] of '*You deserve so
much more than to have been treated like this*', and the PENSIVE FACE 😔
emoji echoes the negative [affect] of '*Sorry that things have imploded.*' The
SALUTING FACE 🫡 emoji also occurs in a number of instances of [echo]. In
both the original post (Text (10.2)) and Text (10.33), 🫡 echoes the positive [af-
fect] directed at the referent in the preceding co-text of the post: '*my dream job*'
and '*you*', respectively. The excerpt did not contain any exemplary instances of
the [harmonise: coalesce] feature as there were no sequences of diverse emoji
at the end of posts. However Text (10.5) illustrates the defining principle of
emoji–language interaction in this feature, as the sequence of 💙 emoji that
conclude the post consolidates and summarises both instances of positive ATTI-
TUDE found in the preceding co-text: the inscribed positive [affect] of '*Sending
you so much love*' and the invoked positive [affect] of '*let me know if I can help
with anything*'.

Emoji coordinating with language to realise the [enmesh: rebound] feature
functioned chiefly to expand on the messages of solidarity with the original
poster or to mock them. The former can be seen across instances of [rebound:
complicate], where emoji serve to add positive attitude targeting the original
poster to a post expressing negative attitude for their leaving Twitter, or vice-
versa. For example, in Text (10.35), the BLUE HEART 💙 emoji establishes
positive attitude targeting the original poster, while the linguistic co-text '*so
sorry the dream had to end like this*' construes negative [affect] targeting the
circumstances of their resignation. Conversely, in Text (10.6) the CRYING
FACE 😢 emoji realises negative attitude targeting the original poster's resignation while the linguistic co-text '*Good luck with what's next*' construes positive
[affect] targeting the original poster. A further instance of [rebound: compli-
cate] occurs in Text (10.12) and functions to mock the original poster. Here
the FACE WITH TEARS OF JOY 😂 emoji indexes the post's author's positive
attitude targeting the implicit negative [affect] realised in the linguistic co-text:
'*Your ass got fired*'.

An example of [rebound: subvert] occurs in Text (10.16) and illustrates
how emoji that realise a meta-commentary function can reverse the interpersonal meaning construed in the linguistic co-text. Here the linguistic co-text
realises an invoked negative [appreciation] of Twitter's ability to operate after
the original poster's resignation, '*It'll muddle through somehow, I'm sure*',
which would suggest the commenter evaluates the original poster as a valuable
employee. However the FACE WITH TEARS OF JOY 😂 emoji that follows
the linguistic co-text reveals its ironic tone, confirming that the commenter in
fact means that Twitter will not suffer from the original poster's resignation,
and thus that the original poster was not an especially valuable employee.
Other posts where emoji index a laughter response such as Text (10.18) and

Text (10.36) can also be interpreted as instances of [rebound: subvert]; however, in these cases the absence of linguistic co-text within the post requires their interpretation in the context of the surrounding posts in the exchange, which we will proceed to discuss in the following section where we address affiliation resources.

Finally, in Text (10.27) we can see an example of the last feature in the RESONANCE system: [position]. Here the question realised in the linguistic co-text '*Why do you all look exactly the same?*' constitutes a resource for heteroglossic expansion, whereby the post acknowledges potential perspectives that might answer this question. Thus the THINKING FACE 😕 emoji coordinates with the linguistic co-text to confirm this dialogic positioning.

Returning to the use of the SALUTING FACE 🫡 emoji noted in the discussion of the [emblematise] feature of emoji–text concurrence, the interpersonal dimension of this emoji's emblematic meaning accrues cumulatively as it is repeatedly used in the excerpt. By evoking the general context of military salutes and referencing more specifically the use of these salutes at funerals, the emoji is loaded with a suite of interpersonal meaning ranging from positive evaluation for the entity being saluted, positive [appreciation] for the institutional context the poster and the entity are part of, and negative evaluation for the entity's departure. As we will see in the description of how bonds are negotiated across this excerpt in the following section, these meanings are referenced and recovered across uses of this emoji to signal particular affiliative stances.

Stepping out of the close analysis of this excerpt to reflect on broader patterns noted across the datasets examined in this book, a salient observation is that insofar as emoji are limited in number, mostly grammatically under-committed (i.e. they cannot be inflected for tense, modalisation, etc.), and not formally defined in dictionaries or thesauruses, they appear to be more sensitive to patterns of collocation than language is. This can be seen in the rapid establishment of 🫡 as signifying a blend of positive [affect] targeting an addressee and negative [affect] targeting their departure in this excerpt, which will be expanded on in the following section on affiliation. Similar examples, however, include many of the surprising or even taboo usages of otherwise innocuous seeming emoji, such as the infamous EGGPLANT 🍆 or PEACH 🍑. What strikes us as noteworthy about these usages is that precisely because emoji have such a broad meaning potential and are not syntagmatically bound to linguistic co-text, they afford a greater degree of creative possibility, which we might compare to the kind of linguistic creativity termed poetic or figurative. Consider the origins of the use of the PEACH 🍑 to symbolise a person's backside: we can assume that this association was born out of use in texts where the emoji's innuendo was unmistakable, and that it was motivated both by the absence of emoji more literally depicting bottoms, and by the very loose similarity in shape between a bottom and a peach. What is surprising about this association, however (again, dedicated corpus work would be required to confirm this), is that PEACH 🍑 emoji's foregrounded region of meaning has shifted from a fruit to a backside. This can only be explained as a response to the overwhelming collocative patterning of this emoji's use in contexts where it is used for this purpose. Of course, language is capable of similar adaptations or even reversals in meaning, as the emergence of slang terms connoting positive evaluation such as 'sick' or 'wicked' attests. Emoji, however, appear to multiply avenues for incongruous meanings and compress the time needed to travel them, producing highly specific vernaculars of emoji use within particular communities.

10.2.2   Emoji and Affiliation

The description of emoji–text convergence in the previous section allows us to make a principled analysis of how emoji are making meaning in coordination with language. However, the full value of this type of analysis is best illustrated when these meanings are coded as couplings that in turn enact social bonds, and when the negotiation of these bonds among interactants is interpreted through the AMBIENT AFFILIATION framework. But before proceeding to the analysis of DIALOGIC AFFILIATION that can be observed among interactants in this excerpt, it is worth considering how the original post realises features of the COMMUNING AFFILIATION system. This may seem an unproductive exercise as, after all, the post was replied to, thus the affiliation resources it realises are best described by the DIALOGIC AFFILIATION system. However, until it received its first reply, the post was simply broadcast to the Twitter audience and thus realised COMMUNING AFFILIATION features. Moreover, by beginning with a COMMUNING AFFILIATION analysis and then progressing to DIALOGIC AFFILIATION for the same text, we can identify points of intersection between the systems that are not so easily seen in typical analyses. We will include the original post here again for ease of reference:

Text (10.2)   guess I just said goodbye to the ghost of my dream job forever? 😢 😢 💙
               Tweeps, you are world-class #LoveWhereYouWorked #OneTeam 🐦
               #NoTeam

In terms of the CONVOKE branch of COMMUNING AFFILIATION resources, the original post realises the [marshal] feature by explicitly naming the community being invited to rally around bonds ('*Tweeps*'). The [designate] feature is realised intermodally through the interaction between the BLUE HEART 💙 emoji, the #Oneteam hashflag 🐦 and the two hashtags, '*#OneTeam*' and '*#NoTeam*'. In coordination with linguistic resources that positively evaluate Twitter employees ('*you are world-class*'), these CONVOKE features specify the community whom the original poster is inviting to affiliate around the bond [TWITTER EMPLOYEE SOLIDARITY].

From the FINESSE branch we can find instances of both [embellish: buttress] and [embellish: spurn]. The [embellish: buttress] feature is realised in relation to the [GOOD OLD TWITTER] bond enacted by '*the ghost of my dream job*', which positively evaluates the original poster's work at Twitter until the change in management. Both the SLAUTING FACE ☺ emoji and '*#LoveWhereYouWorked*' hashtag buttress this bond by referencing bonds associated with the process of saying goodbye to positively evaluated entities, and positive [affect] for past workplaces more generally. The [embellish: spurn] feature is realised by the '*#Noteam*' hashtag, which obliquely references an email sent by Elon Musk to Twitter employees on 16 November 2022, inviting them to click 'Yes' in the email body if they agreed to his proposed new work culture. Twitter employees that rejected this proposal and thus did not click 'Yes' dubbed themselves 'team no', hence the hashtag. Thus the '*#Noteam*' hashtag negates and spurns an implicated [GOOD NEW TWITTER] bond.

Within this post, the [up-scaled] positive evaluation of '*world-class*' serves to [PROMOTE: foster: boost] the [GOOD OLD TWITTER] bond. Complementarily, the up-scaled graduation construed by the repetition of the SALUTING FACE ☺ emoji and the emoji sequence's convergence with linguistically construed positive evaluations serves to realise an instance of [foster: enrich] targeting the [GOOD OLD TWITTER] bond. As with the corpus more generally, this post did not contain any examples of [PROMOTE: modulate]. In summary, across this post we have COMMUNING AFFILIATION resources inviting the audience to rally around the [TWITTER EMPLOYEE SOLIDARITY] and [GOOD OLD TWITTER] bonds and reject a [GOOD NEW TWITTER] bond. As we will see in the DIALOGIC AFFILIATION analysis that follows, this opening broadcast of ambient bonds maps onto the patterns of bonds rallied around by responders to the post.

The original post (Text (10.2)) establishes the main bonds that are negotiated across the remainder of the excerpt. In turn, these bonds are enacted by a number of couplings. The first we encounter is the original poster's positive evaluation for their job at Twitter, inscribed by the linguistic co-text '*dream job*' and the hashtag '*#LoveWhereYouWorked*'; this can be coded as the coupling: [IDEATION: [thing entity] (job at Twitter)/ATTITUDE: positive [appreciation]/[affect]]. We can extrapolate this as contributing to negative evaluation for the original poster's resignation: [IDEATION: [occurrence figure] (original poster's resignation)/ATTITUDE: negative [affect]]. We then also have positive evaluation for the community of Twitter employees, realised linguistically via '*Tweeps, you are world-class*', via the '*#Oneteam*' hashtag and accompanying 🌐 hashflag, and via the SALUTING FACE ☺ ☺ and

BLUE HEART ♥ emoji.[1] This yields the coupling: [IDEATION: [thing entity] (Twitter colleagues)/ATTITUDE: positive [judgement]]. Finally, we have a somewhat more implicit coupling realised by the '*#NoTeam*' hashtag. As noted above, this hashtag references the rejection of the proposed new Twitter work culture; accordingly, we can code this hashtag as realising the coupling: [IDEATION: [thing entity] (Elon Musk's proposed Twitter culture)/ATTITUDE: negative [appreciation]].

The first and most evident bond in this post refers to solidarity within the community of Twitter employees and is enacted by the couplings: [IDEATION: [occurrence figure] (original poster's resignation)/ATTITUDE: negative [affect]] and [IDEATION: [thing entity] (Twitter colleagues)/ATTITUDE: positive [judgement]]. We will label this bond as [TWITTER EMPLOYEE SOLIDARITY]. The second bond has to do with Twitter's historic work culture, and is enacted by the [IDEATION: [thing entity] (job at Twitter)/ATTITUDE: positive [appreciation]/[affect]] and [IDEATION: [thing entity] (Elon Musk's proposed Twitter culture)/ATTITUDE: negative [appreciation]] bonds. We will label this bond as [GOOD OLD TWITTER]. The original poster goes on in Text (10.3) to table a further set of bonds labelled as [NECESSARY RESIGNATION] and [TWITTER ACCOMPLISHMENT PRIDE].

The first response from another user occurs in Text (10.4); here, the BLUE HEART emoji ♥ and linguistic co-text '*you deserve so much more*' realise the coupling [IDEATION: [thing entity] (original poster)/ATTITUDE: positive [judgement]], which serves to table a bond of solidarity with the original poster that we will label [OP SOLIDARITY] (note we have initialised 'original poster' to 'OP'). User 1 goes on to negatively evaluate the change in management at Twitter: '*Sorry that things have imploded.* ☹', which tables a bond that we label [BAD NEW TWITTER].

The following seven posts rally around the [OP SOLIDARITY] bond, in some cases enacted via intermodal couplings of emoji and text, but in others enacted solely by emoji. This latter enactment can be seen in Text (10.8), Text (10.9), Text (10.10), and Text (10.11), where emoji index either generalised negative attitude (e.g. CRYING FACE 😢), generalised positive attitude (e.g. PURPLE HEART 💜, BLUE HEART 💙) or a combination of positive and negative attitude realised metaphorically and emblematically via SALUTING FACE 🫡. What is noteworthy here is how in the context of the exchange, our interpretation of emoji is informed by their use in preceding posts, and by the couplings and bonds of the discourse more generally. Thus, based on the use of emoji hearts alongside linguistic co-text that positively evaluates the original poster, we abduce that the generalised positive attitude realised by the

---

[1] The '#Oneteam' hashtag and 🐦 hashflag refer to the 2020 Twitter #Oneteam conference.

PURPLE HEART 💜 or BLUE HEART 💙 emoji in the absence of linguistic co-text in posts Text (10.9) and Text (10.11) targets the original poster, rather than another ideational target (such as their resignation, which would suggest a rejection of the [OP SOLIDARITY] bond). As such we can begin to see how emoji semiosis is sensitive not only (and primarily) to linguistic resources in their immediate co-text but also to patterns in their usage at expanding scales of discourse.

The co-textual and intertextual mimesis of particular emoji is even more clearly illustrated by the emblematisation of the SALUTING FACE 🫡 noted in the previous section. As discussed, in isolation this emoji evokes the provenance of military service, referencing in particular respect among military personnel and for military institutions, and a combination of admiration and regret for fallen comrades in arms. As instantiated in this excerpt, however, this emoji reflects a suite of meanings drawn from the discourse context of Elon Musk's takeover of Twitter and the ensuing exodus of Twitter employees. Where the SALUTING FACE 🫡 emoji occurs, the surrounding co-text is both infused with meanings associated with military salutes, and the emoji itself is loaded with meanings surrounding the conflict between Musk and Twitter's staff. This process most likely began before the thread shown in the excerpt occurred, and is referenced by the original poster with their use of the SALUTING FACE 🫡 emoji in Text (10.2). In the context of this excerpt, in Text (10.2) the emoji is associated to resignation from Twitter, and thus the process of reciprocal infusion begins: Twitter colleagues are likened to comrades in arms, and resignation from Twitter (presumably following irreconcilable conflicts with the new management) is likened to death in battle. In turn, these associations amplify the solemnity of the [TWITTER EMPLOYEE SOLIDARITY] bond. From here, each successive use of the emoji crystalises this association, with numerous posts (Text (10.10), Text (10.23), and Text (10.40)) comprising solely this emoji, and yet referencing the bonds established in Text (10.2). Thus, we can see how an emoji that evokes a particular provenance can be associated to a different context within a particular discourse setting, and how that association can quickly be taken up and reinforced by other users who wish to express shared community affiliation. Of course, we would also assume that as easily as these associations precipitate, they might also dissipate; however, this micro-example of emoji porously transferring meanings from their provenance to their local context and vice-versa gives us some insight into how more enduring incongruent associations emerge.

Returning to our examination of the bonds negotiated in the excerpt, in Text (10.12) we encounter our first example of a user disaffiliating from the original poster. The main linguistic indicator of this is the description of the original poster's departure from Twitter as their getting '*fired*', the transitivity of which implies it was the company's decision to terminate employment rather than that of the original poster, and thus by extension that the original poster had in some way failed in their professional capacity. The FACE WITH TEARS OF JOY 😂 emoji at the end of this post serves to signal that the poster finds the meaning of the co-text amusing; thus collectively language and emoji are realising the coupling [IDEATION: [occurrence figure] (original poster's loss of job)/ATTITUDE: positive], which in the context of the exchange serves to reject the [OP SOLIDARITY] bond shared in previous posts and table an [OP CRITICISM] bond.

A further instance of disaffiliation occurs in Text (10.16). This post responds to the rallied [OP SOLIDARITY] bond and tabled [BAD NEW TWITTER] bond in a previous post: '*Huge loss for Twitter* 😂', which in turn responds to the original post. In Text (10.16), the linguistic co-text ironically portrays Twitter as negatively impacted by the original poster's resignation, realised primarily via the negative connotations of the term '*muddle*'. The FACE WITH TEARS OF JOY 😂 emoji that follows, however, signals that this portrayal is not intended seriously; rather the poster is suggesting that Twitter will be minimally affected or might even benefit from the original poster's departure. The role of the 😂 here is thus different to Text (10.12), as rather than indicating positive attitude targeting a negative situation, in Text (10.16) the emoji is indicating that linguistically realised negative attitude is not intended seriously. In terms of affiliation, however, Text (10.16) aligns with Text (10.12) insofar as it is rejecting the [OP SOLIDARITY] bond. Moreover, Text (10.16) also [defers] the [BAD NEW TWITTER] bond tabled by the original poster and tables an alternative, [GOOD NEW TWITTER] bond.

The bonds identified above are then negotiated over the remainder of the excerpt (see Table 10.1), and can be quite clearly divided into two, opposing networks of bonds, represented visually in Figure 10.6. In these networks we can tentatively include ambient bonds (shown as connected via dotted arrows) that are relevant to but not explicitly realised in the excerpt, such as the aforementioned [MORAL RESPONSIBILITY OF SOCIAL MEDIA] and [PRIVILEGING FREEDOM OF SPEECH] bonds. We might extrapolate related bonds all the way to broader ideological beliefs loosely congruent with progressive/left wing and conservative/right wing politics too. Naturally, these broader bond networks are speculative and in no way comprehensive; however, we hope that by including these we can illustrate how affiliation analysis of particular stretches of discourse can be interpreted in the context of broader social and cultural meanings.

Returning to our earlier description of AMBIENT AFFILIATION resources in the post, we can see how the original poster's invitation to rally around the [TWITTER EMPLOYEE SOLIDARITY] and [GOOD OLD TWITTER] bonds and reject the [GOOD NEW TWITTER] bond intersects with the bond

Table 10.1 *Twitter resignation excerpt affiliation summary*

Text #	Post Author	Post	Bonds
Text (10.2)	**Original poster:**	guess I just said goodbye to the ▼ghost of my dream job forever? 😢 😢 💜 Tweeps, you are world-class #LoveWhereYouWorked #OneTeam 🐦 #NoTeam	[table] × [TWITTER EMPLOYEE SOLIDARITY] [table] × [GOOD OLD TWITTER]
Text (10.3)	**Original poster:**	Deciding to quit was a tough choice but it was the right one for me. Very proud of the work we did on Embeds and will always love seeing Tweets in the news	[table] × [TWITTER EMPLOYEE SOLIDARITY] [table] × [GOOD OLD TWITTER] [table] × [NECESSARY RESIGNATION] [table] × [TWITTER ACCOMPLISHMENT PRIDE]
Text (10.4)	**User 1:**	💜 💜 💜 You deserve so much more than to have been treated like this. Sorry that things have imploded. 😢 I hope wherever you are next brings joy and a supportive atmosphere.	[table] × [OP SOLIDARITY] [table] × [BAD NEW TWITTER]
Text (10.5)	**User 2:**	Sending you so much love {name}, let me know if I can help with anything💜 💜	[rally] × [OP SOLIDARITY]
Text (10.6)	**User 3:**	😢 Good luck with what's next.	[rally] × [OP SOLIDARITY]
Text (10.7)	**User 4:**	💜 proud of *you*!	[rally] × [OP SOLIDARITY]
Text (10.8)	**User 5:**	😢	[rally] × [OP SOLIDARITY]
Text (10.9)	**User 6:**	💜	[rally] × [OP SOLIDARITY]
Text (10.10)	**User 7:**	😢	[rally] × [OP SOLIDARITY]
Text (10.11)	**User 8:**	💜 😢	[rally] × [OP SOLIDARITY]
Text (10.12)	**User 9:**	Your ass got fired.😂	[reject] × [OP SOLIDARITY] [table] × [OP CRITICISM]
Text (10.13)	**User 10:**	Solidarity.💜	[rally] × [OP SOLIDARITY]
Text (10.14)	**User 11:**	'Solidarity' [GIF of clowns dancing in a circle]	[reject] × [OP SOLIDARITY]
Text (10.15)	**User 12:**	Huge loss for Twitter😢	[rally] × [OP SOLIDARITY] [table] × [BAD NEW TWITTER]
Text (10.16)	**User 13:**	It'll muddle through somehow, I'm sure.😂	[reject] × [OP SOLIDARITY] [defer] × [BAD NEW TWITTER] [table] × [GOOD NEW TWITTER]

Table 10.1 (*cont.*)

Text #	Post Author	Post	Bonds
Text (10.17)	**User 14:**	☹	[dismiss] × [OP SOLIDARITY] [dismiss] × [BAD NEW TWITTER]
Text (10.18)	**User 15:**	😂 😂 😂	[defer] × [OP SOLIDARITY] [defer] × [BAD NEW TWITTER] [rally] × [GOOD NEW TWITTER]
Text (10.19)	**User 16:**	This sucks, this isn't how dream jobs should end🤍	[rally] × [GOOD OLD TWITTER] [rally] × [BAD NEW TWITTER]
Text (10.20)	**User 17:**	Isn't it creepy how they talk about themselves as a world class team etc? They have done a terrible job. 7000 people, and THIS is what they done? #OneTeam 🐦 #noteam	[reject] × [OP SOLIDARITY] [reject] × [GOOD OLD TWITTER] [table] × [BAD OLD TWITTER]
Text (10.21)	**User 18:**	You'll be missed, thanks for being a positive spirit in the london office, making us laugh and pull together when needed🤍	[rally] × [OP SOLIDARITY]
Text (10.22)	**User 19:**	It was tooooo short☹	[rally] × [OP SOLIDARITY]
Text (10.23)	**User 20:**	🥲	[rally] × [OP SOLIDARITY]
Text (10.24)	**User 21:**	Am sorry, {name}! 🤍 If there is anything I can do, am here for you.	[rally] × [OP SOLIDARITY]
Text (10.25)	**User 22:**	I think she's looking for a job😬	[reject] × [OP SOLIDARITY] [rally] × [OP CRITICISM]
Text (10.26)	**User 23:**	She can speak for herself, doesn't need you for directions so🙄	[dismiss] × [OP CRITICISM]
Text (10.27)	**User 24:**	Why do you all look exactly the same? 😶 [image of Elon Musk holding a baby with the face of a crying democratic supporter used in many memes mocking left wing voters]	
Text (10.28)	**User 25:**	New world class eng just dropped✨	[rally] × [OP SOLIDARITY]
Text (10.29)	**Original poster:**	🫂	[table] × [USER 25 AFFECTION]
Text (10.30)	**User 26:**	So sorry. Cheering you onward to happier times.🤍	[rally] × [OP SOLIDARITY]

Table 10.1 (*cont.*)

Text #	Post Author	Post	Bonds
Text (10.31)	**User 27:**	I'm sure there's plenty of openings elsewhere for election manipulators. Good luck	[reject] × [OP SOLIDARITY] [reject] × [GOOD OLD TWITTER]
Text (10.32)	**User 28:**		[rally] × [OP SOLIDARITY]
Text (10.33)	**User 29:**	I am beyond grateful for the time I've had on this bird app. I never realized how many people were behind making sure this thing ran efficiently. Already, just in the past two weeks we've seen the cracks beginning to form in the foundation. You will be missed.	[rally] × [GOOD OLD TWITTER] [rally] × [TWITTER EMPLOYEE SOLIDARITY] [rally] × [BAD NEW TWITTER] [rally] × [OP SOLIDARITY]
Text (10.34)	**User 30:**	You can always learn to code as your next job	[rally] × [OP SOLIDARITY]
Text (10.35)	**User 31:**	so sorry the dream had to end like this	[rally] × [OP SOLIDARITY]
Text (10.36)	**User 32:**		[reject] × [OP SOLIDARITY]
Text (10.37)	**User 33:**		[rally] × [OP SOLIDARITY]
Text (10.38)	**User 34:**		[rally] × [OP SOLIDARITY]
Text (10.39)	**User 35:**	I'm so deeply sad for you	[rally] × [OP SOLIDARITY]
Text (10.40)	**User 36:**	I'm really sorry	[rally] × [OP SOLIDARITY]
Text (10.41)	**User 37:**	Bye bye	[reject] × [OP SOLIDARITY]
Text (10.42)	**User 38:**	I'm so sorry	[rally] × [OP SOLIDARITY]

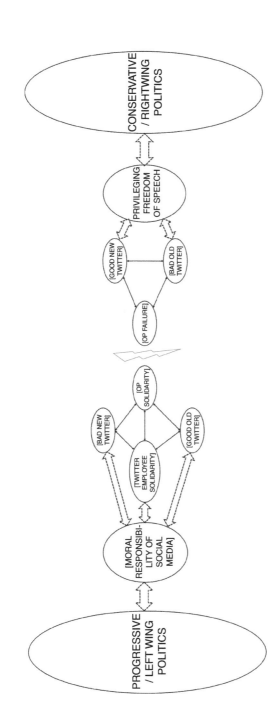

Figure 10.6 Opposing bond networks negotiated in excerpt

networks realised by responding posters' comments. Those who align with the original poster by tabling or rallying around the [OP SOLIDARITY] bond also rally around the [TWITTER EMPLOYEE SOLIDARITY] and [GOOD OLD TWITTER] bonds, while those who table or rally around the [OP FAILURE] bond reject the ambient bonding invitations in the original post. Thus, analysing the affiliation occurring in this excerpt allows us to identify not only the bonds and community memberships negotiated dialogically by interactants, but also how these reflect the original post's broadcast bonds.

10.3   Conclusion

As a concluding note, beyond the theoretical and analytical contributions we have offered in this book, the work we have undertaken underscores the crucial role that linguists might play as emoji and other forms of digital paralanguage increase in cultural prominence. Dürscheid and Meletis (2019, p. 181) have noted the importance of linguists working within the Unicode Consortium: 'Not only do linguists have valuable insight into questions concerning the use of written language, but specialists in the field are also aware of the far-reaching sociolinguistic consequences of the introduction of digital writing in a given community.' There is currently only one linguist working in the consortium, Dr Deborah Anderson, who is a member of the Script Encoding Initiative (SEI). Given the centrality of graphiconic resources to meaning-making in an expanding range of text genres, including some with great public safety and health implications such as online sex-trafficking (Whitney et al., 2018) and illicit drug promotion (Moyle et al., 2019), a principled understanding of their semiosis is essential. Moreover, we would argue that graphicons, especially due to their prominence in social media, need to be included in institutional literacy curricula, so as to equip learners with the necessary understanding to navigate their use. As such, we conclude this book with a general appeal against marginalisation or minimisation of emoji, either as inconsequential semiotically, or limited in terms of the communities or genres they affect; these cute little stylised images are powerful resources for meaning-making, and herald an era of digital discourse where written language is only one among many modes converging to give texts meaning.

References

Abel, J. E. (2019). Not everyone's: or, the question of emoji as 'universal' expression. In E. Giannoulis & L. R. A. Wilde (Eds), *Emoticons, Kaomoji, and Emoji* (pp. 25–43). London: Routledge.

Abercrombie, D. (1968). Paralanguage. *British Journal of Disorders of Communication*, *3*(1), 55–59.

Adami, E., & Jewitt, C. (2016). Special Issue: Social media and visual communication. *Visual Communication*, *15*(3), 263–270.

Ai, W., Lu, X., Liu, X., Wang, N., Huang, G., & Mei, Q. (2017). *Untangling emoji popularity through semantic embeddings*. Paper presented at the Eleventh International AAAI Conference on Web and Social Media, May 15–18, 2017, Montreal, Quebec, Canada.

Al-Rawi, A. (2022). Hashtagged trolling and emojified hate against Muslims on social media. *Religions*, *13*(6), 521.

Al-Rawi, A., Siddiqi, M., Morgan, R., Vandan, N., Smith, J., & Wenham, C. (2020). COVID-19 and the gendered use of emojis on Twitter: infodemiology study. *Journal of Medical Internet Research*, *22*(11). https://www.jmir.org/2020/11/e21646/.

Albert, G. (2020). Beyond the binary: Emoji as a challenge to the image-word distinction. In C. Thurlow, C. Dürscheid, & F. Diémoz (Eds), *Visualizing Digital Discourse* (pp. 65–80). Berlin: De Gruyter Mouton.

Allison, M. (2020). 'So long, and thanks for all the fish!': urban dolphins as ecofascist fake news during COVID-19. *Journal of Environmental Media*, *1*(1). https://intellect discover.com/content/journals/10.1386/jem_00025_1?crawler=true#.

Arviv, E., & Tsur, O. (2021). How to do things without words: modeling semantic drift of emoji. *arXiv preprint* https://arxiv.org/abs/2110.04093.

Baker, P. (2006). *Using Corpora in Discourse Analysis*: New Orleans, IN: A&C Black.

Barbieri, F., Camacho-Collados, J., Ronzano, F. et al. (2018). *Semeval 2018 task 2: multilingual emoji prediction*. Paper presented at the Proceedings of The 12th International Workshop on Semantic Evaluation June, 2018, New Orleans.

Beckett, C. (2016). The rhetoric of the loop: animated gifs and documentary film. *FLOW*. http://www.flowjournal.org/2016/10/the-rhetoric-of-the-loop/, accessed on October 2, 2023.

Bednarek, M. (2009). *Corpora and discourse: a three-pronged approach to analyzing linguistic data*. Paper presented at the Selected Proceedings of the 2008 HCSNet Workshop on Designing the Australian National Corpus, Somerville, MA.

Berard, B. (2018). I second that emoji: the standards, structures, and social production of emoji. *First Monday*, *23*(9). https://doi.org/10.5210/fm.v23i9.9381

Bick, E. (2020). Annotating emoticons and emojis in a German-Danish social media corpus for hate speech research. *RASK–International Journal of Language and Communication*, *52*, 1–20. https://portal.findresearcher.sdu.dk/en/publications/annotating-emoticons-and-emojis-in-a-german-danish-social-media-c

Cappallo, S., Svetlichnaya, S., Garrigues, P., Mensink, T., & Snoek, C. G. (2018). New modality: emoji challenges in prediction, anticipation, and retrieval. *IEEE Transactions on Multimedia*, *21*(2), 402–415.

Cohn, N., Engelen, J., & Schilperoord, J. (2019). The grammar of emoji? Constraints on communicative pictorial sequencing. *Cognitive Research: Principles and Implications*, *4*(1), 33.

Collins, L. C. (2020). Working with images and emoji in the Dukki Facebook Corpus. In S. Rüdiger & D. Dayter (Eds), *Corpus Approaches to Social Media* (Vol. 98, pp. 175–196). Amsterdam: John Benjamins.

Częstochowska, J., Gligorić, K., Peyrard, M. et al. (2022). *On the context-free ambiguity of emoji*. Paper presented at the Proceedings of the International AAAI Conference on Web and Social Media, June 6–9, Atlanta, Georgia.

Dabkowski, M., & Bai, J. (2016). *Proposal for a PRETZEL emoji*. https://unicode.org/L2/L2016/16374-pretzel-emoji.pdf, accessed on October 2, 2023.

Dainas, A., & Herring, S. (2021). Interpreting emoji pragmatics. In C. Xie, F. Yus, & H. Haberland (Eds), *Internet Pragmatics: Theory and Practice* (pp. 107–144). Amsterdam; Philadelphia: John Benjamins Publishing Company.

Dancygier, B., & Vandelanotte, L. (2017). Internet memes as multimodal constructions. *Cognitive Linguistics*, *28*(3), 565–598.

Danesi, M. (2016). *The Semiotics of Emoji: The Rise of Visual Language in the Age of the Internet*. New York: Bloomsbury Publishing.

Daniel, J. (2021). The most frequently used emoji of 2021. https://home.unicode.org/emoji/emoji-frequency/, accessed on October 2, 2023.

Das, A. (2021). How has the coronavirus (COVID-19) pandemic affected global emoji usage? *Journal of Human Behavior in the Social Environment*, *31*(1–4), 425–434.

Davis, M., & Edberg, P. (2018). Unicode Technical Standard# 51: Unicode Emoji, Version 12.0. *The Unicode Consortium*. http://www.unicode.org/reports/tr51/tr51-15.html, accessed on October 2, 2023.

De Seta, G. (2018). Biaoqing: the circulation of emoticons, emoji, stickers, and custom images on Chinese digital media platforms. *First Monday*, *23*(9). https://doi.org/10.5210/fm.v23i9.9391

Djonov, E., & van Leeuwen, T. (2018). Social media as semiotic technology and social practice: the case of ResearchGate's design and its potential to transform social practice. *Social Semiotics*, *28*(5), 641–664.

Doran, Y. J. (2019). Academic formalisms: toward a semiotic typology. In Y. J. Doran, J. R. Martin & Giacomo Figueredo (Eds), *Systemic Functional Language Description* (pp. 331–358). New York: Routledge.

Doran, Y. J., Martin, J. R., & Zappavigna, M. (2024). *Affiliation and Systemic Functional Linguistics: Negotiating Community*. London: Equinox.

Dresner, E., & Herring, S. (2010). Functions of the nonverbal in CMC: emoticons and illocutionary force. *Communication Theory*, *20*(3), 249–268.

Dresner, E., & Herring, S. (2014). Emoticons and illocutionary force. In G. S. Dana Riesenfeld (Ed.), *Perspectives on Theory of Controversies and the Ethics of Communication* (pp. 81–90). Dordrecht: Springer.

Dreyfus, S., Hood, S., & Stenglin, M. (Eds). (2011). *Semiotic Margins: Meaning in Multimodalities*. London: Continuum.

Dürscheid, C., & Haralambous, Y. (2021). Emojis are everywhere: how emojis conquer new contexts. *Grapholinguistics and Its Applications*, (4), 501–512.

Dürscheid, C., & Meletis, D. (2019). Emojis: a grapholinguistic approach. In Y. Haralambous (Ed.), *Grapholinguistics and Its Applications*, (Vol. 1), pp. 167–183. Brest: Fluxus Edition.

Eggins, S., & Slade, D. (1997/2005). *Analysing Casual Conversation*. New York; London: Cassell.

Eisner, B., Rocktäschel, T., Augenstein, I., Bošnjak, M., & Riedel, S. (2016). *Learning emoji representations from their description*. Paper presented at the Proceedings of The Fourth International Workshop on Natural Language Processing for Social Media, Austin, TX, USA, November 1, 2016.

Emojipedia®. (n.d.). Eyes emoji. https://emojipedia.org/eyes/, accessed on October 2, 2023.

Escouflaire, L. (2021). Signaling irony, displaying politeness, replacing words: the eight linguistic functions of emoji in computer-mediated discourse. *Lingvisticæ Investigationes*, *44*(2), 204–235.

Etaywe, A., & Zappavigna, M. (2022). Identity, ideology and threatening communication: An investigation of patterns of attitude in terrorist discourse. *Journal of Language Aggression and Conflict*, *10*(2), 315–350.

Fan, Y. (2022). Analyzing the semiotic nature of GIFs: visual nominalization and visual telicity. *Language and Semiotic Studies*, *8*(3), 45–65.

Fernández-Gavilanes, M., Juncal-Martínez, J., García-Méndez, S., Costa-Montenegro, E., & González-Castano, F. J. (2018). Creating emoji lexica from unsupervised sentiment analysis of their descriptions. *Expert Systems with Applications*, *103*, 74–91. https://www.sciencedirect.com/science/article/pii/S0957417418301222

Fitzpatrick, T. B. (1988). The validity and practicality of sun-reactive skin types I through VI. *Archives of Dermatology*, *124*(6), 869–871.

Gawne, L., & Daniel, J. (2021). *The past and future of hand emoji*. Paper presented at the Proceedings of the 4th International Workshop on Emoji Understanding and Applications in Social Media, June 7–8, 2021, Atlanta, GA, United States.

Gawne, L., & McCulloch, G. (2019). Emoji as digital gestures. *Language@ Internet*, *17*(2). https://www.languageatinternet.org/articles/2019/gawne

Ge, J. (2019). *Emoji sequence use in enacting personal identity*. Paper presented at the Companion Proceedings of the 2019 World Wide Web Conference, May 13–17, 2019, San Francisco.

Ge, J., & Herring, S. (2018). Communicative functions of emoji sequences on Sina Weibo. *First Monday*, *23*(11). https://doi.org/10.5210/fm.v23i11.9413

Gibson, J. J. (1979). *The Ecological Approach to Perception*. Boston: Houghton Mifflin.

Gibson, W., Huang, P., & Yu, Q. (2018). Emoji and communicative action: the semiotics, sequence and gestural actions of 'face covering hand'. *Discourse, Context & Media*, *26*, 91–99.

Gn, J. (2018). Emoji as a 'language' of cuteness. *First Monday*, *23*(9). https://doi .org/10.5210/fm.v23i9.9396, accessed on October 2, 2023.

Gray, K., & Holmes, S. (2020). Tracing ecologies of code literacy and constraint in emojis as multimodal public pedagogy. *Computers and Composition*, *55*. https:// www.sciencedirect.com/science/article/pii/S875546152030013X

Guibon, G., Ochs, M., & Bellot, P. (2018). *From emoji usage to categorical emoji prediction.* Paper presented at the 19th International Conference on Computational Linguistics and Intelligent Text Processing (CICLING 2018), March 18–24, 2018, Hanoi, Vietnam.

Halliday, M. A. K. (1976). Anti-languages. *American Anthropologist, 78*(3), 570–584.

Halliday, M. A. K. (1978). *Language as Social Semiotic: The Social Interpretation of Language and Meaning.* London: Edward Arnold.

Halliday, M. A. K. (1979). Modes of meaning and modes of expression: types of grammatical structure, and their determination by different semantic functions. In D. J. Allerton, E. Carney, & D. Holdcroft (Eds), *Function Context in Linguistic Analysis: Essays Offered to William Haas* (Vol. 1, pp. 57–79). Cambridge: Cambridge University Press.

Halliday, M. A. K. (1989). *Spoken and Written Language.* Oxford: Oxford University Press.

Halliday, M. A. K., & Hasan, R. (1985). *Language, Context and Text: Aspects of Language in a Social Semiotic Perspective.* Geelong, Victoria: Deakin University Press.

Halliday, M. A. K., & Martin, J. R. (2003). *Writing Science: Literacy and Discursive Power.* London: Routledge.

Halliday, M. A. K., & Matthiessen, C. M. I. M. (1999/2006). *Construing Experience Through Meaning: A Language-Based Approach to Cognition.* London: Cassell.

Halliday, M. A. K., & Matthiessen, C. M. I. M. (2004). *An Introduction to Functional Grammar* (3rd ed.). London: Hodder Education Publishers.

Halliday, M. A. K., & Matthiessen, C. M. I. M. (2014). *An Introduction to Functional Grammar* (4th ed.). London: Routledge.

Hao, J. (2015). *Construing biology: An ideational perspective.* (PhD Thesis). Sydney: University of Sydney. https://ses.library.usyd.edu.au/handle/2123/13955, accessed on October 2, 2023.

Hao, J. (2020). *Analysing Scientific Discourse from a Systemic Functional Linguistic Perspective: A Framework for Exploring Knowledge Building in Biology.* London: Routledge.

Hao, J., & Humphrey, S. (2009). The role of 'coupling' in biological experimental reports. *Linguistics & the Human Sciences, 5*(2). https://www.researchgate.net/publication/270415254_The_Role_of_'Coupling'_in_Biological_Experimental_Reports/citation/download

He, J. (2022). Sharing emotions or/and making allies: emoji's interpersonal function in Chinese social media news comments. *Social Semiotics,* 1–16. https://www.tandfonline.com/action/showCitFormats?doi=10.1080%2F10350330.2021.2025355

Herring, S., & Dainas, A. (2017). *'Nice picture comment!' Graphicons in Facebook comment threads.* Paper presented at the Proceedings of the 50th Hawaii International Conference on System Sciences, January 4–7, 2017, Waikoloa Village, Hawaii.

Herring, S., Dainas, A., & Tang, Y. (2021). *'MEOW! Okay, I shouldn't have done that': factors influencing vocal performance through animoji.* Paper presented at the 15th International AAAI Conference on Web and Social Media, held virtually from June 7 to 10, 2021.

Hood, S. (2010). *Appraising Research: Evaluation in Academic Writing.* New York: Palgrave Macmillan.

Hutchby, I. (2001). Technologies, texts and affordances. *Sociology, 35*(2), 441–456.

Iconfactory. (2022). Twitter emoji. https://design.iconfactory.com/twitter-emoji/, accessed on October 2, 2023.

Inwood, O., & Zappavigna, M. (2021). Ambient affiliation, misinformation and moral panic: negotiating social bonds in a YouTube internet hoax. *Discourse & Communication, 15*(3), 281–307.

Inwood, O., & Zappavigna, M. (2022). A systemic functional linguistics approach to analyzing white supremacist and conspiratorial discourse on YouTube. *The Communication Review,* 25(3–4), 204–234.

Jovanovic, D., & van Leeuwen, T. (2018). Multimodal dialogue on social media. *Social Semiotics, 28*(5), 683–699.

Kaiser, E. (2021). *Focus marking with emoji: on the relation between information structure and expressive meaning.* Paper presented at the Colloque de syntaxe et sémantique á Paris (CSSP), Paris, France, December 9–11, 2021.

Kaiser, E., & Grosz, P. G. (2021). *Anaphoricity in emoji: an experimental investigation of face and non-face emoji.* Paper presented at the Proceedings of the Linguistic Society of America, virtually, January 7–10, 2021.

Katsumata, Y. (2022). How many more emoji do we need? In B. Cammaerts & L. Derand (Eds), *Media@LSE MSc Dissertation Series* (pp. 1–43). London: Media@ LSE, London School of Economics and Political Science.

Katsuno, H., & Yano, C. R. (2002). Face to face: on-line subjectivity in contemporary Japan. *Asian Studies Review, 26*(2), 205–231.

Kehoe, A., & Gee, M. (2019). *Analysing emojis in context in a corpus of Twitter data.* Paper presented at the 8th Biennial International Conference on the Linguistics of Contemporary English, University of Bamberg, Germany, September 26–28, 2019.

Kimura, M., & Katsurai, M. (2017). *Automatic construction of an emoji sentiment lexicon.* Paper presented at the Proceedings of the 2017 IEEE/ACM International Conference on Advances in Social Networks Analysis and Mining, Sydney, Australia, July 31–August 03, 2017.

Knight, N. K. [naomiknight_realestate]. (2022). A Townhouse bright and cheery for your Morning Coffee! https://www.instagram.com/naomiknight%5Frealestate/, accessed on October 2, 2023.

Knight, N. K. (2008). 'Still cool … and American too!': an SFL analysis of deferred bonds in internet messaging humour. In N. Nørgaard (Ed.), *Systemic Functional Linguistics in Use, Odense Working Papers in Language and Communication* (Vol. 29). Odense: Institute of Language and Communication, University of Southern Denmark.

Knight, N. K. (2010a). *Laughing our bonds off: conversational humour in relation to affiliation.* (PhD Thesis). Sydney: University of Sydney. https://ses.library.usyd.edu .au/handle/2123/6656.

Knight, N. K. (2010b). Wrinkling complexity: concepts of identity and affiliation in humour. In M. Bednarek & J. R. Martin (Eds), *New Discourse on Language: Functional Perspectives on Multimodality, Identity, and Affiliation* (pp. 35–58). London: Continuum.

Knight, N. K. (2013). Evaluating experience in funny ways: how friends bond through conversational humour. *Text & Talk, 33*(4–5), 553–574. doi:10.1515/text-2013-0025

Konrad, A., Herring, S., & Choi, D. (2020). Sticker and emoji use in Facebook Messenger: implications for graphicon change. *Journal of Computer-Mediated Communication, 25*(3), 217–235.

Kralj Novak, P., Smailović, J., Sluban, B., & Mozetič, I. (2015). Sentiment of emojis. *PloS One, 10*(12). https://doi.org/10.1371/journal.pone.0144296, accessed on October 2, 2023.

Kress, G. R. (2010). *Multimodality: A Social Semiotic Approach to Contemporary Communication*. London: Routledge.

Kress, G. R., Jewitt, C., Ogborn, J., & Tsatsarelis, C. (2006). *Multimodal Teaching and Learning: The Rhetorics of the Science Classroom*. London: Bloomsbury Publishing.

Kress, G. R., & van Leeuwen, T. (2001). *Multimodal Discourse: The Modes and Media of Contemporary Communication*. London: Edward Arnold.

Kress, G. R., & van Leeuwen, T. (2006). *Reading Images: The Grammar of Visual Design* (2nd ed.). London: Psychology Press.

Lazzini, A., Lazzini, S., Balluchi, F., & Mazza, M. (2022).Emotions, moods and hyperreality: social media and the stock market during the first phase of COVID-19 pandemic. *Accounting, Auditing & Accountability Journal, 35*(1), 199–215.

Lemke, J. L. (1998). Multiplying meaning: visual and verbal semiotics in scientific text. In J. R. Martin & R. Veel (Eds), *Reading Science: Critical and Functional Perspectives on Discourses of Science* (pp. 87–113). London: Routledge.

Li, L., & Yang, Y. (2018). Pragmatic functions of emoji in internet-based communication: a corpus-based study. *Asian-Pacific Journal of Second and Foreign Language Education, 3*(1), 1–12.

Li, M., Guntuku, S., Jakhetiya, V., & Ungar, L. (2019). *Exploring (dis-) similarities in emoji-emotion association on twitter and weibo*. Paper presented at the Companion Proceedings of The 2019 World Wide Web Conference. https://doi.org/10.1371/journal.pone.0144296, accessed on October 2, 2023.

Lieber Milo, S. (2017). *The macro and micro aspects and effects of kawaii*. (PhD). Osaka University.

Lim, S. S. (2015). On stickers and communicative fluidity in social media. *Social Media+ Society, 1*(1), 2056305115578137.

Littlemore, J., & Tagg, C. (2018). Metonymy and text messaging: a framework for understanding creative uses of metonymy. *Applied Linguistics, 39*(4), 481–507.

Liu, F. (2018). Lexical metaphor as affiliative bond in newspaper editorials: a systemic functional linguistics perspective. *Functional Linguistics, 5*(1), 1–14. doi:10.1186/s40554-018-0054-z

Logi, L. (2021). *Impersonation, expectation and humorous affiliation: how intermodal impersonation and linguistic expectation are employed by stand-up comedians to create humour*. (PhD thesis). Sydney: UNSW. https://unsworks.unsw.edu.au/entities/publication/5d9c5bbf-3ace-4085-91d0-49a3c58e3b90

Logi, L., & Zappavigna, M. (2019). Dialogic resources in interactional humour. *Journal of Pragmatics, 153*, 1–14.

Logi, L., & Zappavigna, M. (2021a). Impersonated personae: paralanguage, dialogism and affiliation in stand-up comedy. *HUMOR: International Journal of Humor Research, 34*(3), 339–373.

Logi, L., & Zappavigna, M. (2021b). A social semiotic perspective on emoji: how emoji and language interact to make meaning in digital messages. *New Media & Society*. https://doi.org/10.1177/14614448211032

Logi, L., & Zappavigna, M. (2022). Affiliation: an appliable framework for exploring community and identity in discourse. In D. Caldwell, J. R. R. Martin, & J. S. Knox

(Eds), *Appliable Linguistics and Social Semiotics: Developing Theory from Practice* (pp. 325–340). London: Bloomsbury.

Logi, L., Zappavigna, M., & Martin, J. R. (2022). Bodies talk: modelling paralanguage in Systemic Functional Linguistics. In D. Caldwell, J. R. Martin, & J. S. Knox (Eds), *Developing Theory: A Handbook in Appliable Linguistics and Semiotics* (pp. 487–506). London: Bloomsbury.

Loomis, S. R., Winstein, K., & Lee, J. (2016). Coded hashes of arbitrary images (or: the last frontier of emoji encoding). http://www.unicode.org/L2/L2016/16105-unicode-image-hash.pdf, accessed on February 6, 2023.

Lu, Q. (2019). Computers and Chinese writing systems. In C. Huang, J. Zhuo, & B. Meisterernst (Eds), *The Routledge Handbook of Chinese Applied Linguistics* (pp. 461–482). London: Routledge.

Makki, M., & Zappavigna, M. (2022). Out-grouping and ambient affiliation in Donald Trump's tweets about Iran: exploring the role of negative evaluation in enacting solidarity. *Pragmatics, 32*(1), 104–130.

Martin, J. R. (1992). *English Text: System and Structure*. Amsterdam; Philadelphia: John Benjamins Publishing Company.

Martin, J. R. (2001). Fair trade: negotiating meaning in multimodal texts. In P. Coppock (Ed.) *The Semiotics of Writing: Transdisciplinary Perspectives on the Technology of Writing*, (pp. 311–338). Turnhout, Belgium: Brepols.

Martin, J. R. (2004). Mourning: how we get aligned. *Discourse & Society, 15*(2–3), 321–344.

Martin, J. R. (2008a). Innocence: realisation, instantiation and individuation in a Botswanan town. In A. Mahboob & N. K. Knight (Eds), *Questioning Linguistics* (pp. 32–76). Newcastle: Cambridge Scholars Publishing.

Martin, J. R. (2008b). Intermodal reconciliation: mates in arms. In L. Unsworth (Ed.), *New Literacies and the English Curriculum: Multimodal Perspectives* (pp. 112–148). London: Continuum.

Martin, J. R. (2010). Semantic variation: modelling realisation, instantiation and individuation in social semiosis. In J. R. Martin & M. Bednarek (Eds), *New Discourse on Language: Functional Perspectives on Multimodality, Identity, and Affiliation* (pp. 1–34). New York; London: Continuum.

Martin, J. R. (2011). Multimodal semiotics: theoretical challenges. In S. Dreyfus, S. Hood, & M. Stenglin (Eds), *Semiotic Margins: Meaning in Multimodalities* (pp. 243–270). London: Bloomsbury.

Martin, J. R. (2013). *Systemic Functional Grammar: A Next Step into the Theory-Axial Relations* (第1版. Di 1 ban. ed.). Beijing: Beijing Shi: Gao deng jiao yu chu ban she.

Martin, J. R. (2014). Evolving systemic functional linguistics: beyond the clause. *Functional Linguistics, 1*(1), 3.

Martin, J. R., & Rose, D. (2003). *Working with Discourse: Meaning Beyond the Clause* (1st ed.). London: Continuum.

Martin, J. R., & Rose, D. (2007). *Working with Discourse: Meaning Beyond the Clause* (2nd ed.). London: Bloomsbury.

Martin, J. R., & Stenglin, M. (2006). Materializing reconciliation: negotiating difference in a transcolonial exhibition. In T. Royce & B. W. (Eds), *New Directions in the Analysis of Multimodal Discourse* (pp. 215–238). Mahwah, NJ: Lawrence Erlbaum Associates.

Martin, J. R., & White, P. R. R. (2005). *The Language of Evaluation: Appraisal in English*. Basingstoke: Palgrave Macmillan.

Martin, J. R., & Zappavigna, M. (2019). Embodied meaning: a systemic functional perspective on paralanguage. *Functional Linguistics, 6*(1), 1.

McCulloch, G., & Gawne, L. (2018). *Emoji grammar as beat gestures.* Paper presented at the Proceedings of the 1st International Workshop on Emoji Understanding and Applications in Social Media, Standford, June 25, 2018.

McGrenere, J., & Ho, W. (2000). *Affordances: clarifying and evolving a concept.* Paper presented at the Graphics Interface, May 15–17, Montréal, Québec, Canada.

McIvor, M., & Amesbury, R. (2017). Emoji dei: religious iconography in the digital age. *Bulletin for the Study of Religion, 46*(3–4), 56–61.

McKay, I. (2020). Some distributional patterns in the use of typed laughter-derived expressions on Twitter. *Journal of Pragmatics, 166*, 97–113. https://www.science direct.com/science/article/pii/S0378216620301211

McNeill, D. (1992). *Hand and Mind: What Gestures Reveal About Thought.* Chicago: University of Chicago Press.

Medlock, B., & McCulloch, G. (2016). *The linguistic secrets found in billions of emoji.* Paper presented at the SXSW, March 11–19, Austin, TX.

Miller, H., Thebault-Spieker, J., Chang, S., Johnson, I., Terveen, L., & Hecht, B. (2016). *'Blissfully happy' or 'ready to fight': varying interpretations of emoji.* Paper presented at the Proceedings of the International AAAI Conference on Web and Social Media, May 17–20, 2016, Cologne, Germany.

Miller Hillberg, H., Levonian, Z., Kluver, D., Terveen, L., & Hecht, B. (2018). What I see is what you don't get: the effects of (not) seeing emoji rendering differences across platforms. *Proceedings of the ACM on Human-Computer Interaction, 2*(CSCW), 1–24.

Miltner, K. M. (2020). 'One part politics, one part technology, one part history': racial representation in the Unicode 7.0 emoji set. *New Media & Society 23*(3).

Miltner, K. M., & Highfield, T. (2017). Never gonna GIF you up: analyzing the cultural significance of the animated GIF. *Social Media+ Society, 3*(3).

Miyake, K. (2020). Evolution of emoji and beyond: a diachronic observation of visual representations in Japanese mobile media. 東洋大学人間科学総合研究所紀要 *[Bulletin of the Research Institute for Human Sciences, Toyo University], 22*, 1–15.

Moschini, I. (2016). The 'face with tears of joy' emoji: a socio-semiotic and multi-modal insight into a Japan-America mash-up. *HERMES – Journal of Language and Communication in Business*, (55), 11–25.

Moyle, L., Childs, A., Coomber, R., & Barratt, M. J. (2019). #Drugsforsale: an explor-ation of the use of social media and encrypted messaging apps to supply and access drugs. *International Journal of Drug Policy, 63*, 101–110.

Ngo, T., Martin, J. R., Hood, S., Painter, C., Smith, B. A., & Zappavigna, M. (2021). *Modelling Paralanguage Using Systemic Functional Semiotics: Theory and Application.* London: Bloomsbury Academic.

Norman, D. A. (1988). *The Psychology of Everyday Things.* New York: Basic Books.

O'Halloran, K. (1999). Interdependence, interaction and metaphor in multisemiotic texts. *Social Semiotics, 9*(3), 317–354.

O'Halloran, K. (2004). *Multimodal Discourse Analysis: Systemic Functional Perspectives.* London: Bloomsbury.

Oomori, K., Shitara, A., Minagawa, T., Sarcar, S., & Ochiai, Y. (2020, October). A preliminary study on understanding voice-only online meetings using emoji-based captioning for deaf or hard of hearing users. In Huang Guo Wen (Ed.), *Proceedings of the 22nd International ACM SIGACCESS Conference on Computers and Accessibility* (pp. 1–4). Lisbon: University of Lisbon. https://dl.acm.org/doi/10.1145/3373625.3418032

Page, R., Barton, D., Unger, J. W., & Zappavigna, M. (2014). *Researching Language and Social Media: A Student Guide*. London: Routledge.

Painter, C., & Martin, J. R. (2012). Intermodal complementarity: modelling affordances across verbiage and image in children's picture books. In G. W. Huang (Ed.), *Studies in Systemic Functional Linguistics and Discourse Analysis (III)* (pp. 132–158). Beijing: Higher Education Press.

Painter, C., Martin, J. R., & Unsworth, L. (2013). *Reading Visual Narratives: Image Analysis of Children's Picture Books*. London: Equinox.

Panckhurst, R., & Frontini, F. (2020). Evolving interactional practices of emoji in text message. In Crispin Thurlow, Christa Dürscheid & Federica Diémoz (Eds), *Visualizing Digital Discourse* (pp. 81–103). Berlin: De Gruyter.

Parkwell, C. (2019). Emoji as social semiotic resources for meaning-making in discourse: mapping the functions of the toilet emoji in Cher's tweets about Donald Trump. *Discourse, Context & Media, 30*.

Pavalanathan, U., & Eisenstein, J. (2016). More emojis, less:) The competition for paralinguistic function in microblog writing. *First Monday, 21*(11). https://doi.org/10.5210/fm.v21i11.6879

Pellitteri, M. (2018). Kawaii aesthetics from Japan to Europe: theory of the Japanese 'cute' and transcultural adoption of its styles in Italian and French comics production and commodified culture goods. *Arts, 7*(3), 24.

Pérez-Sabater, C. (2019). Emoticons in relational writing practices on WhatsApp: some reflections on gender. In P. Bou-Franch & P. Garcés-Conejos Blitvich (Eds), *Analyzing Digital Discourse: New Insights and Future Directions* (pp. 163–189). Cham: Palgrave Macmillan.

Reifman, A., Ursua-Benitez, M., Niehuis, S., Willis-Grossmann, E., & Thacker, M. (2020). # HappyAnniversary: gender and age differences in spouses' and partners' Twitter greetings. *Interpersona: An International Journal on Personal Relationships, 14*(1), 54–68.

Rettberg, J. W. (2017). Hand signs for lip-syncing: the emergence of a gestural language on musical.ly as a video-based equivalent to emoji. *Social Media+ Society, 3*(4), 2056305117735751.

Robertson, A., Liza, F. F., Nguyen, D., McGillivray, B., & Hale, S. A. (2021). Semantic journeys: quantifying change in emoji meaning from 2012–2018. *arXiv preprint arXiv:2105.00846*.

Robertson, A., Magdy, W., & Goldwater, S. (2021). Black or white but never neutral: how readers perceive identity from yellow or skin-toned emoji. *Proceedings of the ACM on Human-Computer Interaction, 5*(CSCW2), 1–23.

Rothenberg, M. (2013). Emojitracker. http://www.emojitracker.com/

Royce, T., & Bowcher, W. (Eds). (2007). *New Directions in the Analysis of Multimodal Discourse*. Mahwah, NJ: Lawrence Erlbaum Associates.

Sampietro, A. (2016). Exploring the punctuating effect of emoji in Spanish Whatsapp chats. *Lenguas Modernas, (47)*, 91–113.

Sampietro, A. (2019). Emoji and rapport management in Spanish WhatsApp chats. *Journal of Pragmatics*, *143*, 109–120.

Sampietro, A., Felder, S., & Siebenhaar, B. (2022). Do you kiss when you text? Cross-cultural differences in the use of the kissing emojis in three WhatsApp corpora. *Intercultural Pragmatics*, *19*(2), 183–208.

Sasamoto, R. (2022). Perceptual resemblance and the communication of emotion in digital contexts: a case of emoji and reaction GIFs. *Pragmatics*, *33*(3), 393–417. https://doi.org/10.1075/prag.21058.sas

Seargeant, P. (2019). *The Emoji Revolution: How Technology Is Shaping the Future of Communication*. Cambridge: Cambridge University Press.

Shardlow, M., Gerber, L., & Nawaz, R. (2022). One emoji, many meanings: a corpus for the prediction and disambiguation of emoji sense. *Expert Systems with Applications*, *198*.

Shiha, M., & Ayvaz, S. (2017). The effects of emoji in sentiment analysis. *International Journal of Electrical and Computer Engineering (IJCEE)*, *9*(1), 360–369.

Shonenkov, A., Bakshandaeva, D., Dimitrov, D., & Nikolich, A. (2021). Emojich–zero-shot emoji generation using Russian language: a technical report. *arXiv preprint arXiv*:2112.02448.

Siever, C. M. (2019). 'Iconographetic communication' in digital media: emoji in WhatsApp, Twitter, Instagram, Facebook – from a linguistic perspective. In Elena Giannoulis & Lukas R. A. Wilde (Eds), *Emoticons, Kaomoji, and Emoji* (pp. 127–147). London: Routledge.

Siever, C. M., Siever, T., & Stöckl, H. (2020). Emoji–text relations on Instagram: empirical corpus studies on multimodal uses of the iconographetic mode. In Hartmut Stöckl, Helen Caple & Jana Pflaeging (Eds), *Shifts Toward Image-Centricity in Contemporary Multimodal Practices* (pp. 177–203). London: Routledge.

Solomon, B. (2021). demoji 1.1.0, Version 1.x. https://pypi.org/project/demoji/

Spina, S. (2019). Role of emoticons as structural markers in Twitter interactions. *Discourse Processes*, *56*(4), 345–362.

Stark, L. (2018). Facial recognition, emotion and race in animated social media. *First Monday*. https://doi.org/10.1177/2056305120933285

Steinberg, M. (2020). LINE as super app: platformization in East Asia. *Social Media+ Society*, *6*(2), 2056305120933285.

Stenglin, M. (2008). Interpersonal meaning in 3D space: how a bonding icon gets its 'charge'. In Len Unsworth (Ed.), *Multimodal Semiotics: Functional Analysis in Contexts of Education* (pp. 50–66). London: Bloomsbury.

Stenglin, M. (2012). *Transformation & transcendence: bonding through ritual*. Paper presented at the International Systemic Functional Linguistics Conference, University of Technology, Sydney July 16–20, 2012.

Stöckl, H., Caple, H., & Pflaeging, J. (2020). *Shifts Towards Image-Centricity in Contemporary Multimodal Practices*. London: Routledge.

Sutton, S., & Lawson, S. (2017). *A provocation for rethinking and democratising emoji design*. Paper presented at the Proceedings of the 2017 ACM Conference Companion Publication on Designing Interactive Systems, New York.

Sweeney, M. E., & Whaley, K. (2019). Technically white: emoji skin-tone modifiers as American technoculture. *First Monday*, *24*(7). http://dx.doi.org/10.5210/fm.v24i7.10060

Szenes, E. (2016). *The linguistic construction of business reasoning: Towards a language-based model of decision-making in undergraduate business.* (PhD thesis). Sydney: University of Sydney. https://ses.library.usyd.edu.au/handle/2123/16815, accessed on October 2, 2023.

Szenes, E. (2021). The linguistic construction of business decisions: a systemic functional linguistic perspective. *Language, Context and Text, 3*(2), 335–366.

Tagg, C., & Lyons, A. (2021). Repertoires on the move: exploiting technological affordances and contexts in mobile messaging interactions. *International Journal of Multilingualism, 18*(2), 244–266.

Thurlow, C., Dürscheid, C., & Diémoz, F. (2020). *Visualizing Digital Discourse: Interactional, Institutional and Ideological Perspectives* (Vol. 21). Berlin, Boston: De Gruyter.

Twitter. (2020). Twemoji. https://github.com/twitter/twemoji, accessed on October 2, 2023.

Unicode Consortium. (2020). Emoji ordering, v13.0. https://unicode.org/emoji/charts-13.0/emoji-ordering.html

Unicode Consortium. (2021a). Unicode members. https://home.unicode.org/membership/members/, accessed on October 2, 2023.

Unicode Consortium. (2021b). Unicode Standard. http://www.unicode.org/versions/latest/

Unicode Consortium. (2022a). Emoji names and keywords. https://cldr.unicode.org/translation/characters/short-names-and-keywords

Unicode Consortium. (2022b). Guidelines for Submitting Unicode® Emoji Proposals. https://www.unicode.org/emoji/proposals.html

Unicode Consortium. (2022c). Unicode® Technical Standard #51: Longer Term Solutions. https://unicode.org/reports/tr51/

Unsworth, L. (2006). Towards a metalanguage for multiliteracies education: describing the meaning-making resources of language-image interaction. *English Teaching: Practice and Critique, 5*(1), 55–76.

van Leeuwen, T. (2008). New forms of writing, new visual competencies. *Visual Studies, 23*(2), 130–135.

van Leeuwen, T. (2011). Rhythm and multimodal semiosis. In S. Dreyfus, S. Hood, & M. Stenglin (Eds), *Semiotic Margins: Meanings in Multimodalities* (pp. 168–176). London: Bloomsbury Publishing.

Wallestad, T. J. (2013). Developing the visual language of comics: the interactive potential of Japan's contributions. *Hyōgen Bunka, 7,* 3–12.

White, P. R. R. (2020). Attitudinal alignments in journalistic commentary and social-media argumentation: the construction of values-based group identities in the online comments of newspaper readers. In M. Zappavigna & S. Dreyfus (Eds), *Discourses of Hope and Reconciliation: On JR Martin's Contribution to systemic Functional Linguistics* (pp. 21–49). London: Bloomsbury.

Whitney, J., Jennex, M., Elkins, A., & Frost, E. (2018). *Don't want to get caught? don't say it: the use of emojis in online human sex trafficking ads.* Paper presented at the Proceedings of the 51st Hawaii International Conference on System Sciences.

Wicke, P., & Bolognesi, M. (2020). Emoji-based semantic representations for abstract and concrete concepts. *Cognitive Processing, 21*(4), 615–635.

Wiese, H., & Labrenz, A. (2021). Emoji as graphic discourse markers: functional and positional associations in German WhatsApp® messages. In D. Van Olmen & J.

Šinkūnienė (Eds), *Pragmatic Markers and Clause Peripheries* (pp. 277–302). Amsterdam: John Benjamins.

Wilde, L. R. A. (2019). The elephant in the room of emoji research: or, pictoriality, to what extent? In Elena Giannoulis & Lukas R. A. Wilde (Eds), *Emoticons, Kaomoji, and Emoji* (pp. 171–196). London: Routledge.

Wolny, W. (2016). Sentiment analysis of Twitter data using emoticons and emoji ideograms. *Studia Ekonomiczne, 296*, 163–171.

Yang, X., & Liu, M. (2021). The pragmatics of text-emoji co-occurrences on Chinese social media. *Pragmatics, 31*(1), 144–172.

Yimam, S. M., Gurevych, I., de Castilho, R. E., & Biemann, C. (2013). *Webanno: a flexible, web-based and visually supported system for distributed annotations.* Paper presented at the Proceedings of the 51st Annual Meeting of the Association for Computational Linguistics: System Demonstrations.

Yus, F. (2021). Smartphone communication. Interactions in the app ecosystem. London: Routledge.

Zappavigna, M. (2011). Ambient affiliation: a linguistic perspective on Twitter. *New Media & Society, 13*(5), 788–806.

Zappavigna, M. (2012). *Discourse of Twitter and Social Media: How We Use Language to Create Affiliation on the Web.* London: Bloomsbury.

Zappavigna, M. (2014a). Coffeetweets: bonding around the bean on Twitter. In P. Seargeant & C. Tagg (Eds), *The Language of Social Media: Identity and Community on the Internet* (pp. 139–160). London: Palgrave Macmillan.

Zappavigna, M. (2014b). Enacting identity in microblogging through ambient affiliation. *Discourse & Communication, 8*(2), 209–228.

Zappavigna, M. (2014c). Enjoy your snags Australia … oh and the voting thing too# ausvotes# auspol: iconisation and affiliation in electoral microblogging. *Global Media Journal: Australian Edition, 8*(2), 1–16.

Zappavigna, M. (2015). Searchable talk: the linguistic functions of hashtags. *Social Semiotics, 25*(3), 274–291.

Zappavigna, M. (2017a). Evaluation. In C. R. Hoffmann & W. Bublitz (Eds), *Pragmatics of Social Media* (pp. 435–459). Berlin and Boston: De Gruyter Mouton

Zappavigna, M. (2017b). 'Had enough of experts' intersubjectivity and the quoted voice in microblogging. In E. Friginal (Ed.), *Studies in Corpus-Based Sociolinguistics* (pp. 321–343). London: Routledge.

Zappavigna, M. (2018). *Searchable Talk: Hashtags and Social Media Metadiscourse*: London: Bloomsbury Publishing.

Zappavigna, M. (2019a). Ambient affiliation and #brexit: negotiating values about experts through censure and ridicule. In V. Koller, S. Kopf, & M. Miglbauer (Eds), *Discourses of Brexit* (pp. 48–68). London: Routledge.

Zappavigna, M. (2019b). Language and social media: enacting identity through ambient affiliation. In G. Thompson, W. Bowcher, L. Fontaine, & J. Y. Liang (Eds), *The Cambridge Handbook of Systemic Function Linguistics* (pp. 714–737). London: Cambridge University Press.

Zappavigna, M. (2020). 'And then he said … no one has more respect for women than i do': intermodal relations and intersubjectivity in image macros. In Hartmut Stöckl, Helen Caple & Jana Pflaeging (Eds), *Shifts toward Image-Centricity in Contemporary Multimodal Practices* (pp. 204–225). London: Routledge.

Zappavigna, M. (2021). Ambient affiliation in comments on YouTube videos: communing around values about ASMR. 外国语, 44(1), 21–40.

Zappavigna, M., Cleirigh, C., Dwyer, P., & Martin, J. R. (2010). The coupling of gesture and phonology. In M. Bednarek & J. R. Martin (Eds), *New Discourse on Language: Functional Perspectives on Multimodality, Identity, and Affiliation* (pp. 219–236): London: Bloomsbury.

Zappavigna, M., Dwyer, P., & Martin, J. R. (2008). Syndromes of meaning: exploring patterned coupling in a NSW Youth Justice Conference. In A. Mahboob & N. K. Knight (Eds), *Questioning Linguistics* (pp. 165–187): Newcastle: Cambridge Scholars.

Zappavigna, M., & Logi, L. (2021). Emoji in social media discourse about working from home. *Discourse, Context & Media, 44*, 100543.

Zappavigna, M., & Martin, J. R. (2018). #Communing affiliation: Social tagging as a resource for aligning around values in social media. *Discourse, Context & Media, 22*, 4–12. doi:10.1016/j.dcm.2017.08.001

Zhang, Y., Wang, M., & Li, Y. (2021). More than playfulness: emojis in the comments of a WeChat official account. *Internet Pragmatics, 4*(2), 247–271.

Zhao, S. (2011). *Learning through multimedia interaction: the construal of primary social science knowledge in web-based digital learning materials.* (PhD Thesis). University of Sydney, Australia.

Zhao, S., Djonov, E., & van Leeuwen, T. (2014). Semiotic technology and practice: a multimodal social semiotic approach to PowerPoint. *Text & Talk, 34*(3), 349–375.

Glossary

1 Glossary of Technical Terms from Systemic Functional Linguistics

[Affect] An APPRAISAL system feature describing the construal of emotions and emotional states.

Affiliation A framework for describing how social bonds are construed as values in language.

Affordances The particular properties of a semiotic mode in terms of how its attendant resources can make meaning in light of constraints such as the nature of the medium. Affordance is a term also used to describe the capacities of particular kinds of semiotic technologies in terms of how they enable and constrain particular kinds of meaning-making.

Ambient affiliation An extended for describing how social bonds are construed as values in language that account for both dialogic interaction and communing without direct interaction.

APPRAISAL The discourse semantic system describing how evaluative meanings are construed in language.

[Appreciation] An APPRAISAL system feature describing the construal of social and aesthetic valuations of objects and things.

ATTITUDE An APPRAISAL system describing the construal of feelings, and opinions.

Bonding icon An emblem that takes on interpersonal significance for a community such that its ideational meaning is backgrounded, and its interpersonal meaning is foregrounded and shared among the community.

Bond A social relation that can be realised in discourse through couplings, e.g. ideation-attitude couplings.

Bond network A set of relations between different bonds (e.g. those shared by a particular sub-community).

Co-text The written text that accompanies other kinds of semiotic resources in a social media post. Also referred to as written text and verbiage.

COMMUNING AFFILIATION A form of affiliation involving bonding without direct interaction between interlocutors (e.g. in online and broadcast contexts).

CONCURRENCE CONVERGENCE in the form of a relation between ideational meanings made in language and paralanguage.

CONVERGENCE The relation between meanings made in language and paralanguage.

Coupling An association between two semiotic variables (e.g. an instance of ATTITUDE and an instance of IDEATION).

DIALOGIC AFFILIATION A form of affiliation where values are negotiated interactively.

Discourse semantics   One of the linguistic strata in Systemic Functional Linguistics, defined as a pattern of patterns of the strata beneath (i.e. a pattern of lexicogrammatical patterns). See Figure 3.1 in Chapter 3.

ENGAGEMENT   An APPRAISAL system describing the how voices are managed in discourse.

[Element]   Part of a figure in terms of the discourse semantic system of IDEATION. There are three main types of [elements]: [entities] (items participating in an activity), [occurrences] (happenings), and [qualities] (properties).

[Entity]   A type of [element] in the discourse semantic system of IDEATION. [Entities] include [thing entities] (e.g. a cup of coffee) and [semiotic entities] (e.g. a discussion).

Field   A register variable about how language construes a domain of experience (e.g. the processes, events, and activities in which participants are involved).

[Figure]   A change or a state (involving one or more elements) in terms of the discourse semantic system of IDEATION.

GRADUATION   An APPRAISAL system describing how ATTITUDES are scaled up and down in terms of intensity or typicality.

IDEATION   The discourse semantic system modelling how [sequences], [figures], and [elements] represent experience as activities and states.

IDEATION-ATTITUDE **coupling**   An association between attitudinal meaning (e.g. an evaluation) and IDEATION (e.g. the target of an evaluation). One or more couplings form the discursive realisation of a social bond.

Ideational metafunction   How language meanings involved in construing experience.

Instantiation   The process by which a discursive feature is construed in a text.

Intermodal coupling   An interaction between two semiotic variables in different modalities (e.g. image and language).

Interpersonal metafunction   How language construes meanings involved in enacting relationships (e.g. evaluative meanings).

Intersemiotic complementarity   How meanings across different modalities (e.g. image and verbiage) coordinate to make coherent meaning within a single text.

[Judgement]   An APPRAISAL system feature describing the construal of social and ethical judgements of people and their behaviour.

Lexicogrammar   The stratum above phonology/graphology and below discourse semantics in the SFL model of language. See Figure 3.1 in Chapter 3.

Metafunctions   The high-level functions that Halliday ascribes to language (see ideational, interpersonal, and textual metafunctions).

Minimum mapping principle   A principle for assessing emoji–text CONVERGENCE that considers whether the emoji and the language can be said to construe a cohesive dimension of field or tenor.

Mode   A register variable about the role language is playing in a text (e.g. the organisation of information flow).

[Occurrence]   An [element] that construes an event or activity.

[Occurrence figure]   A [figure] that includes an [occurrence] construing an event or activity.

Paralanguage   Semiotic resources that are dependent on language for making meaning (e.g. gesture).

Prosodic correspondence   A principle for assessing emoji–text CONVERGENCE that considers where emoji coordinate together prosodically, for instance, shifting together with changes in attitudinal meaning across the text.

Proximity principle   A principle for assessing emoji–text CONVERGENCE that considers the adjacency of an emoji to particular language features in the unfolding text.

[Quality]   An [element] that construes a description or assessment.

Realisation   A hierarchy of abstraction through which each stratum of language is realised as patterns of patterns of the stratum below.

Register   A stratum of context in terms of the SFL model of language.

RESONANCE   CONVERGENCE in the form of a relation between interpersonal meanings made in language and paralanguage.

[Sequence]   One or more [figures] realised by a clause or clause complex.

[State figure]   A [figure] that does not include an [occurrence] and instead features relational or existential processes describing a state of affairs.

SYNCHRONICITY   CONVERGENCE in the form of a relation between textual meanings made in language and paralanguage.

System network   A formalism developed within Systemic Functional Linguistics in the form of a graphical notation format, wherein a 'system' is a particular region of meaning realised through particular linguistic choices. An 'or' choice is represented through square brackets and an 'and' relation through curly brackets (a brace).

Tenor   A register variable about how language enact social relationships (e.g. the degree of contact and solidarity among participants).

Textual metafunction   How language organises ideational and interpersonal meanings to forge cohesive and coherent texts.

2 CONVERGENCE **System Network with Feature Glossary**

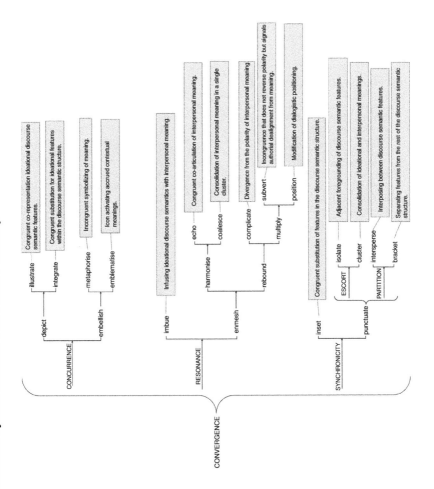

CONVERGENCE

CONCURRENCE

depict — illustrate — Congruent co-representation ideational discourse semantic features.
— integrate — Congruent substitution for ideational features within the discourse semantic structure.

embellish — metaphorise — Incongruent symbolizing of meaning.
— emblematise — Icon activating accrued contextual meanings.

RESONANCE

imbue — Infusing ideational discourse semantics with interpersonal meaning.

enmesh — harmonise — echo — Congruent co-articulation of interpersonal meaning.
— coalesce — Consolidation of interpersonal meaning in a single cluster.
— rebound — complicate — Divergence from the polarity of interpersonal meaning
— multiply — subvert — Incongruence that does not reverse polarity but signals authorial dealignment from meaning.
— position — Modification of dialogistic positioning.

SYNCHRONICITY

inset — Congruent substitution of features in the discourse semantic structure.

punctuate — ESCORT — isolate — Adjacent foregrounding of discourse semantic features.
— cluster — Consolidation of ideational and interpersonal meanings.
— PARTITION — intersperse — Interposing between discourse semantic features.
— bracket — Separating features from the rest of the discourse semantic structure.

Index

For EU product safety concerns, contact us at Calle de José Abascal, 56–1°, 28003 Madrid, Spain or eugpsr@cambridge.org.

* 9 7 8 1 0 0 9 1 7 9 8 0 5 *